ESSENTIAL
MANAGERS

MANAGEMENT
HANDBOOK

ESSENTIAL
MANAGERS

MANAGEMENT
HANDBOOK

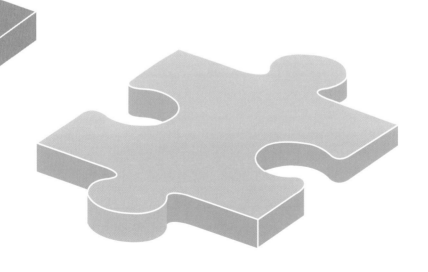

Produced for DK by
Dynamo Limited
1 Cathedral Court, Southernhay East, Exeter, EX1 1AF

Senior Editor Chauney Dunford
Senior Art Editor Helen Spencer
Managing Editor Gareth Jones
Senior Managing Art Editor Lee Griffiths
Producer Nancy-Jane Maun
Production Editor Kavita Varma
Jacket Designer Juhi Sheth
DTP Designer Rakesh Kumar
Senior Jackets Coordinator Priyanka Sharma-Saddi
Associate Publishing Director Liz Wheeler
Art Director Karen Self
Design Director Philip Ormerod
Publishing Director Jonathan Metcalf

Content previously published in Essential Managers (EM) Managing People (2009, 2015, 2021),
EM Flexible Working (2021), EM Leadership (2008, 2015, 2021),
EM Achieving High Performance (2009, 2015, 2022), EM Effective Communication (2009, 2015, 2022),
EM Presenting (2008, 2015, 2022), and EM Negotiating (2009, 2015, 2021)

First published in Great Britain in 2016. This edition in 2022 by
Dorling Kindersley Limited, DK, One Embassy Gardens,
8 Viaduct Gardens, London, SW11 7BW

The authorised representative in the EEA is
Dorling Kindersley Verlag GmbH. Arnulfstr. 124,
80636 Munich, Germany

Copyright © 2022 Dorling Kindersley Limited
A Penguin Random House Company
10 9 8 7 6 5
009-325056-Jun/2022

A CIP catalogue record for this book
is available from the British Library.
ISBN: 978-0-2415-1579-2

Printed and bound in China

For the curious
www.dk.com

This book was made with Forest
Stewardship Council ™ certified paper—
one small step in DK's commitment
to a sustainable future. For more
information, go to www.dk.com/our-
green-pledge

Contents

Introduction

A managerial role is an exciting, but daunting challenge. You are responsible for making sure your team is working together, achieving results, and that overall your department is running smoothly even when working remotely. There is no single technique to becoming an excellent manager, but the **Essential Managers Handbook** provides indispensable advice on six of the key areas of management.

Lead your team

Managing People is essential to building a high-performing team. A successful manager must learn to set targets, plan work, delegate tasks, motivate employees, be inclusive, appraise performance, and solve problems, whether working together in an office with their team or remotely. Managing people is a process that is always evolving to reflect the complex, diverse, and flexible modern workspace, but by learning the core skills in this section, you will be well prepared to accommodate change. In order to run your team successfully, it is critical to be seen as a good leader. **Leadership** is the ability to create an environment where each individual feels totally committed to doing a great job. This section provides advice to help you to develop your leadership skills, allowing you to realize both your own and your team's full potential.

Achieve your potential

Achieving this potential occurs through a combination of becoming more creative and confident, and improving your communication skills. In **Achieving High Performance**, you will be given the tools to understand yourself, and learn how to play to your strengths and overcome your weaknesses. The **Effective Communication** section of this book focuses on a range of topics, from planning a strategy to analysing your audience. You will learn to communicate and listen well, both to your team and to your intended market.

Improve your business skills

A good manager also needs to be a successful presenter, as presentations have become an essential tool for business communication around the world,

elivered either in-person or
emotely. Whether you are
elivering a formal speech, giving
n informal address to your staff,
r communicating with the media,
e elements of great presentations
re described in the **Presenting**
ection in clear, concise, and
ractical detail. **Negotiating** is
hallenging, complex, and exciting,
nd another important skill that
l managers should master. This
ection outlines various techniques
at can help to make you a more
uccessful negotiator in every
tuation you face; from teaching
ou how to manage your own
motions, to understanding
ur negotiation style.

Throughout this book, you will
find many features aimed at
helping you to learn the essentials
of being a manager quickly and
efficiently. "Ask Yourself" boxes
allow you to review your situation
and assess how you can improve
your skills, while "Tip" boxes
provide expert advice. Case
studies demonstrate real-life
examples for you to learn from,
and "Do's and Don'ts" boxes
provide at-a-glance advice on
key topics.

MANAGING PEOPLE

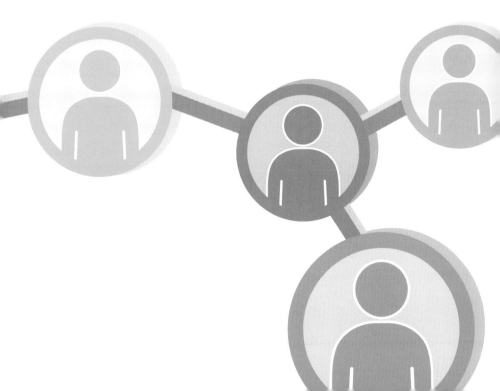

Understanding
yourself

Knowing yourself will give you valuable insights into your aptitude for managing others. It allows you to understand how you are perceived, why people respond to you in the way they do, and how to get the best out of them.

Developing self-awareness

Awareness of your emotions, personality, what you enjoy and dislike, what motivates you, and what comes easily or poses challenges is a key precursor to developing effective managerial ability. Quite simply, if you can't manage yourself, you will not be able to manage anyone else.

Keeping moving

The best way to enhance your self-awareness is to learn in a systematic way from your own experiences. Start by reflecting on situations in your working life, your actions in response to them, and the outcomes of these events. Schedule a regular time to do this, either at the beginning or end of a workday, when you are not in the thick of the action. Give yourself space to reflect, and make sure you can be alone and uninterrupted for a good 20 minutes or so. Try to gain a better understanding of what happened and think about how you can learn from each situation.

Take time to **reflect on situations** in your working life, **your actions** in response to them, and **the outcomes** of these events

Analyzing your performance

Assessing your progress towards your goals can help you gain a fuller understanding of your strengths and weaknesses. Whenever you make a key decision or take a key action, write down what you expect will happen. Then, every three or four months, compare the actual results with your expectations. If you practise this method consistently, it will help you discover what you are doing, or failing to do, that deprives you of the full benefits of your strengths, and will demonstrate areas in which you are not particularly competent and cannot perform adequately.

> ### Tip
>
> **MAKE NOTES**
> Use your journal to **"think on paper"** about what you have read about management in this or other books, or **your experiences** in management training programmes.

In focus

FIND FEEDBACK

It is important to find at least one person in your life who will give you honest, gut-level feedback, to help you gain perspective on your experiences and learn from them. This should be someone you trust enough to go to when you have real problems and ask, "Am I off base here? Am I crazy?" This person could be a partner, a mentor, a best friend, a co-worker, a therapist, or a personal coach. Today, many organizations are providing their managers with 360-degree feedback, allowing them to receive insights on their strengths and weaknesses from other members of staff.

Keeping a journal

Keeping a journal is a good way to help you learn from experience. Journals are similar to diaries, but include entries that address critical aspects of your managerial experiences and reflect on interactions with bosses, employees, and team-mates. If you want to solicit feedback, post your journal as an online blog.

Journal entries could describe:

- ✓ A good (or bad) way someone handled a situation

- ✓ A problem in the making

- ✓ The different ways people react to situations

- ✓ Comments about insightful or interesting quotations

- ✓ Anecdotes, news articles, or even humorous cartoons

- ✓ Your thoughts on people in the news, or in books or films

Using emotional intelligenc

Emotional intelligence (EI) is the ability to monitor and work with your and others' emotions. It is measured in EQ, which is the emotional equivalent of IQ. Daniel Goleman – author of the bestselling *Emotional Intelligence* – and other writers suggest that a technically proficient manager with a high EQ will be more successful than a manager who has only a high IQ.

Understanding EQ

Your EQ is the measure of your ability to understand and interact with others and becomes more important the more people you deal with. EQ does not measure personality traits or cognitive capacity. Emotional intelligence can be developed over time and can be improved through training and therapy. Those with a high EQ will be better able to control their own emotions, while at the same time using them as a basis for action. Working with emotions, rather than being at the mercy of them, makes individuals more successful in dealing with the demands of the environment around them. They are better able to control impulses and deal with stress, and better at problem solving. All of these qualities help the individual to perform more competently at work.

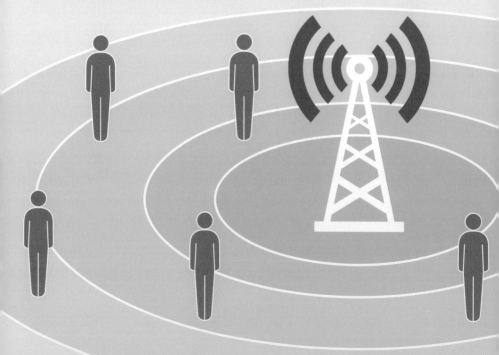

CHECKLIST...
Applying emotional intelligence   **YES** **NO**

1 Am I **aware of my feelings** and do I act accordingly? .... ☐ ☐

2 Can I **share my feelings** in a straightforward, composed manner? .... ☐ ☐

3 Do I **treat others** with compassion, sensitivity, and kindness? .... ☐ ☐

4 Am I **open to the opinions and ideas** of others? .... ☐ ☐

5 Can I **decisively confront** conflict? .... ☐ ☐

6 Do I **maintain a balance** between my personal life and work? .... ☐ ☐

Using EI at work
To be a successful manager in today's business world, a high EQ may be more important than sheer intellectual or technical ability. A manager who leads a project team of diverse people will need to understand and interact successfully with others. Applying emotional intelligence at work means you are open to the ideas of others and can build and mend relationships with them. You are aware of your feelings and act accordingly, articulating ideas so that others can understand them, developing rapport, building trust, and working towards consensus. Managers who are attuned to their own feelings and the feelings of others use this understanding to enhance personal, team, and organizational performance.

Managing emotions

Emotional intelligence has two aspects: one inward facing and one outward facing. The first of these is your emotional self-awareness and your ability to manage your own emotions. The second is your degree of empathy, or awareness of others' emotions, and your ability to productively manage relationships with others. Both inward- and outward-facing aspects of emotional intelligence are made up of a number of skills or competencies.

The four competencies of emotional intelligence

INWARD COMPETENCIES

SELF-AWARENESS

O Emotional self-awareness

O Accurate self-assessment

O Self-confidence

SELF-MANAGEMENT

O Emotional self-control

O Trustworthiness

O Conscientiousness

O Achievement orientation

O Adaptability

O Optimism

O Initiative

RELATIONSHIP MANAGEMENT
- Development of others
- Inspirational leadership
- Influence
- Communication
- Effecting change
- Conflict management
- Bond building
- Teamwork and collaboration

OUTWARD COMPETENCIES

SOCIAL AWARENESS
- Empathy
- Organizational awareness
- Service orientation

71%
of managers value EQ **more highly** than IQ in their **employees**

Applying assertiveness

An effective manager needs to behave in an active and assertive manner to get things done. Assertive managers are able to express their feelings and act with appropriate degrees of openness and candour, but still have a regard for the feelings or rights of others.

Understanding personality types

Assertiveness and the ability to express feelings are skills that people possess to different extents. Some are aggressive, direct, and blunt, and can appear domineering, pushy, or self-centred. Some people tend to be passive, inhibited, and submissive; they bottle up their feelings and fail even to stand up for their legitimate rights. Passive individuals seek to avoid conflicts and tend to sublimate their own needs and feelings in order to satisfy others.

Assertive behaviour for effective management

Most people fall between the extremes of passive and aggressive. At these extremes, passive and aggressive behaviours hinder effective managerial relations because neither encourages openness. Effective managers need to be assertive, express their ideas and feelings openly, and stand up for their rights, and all in a way that makes it easier for those they are managing to do the same. The assertive manager is straightforward yet sensitive to the

Becoming more assertive

STATE YOUR CASE

Try beginning your conversations with "I" phrases, such as **"I think"**, **"I believe"**, or **"I need"**.

BE PREPARED

Prepare for tricky encounters: have all the **facts to hand**, and try to anticipate the other person's replies.

USE OPEN QUESTIONS

If you are finding it hard to get a person to talk to you, use open questions that cannot be answered with a **simple "yes"** or **"no"** answer.

ASK YOURSELF...
Am I assertive enough?

	YES	NO
1 Does my response **accurately reflect** how I feel if I'm given a compliment about my work?	☐	☐
2 Am I **able to speak up** when I'm in a group of strangers?	☐	☐
3 If others interrupt me when I am talking, can I **hold my ground**?	☐	☐
4 Do I **avoid being taken advantage of** by other people?	☐	☐
5 Am I able to **criticize others' work** if I think they might react badly?	☐	☐

eeds of others; he or she does not eek to rule over less assertive people. eeking dominance may produce hort-term results but will not make the est use of the team-members' abilities.

> The **assertive** manager is straightforward yet sensitive to the **needs of others**

VISUALIZE YOURSELF

Try assertive role play with a trusted colleague to help you to see yourself as an **assertive person**.

GET PERSPECTIVE

Try to see a situation from the other person's **point of view**. Most workplace bullies, for example, are hiding their own insecurities or an inability to do the job.

BE PATIENT

You'll need **time and practice** to become comfortable with the **new behaviour**. Recognize that those around you may initially be uncomfortable when you start to **become more assertive**.

Examining your assumptions

Managers tend to treat their teams according to assumptions they hold about what motivates people. These assumptions create self-fulfilling prophecies in the behaviour of the team. Managers reward what they expect, and consequently only get what they expect. Challenging your own assumptions is one of the first steps in becoming a better manager

X-style managers

Prominent management theorist Douglas McGregor distinguished two management styles – X and Y – based on the assumptions held by managers about the motives of their team. X-style managers believe that workers need to be coerced and directed. They tend to be strict and controlling, giving their workers little latitude and punishing poor performance. They use few rewards and typically give only negative feedback. These managers see little point in workers having autonomy, because they think that the workforce neither expects nor desires cooperation.

Y-style managers

Y-style assumptions reflect a much more optimistic view of human nature. Y-style management contends that people will gladly direct themselves towards objectives if their efforts are appropriately rewarded. Managers who hold Y assumptions assume a great deal of confidence in their workers. They are less directive and empower workers, giving them more responsibilities and freedom to accomplish tasks as they deem appropriate.

Shaping the environment

Organizations that are designed based on X-style assumptions are very differe to those designed by Y-style managers. For example, because they believe that their workers are motivated to help the organization reach its goals, Y-style managers will decentralize authority and give more control to workers than X-style managers will. A Y-style manage realizes that most people are not resistant to organizational needs by nature, but may have become so as a result of negative experiences. Y-style managers strive to design structures that involve the team members in

Tip

ANALYZE YOURSELF
Honestly review every **decision you make** and every **task you delegate**. In each case, ask yourself what you assumed those involved would think, and how you expected them to behave. Remember that **positive expectations** help to produce positive outcomes.

xecuting their work roles, such as articipative management and joint goal etting. These approaches allow team members to exercise some self-direction nd self-control in their work lives.

In Y-style management, although ndividuals and groups are still ccountable for their activities, the role f the manager is not to exert control but to provide support and advice, and to make sure that workers have the resources they need to effectively perform their jobs. By contrast, X-style managers consider their role to be to monitor workers to ensure that they contribute to the production process and do not threaten product quality.

X and Y assumptions

X-STYLE MANAGERS

O Team members inherently dislike work and will attempt to avoid it.

O Workers must be coerced, controlled, or threatened with punishment to achieve goals.

O Team members will shirk responsibility and seek formal direction.

O Most workers place security above all other factors associated with work and will display little ambition.

Y-STYLE MANAGERS

O People can enjoy work and can view it as being as natural to them as rest or play.

O People will exercise self-direction and self-control if they are committed to the objectives behind tasks.

O The average person can learn to accept and seek responsibility.

O Most workers place job satisfaction and career fulfilment high on their list of priorities.

Clarifying your values

Values are stable and enduring beliefs about what is good, right, and worthwhile, and about the behaviour that is desirable for achieving wha is worthwhile. To be an effective manager, it is necessary to have a good understanding of what your values are and to act accordingly.

Defining values
Values are formed early in our lives, from the influence of our parents, teachers, friends, religious leaders, and media role-models. Some may change as we go through life and experience different behaviours. Your values manifest themselves in everything you do and the choices that you make. If you are someone who particularly values promptness, for example, you will make sure that you always behave in ways that mean you are on time for appointments. The thought of being late will stimulate feelings of stress in you, and induce a subsequent adrenaline rush as you hurry to be at the appointment on time. As a manager, it is important for you to clarify your values, so that you can determine what your goals are and how you want to manage yourself and others to achieve them.

Clarifying your personal values
It may sound strange, but one of the best ways to clarify your personal values and gain a clear understanding of what is important to you is to think about how you would like to be remembered in your eulogy. Sit quietly and consider how you want your friends and family to remember you, and what you want your work colleagues to

say they thought of you. Also think of your broader contributions – how would you like to be remembered in the communities you are a part of? Make notes, and use the information you write down to identify the values that are most important to you.

Dealing with conflicts
It can be challenging when your personal values conflict with those of your organization, or when there are conflicting values between individuals o sub-groups. Value differences can exist, for example, about how to perform jobs,

ASK YOURSELF...
About your influences   **YES   NO**

1 Can I identify the individuals and the events that
influenced the development of my **value system**? .... ☐   ☐

2 Are these sources of influence **still as important to me**
as recent events and people who influence me now? .... ☐   ☐

3 Are my values **still appropriate** as guides of behaviour
in the world I live in today? .... ☐   ☐

4 Should I consider changing some of my values to make
them **more relevant**? .... ☐   ☐

he nature of reward systems, or the egree of intimacy in work relationships. aving a clear understanding of your wn personal value set will help you manage these conflict situations. If ou are clear about your own values, you an act with integrity and practise what ou preach regardless of emotional or ocial pressure. To address a conflict tuation, first make sure you are aware f, understand, and are tolerant of the value differences held by the other parties. This will help you to determine whether the value conflict is, in fact, irresolvable and will require personnel changes, or whether compromises and adjustments can be made to accommodate the different perspectives.

In focus

TYPES OF VALUE
Values can be classified into two types: terminal and instrumental. **Terminal values** (your "ends" in life) are desirable ends or goals, such as a comfortable, prosperous life, world peace, great wisdom, or salvation. **Instrumental values** (the "means" to those ends) are beliefs about what behaviours are appropriate in striving for desired goals and ends. Consider a manager who works extra hours to help deliver a customer's rush order. The attitude displayed is a willingness to help a customer with a problem. The value that serves as the foundation of this attitude might be that of service to others.

Developing your personal mission statement

A personal mission statement provides you with the long-term vision and motivation to manage yourself and others in your team according to your own values. It also allows you to establish your purpose and goals as a manager and sets a benchmark for self-evaluation.

Defining your future

Your personal mission statement spells out your managerial philosophy. It defines the type of manager you want to be (your character), what you want to accomplish (your contributions), and what principles guide your behaviour (your values). It provides you with the vision and values to direct your managerial life – the basis for setting long- and short-term goals, and how best to deploy your time.

Setting out your philosophy

Make sure that your personal mission statement is an accurate reflection of your values, goals, and aspirations for

SEE THE FUTURE
Develop a vision of what it will be like when you achieve your goals. Your vision of a desirable future can be **a powerful motivating force**.

EVALUATE PROGRESS
Continually evaluate your performance against your **mission statement**. When things don't work out, be honest with yourself about wh

Tip

LEARN FROM SETBACKS
Things will not always work out as you have planned. When you face setbacks, **be honest with yourself** about what happened and why, and think carefully about whether you need to **re-evaluate your goals**.

success. A personal statement might read: "My career goals are to effectively manage my team to achieve respect and knowledge, to use my talents as a manager to help others, and to play an active role in this organization." Another individual's statement might have a very different focus: "As a manager in this creative firm, I want to establish a fault-free, self-perpetuating learning environment." Re-evaluate your mission statement on a regular basis – annually, at least – to ensure that it still describes your overall vision for your future as a manager

Setting and attaining your personal managerial goals

BE SMART
Set goals that are **Specific**, **Measurable**, **Attainable**, **Realistic**, and **Time-bound**. You are more likely to achieve goals that are well defined and within reach.

REWARD YOURSELF
Reward yourself for small wins. When you achieve **incremental progress** towards your goals, treat yourself to a reward, such as a night out or some recreational activity.

GET SUPPORT
Develop a support group of people who will **help you in achieving your goals**. Your support group should include those with the resources you need to be successful.

SET YOUR GOALS
Personalize your goals. You will be **far more committed** to goals that you have set yourself, rather than those that have been set for you by someone else.

Managing
a team

Teams are the cornerstones of many organizations. Successful team leaders understand what makes a team effective and what can lead to failure. To be a successful manager, you need to be able to plan and design the work of your team, delegate tasks effectively, monitor progress, and motivate your team to excel.

02

Setting goals and planning

Planning is a key skill for any manager and starts with having a good understanding of the organization's objectives. It involves establishing a strategy for achieving those goals using the personnel available, and developing the means to integrate and coordinate necessary activities.

Knowing your goals

Planning is concerned with ends (what needs to be done) and means (how those ends are to be achieved). In order to create a plan, managers must first identify the organization's goals – what it is trying to achieve.

Planning and monitoring

Goals are the foundation of all other planning activities. They refer to the desired outcomes for the entire organization, for groups and teams within the organization, and for individuals. In the best organizations, employees and teams work closely with their managers to set their own goals and plan courses of action. Goals provide the direction for all management decisions and form the criteria against which actual accomplishments can be measured.

Tip

LOOK TO THE FUTURE
Write down three SMART goals that you **want your team to achieve** in the next five years, and then **plan how you will reach them**.

How to develop and implement a plan

Define your overall goals, by asking questions such as **"Why do we exist?"** and **"What do we do?"**

Thoroughly analyze your working environment, to **identify opportunities** you can exploit **and threats** you may encounter.

Use the results to **set objectives** that you want to meet. These will create a standard against which to **measure your progress**.

Setting your goals

There are five basic rules that can help you set effective goals. Always make your goals SMART: Specific, Measurable, Aligned, Reachable, and Time-bound.

S **Specific** Goals are meaningful only when they are specific enough to be measured and verified.

M **Measurable** Goals need to have a clear outcome that can be objectively assessed. They also need to have clear benchmarks that can be checked along the way.

A **Aligned** Goals should contribute to the mission, vision, and strategic plan of the organization and be congruent with the values and objectives of the employee implementing them.

R **Reachable** Goals should require you to stretch to reach them, but not be set unrealistically high.

T **Time-bound** Open-ended goals can be neglected because there is no sense of urgency to complete them. Whenever possible, goals should include a time limit.

Goals are the **desired outcomes** for the whole organization, for groups within it, and for individuals

Monitor your progress to **ensure you are on the right track**.

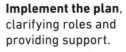

Formulate a plan to achieve those objectives – what needs to be done, by whom, and by when.

Implement the plan, clarifying roles and providing support.

Designing work

Job design refers to the way tasks are combined to form complete jobs. It involves trying to shape the right jobs to conform to the right people, taking into account both the organization's goals and the employees' satisfaction. Well-designed jobs lead to high motivation, high-quality performance, high satisfaction, and low absenteeism and turnover.

Defining jobs

Jobs vary considerably: a lifeguard, for example, will have very different day-to-day responsibilities from an accountant or a builder. However, any job can be described in terms of five core job dimensions:

- **Skill variety:** the degree to which a job requires a variety of different activities so that the worker can employ a number of different skills and talents.
- **Task identity:** the degree to which a job requires completion of a whole and identifiable piece of work.
- **Task significance:** the degree to which a job has an impact on the lives of other people.
- **Autonomy:** the degree to which a job provides freedom and discretion to workers in scheduling their tasks and in determining how the work will be carried out.
- **Feedback:** the degree to which workers get direct and clear information about the effectiveness of their performance.

As a manager, you can maximize your team's performance by enhancing these five dimensions. Skill variety, task identity, and task significance combine to create meaningful work. Jobs with these characteristics will be perceived as important, valuable, and worthwhile.

Jobs that possess autonomy give workers a sense of responsibility for their results. Jobs that provide feedback indicate to the employee how effectively he or she is performing.

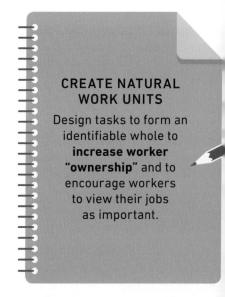

CREATE NATURAL WORK UNITS
Design tasks to form an identifiable whole to **increase worker "ownership"** and to encourage workers to view their jobs as important.

Skill variety, task identity, and task significance combine to **create jobs** that are seen as important, valuable, and worthwhile

COMBINE TASKS

Put existing fragmented tasks together to form larger modules of work. This can help to **increase skill variety** and task identity.

Tip

RESPECT DECISIONS

If you have empowered a team member to make a decision, try not to reverse it – unless it really puts the organization in danger. Repeatedly undoing your team members' decisions reduces trust and their sense of autonomy.

Ways to design work by enhancing the five dimensions

EXPAND JOBS VERTICALLY

Giving employees responsibilities formerly reserved for managers closes the gap between the "doing" and "controlling" aspects of the job and **increases autonomy**.

ESTABLISH CLIENT RELATIONSHIPS

Building **direct relationships** between the worker and the client – the user of the product or the service that the employee works on – **increases skill variety**, autonomy, and feedback.

IMPROVE FEEDBACK CHANNELS

Feedback tells team members **how well they are performing**, and whether their performance is improving, deteriorating, or remaining constant. Employees should receive feedback directly as they do their jobs.

Driving performance

As Lee Iacocca, former CEO of Chrysler Corporation, said: "All business operations can be reduced to three words: people, product, and profit. People come first. Unless you've got a good team, you can't do much with the other two." Successful managers are those who create, work with, and manage successful teams.

Defining high-performing teams

A team is two or more people who meet regularly (whether in person or remotely), perceive themselves as a unit distinguishable from others, have complementary skills, and are committed to a common purpose, a set of performance goals, and an approach for which they hold themselves mutually accountable.

High-performing teams engage in collective work produced by coordinated joint efforts that result in more than the sum of the individual efforts. Research and practical experience have shown that teams with many more than 12 members tend to lack cohesion and struggle to make fast and effective decisions.

Understanding team performance

WHO ARE WE?

Sharing strengths, weaknesses, work preferences, and values allows the establishment of a **set of common beliefs** for the team, creating a group identity and a feeling of **"what we stand for"**.

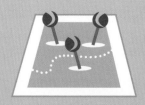

WHERE ARE WE NOW?

Understanding the current position means that a team can **reinforce its strengths**, improve on its weaknesses, and **identify opportunities** to capitalize on and threats to be aware of.

WHERE ARE WE GOING?

Teams need to have a **vision** of the pot of gold at the end of the rainbow. They also need a **mission**, a **purpose**, and a set of **specific team goals** that they are all excited about.

MUTUAL TRUST

A climate of mutual trust is essential in a high-performing team – each member of the team needs to know they can depend on the others. Successful managers build mutual trust by creating a climate of openness in which employees are free to discuss problems without fear of retaliation. They are approachable, respectful, and listen to team members' ideas, and develop a reputation for being fair, objective, and impartial in their treatment of others. Consistency and honesty are key, so these managers avoid erratic and unpredictable behaviour and always follow through on any explicit and implied promises they make.

Communication is at the heart of building and maintaining mutual inter-dependence between members of a team. Managers of high-performing teams keep team members informed about upper-management decisions and policies and give accurate feedback on their performance. They are also open and candid about their own problems and limitations.

HOW WILL WE GET THERE?

Team members must understand who will do what and when to **accomplish team goals**, and must be clear about their job description, **roles on the team**, responsibilities, and areas of authority and accountability.

WHAT SUPPORT DO WE GET/NEED?

Reviewing each member's training and development needs can set the stage for **individual training, counselling, and mentoring** that will strengthen both the individual and the team.

HOW EFFECTIVE ARE WE?

Regular performance reviews of quantity and quality outputs and the team process – with recognition and **reward for success** – ensure achievement of team goals and provide members with standards.

Achieving good teamwork

To help your teams perform to the best of their ability, create clear goals. All team members need to have a thorough understanding of the goals of the team and a belief that these goals embody a worthwhile result. This encourages team members to sublimate personal concerns to those of the team. Members need to be committed to the team's goals, know what they are expected to accomplish, and understand how they will work together to achieve these goals.

However, these goals must be attainable; team members can lose morale if it seems that they are not.

To avoid this, set smaller interim milestones in the path to your overall goal. As these smaller goals are attained your team's success is reinforced. Cohesiveness is increased, morale improves, and confidence builds.

As the manager of a team, it is your job to provide the resources and support that the members need to achieve success. Offer skills training where needed, either personally or by calling in specialists within your organization or outside training services.

Steering your team

Team members should all share in the glory when their team succeeds, but also share the responsibility when the team fails. However, members need to know that they cannot ride on the backs of others.

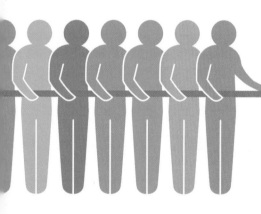

6–12

members is the **ideal number** for a team to work at optimal effectiveness

Identify what each member's contribution to the team's work should be and make it a part of his or her overall performance appraisal. To help monitor performance select members of the team to act as participant–observers. While a team is working, the role of the participant–observer is to focus on the processes being used – the sequence of actions that takes place between team members to achieve a goal. Periodically, the participant–observer should stop the team from working on its task and discuss the process members are engaged in. The objectives of the participant–observer are to improve the team's functioning by discussing the processes being used and creating strategies for improving them.

CHECKLIST...

Creating a team performance agreement   **YES   NO**

1 Have I identified **what is to be done** and when? .... ☐ ☐

2 Have I **specified the boundaries** (guiding rules of behaviour)
or the means for accomplishing results? .... ☐ ☐

3 Have I identified the human, financial, technical, or
organizational support available to help **achieve the results?** ... ☐ ☐

4 Have I established the **standards of performance** and the time
intervals for evaluation? .... ☐ ☐

5 Have I specified what will happen in **performance evaluations**
and the consequences of not meeting the standards? .... ☐ ☐

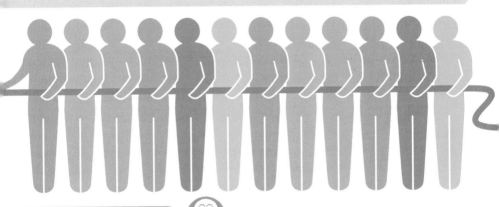

Tip

CHANGE PERSONNEL
If your teams get bogged
down in their own inertia or
internal fighting, **rotate the
members**. Consider how
certain personalities will
mesh and **re-form your
teams** in ways that will
better complement skills.

Setting standards

Create a performance agreement to
record the details of what the team
is aiming to achieve, what is required
and expected of every team member, and
what support will be available to them.
Setting out the framework for team
success clearly helps to ensure that
there is a mutual understanding and
common vision of the desired results
and emphasizes the standards that you
expect from every team member.

Valuing diversity

Bonding with people at work who are similar can be challenging enough but bridging the gap and authentically connecting with people who are different demands a specific skill set. As workplaces become more diverse and business becomes more global, managers must understand how cultural diversity affects the expectations and behaviour of everyone in the organization.

Understanding the changes

The labour market is dramatically changing. Most countries are experiencing an increase in the age of their workforce, increased immigration, and, in many, a rapid increase in the number of working women. At the same time, more businesses are selling and manufacturing products and services abroad. As a result, managers must be able to work with people of all backgrounds both inside and outside their organizations, and ensure that their employees can do the same. Workers who believe they are not merely tolerated but valued by their employer are more likely to be loyal, productive, and committed.

Tip

LET EVERYONE KNOW
Make a public commitment to valuing diversity – this will ensure that you are **accountable for your actions**, and may attract potential employees who prefer to work for someone who values **equal opportunities** for all.

Capitalizing on diversity

There's a strong case for boosting diversity and inclusion (D&I). A 2020 study by McKinsey & Company showed that from 2014 to 2019 firms with higher levels of gender, ethnic, and cultural diversity were more likely to earn higher profits than those with lower diversity. Organizations with more than 30 per cent female executives outperformed less gender-diverse ones, while the most technically and culturally diverse firms were 36 per cent more profitable. D&I helps organizations avoid "groupthink" and to connect with a wider customer base. But it's about more than hiring diverse talent. It's how people from underrepresented backgrounds feel about their workplace that affects if they stay and advance. Even in diverse firms, managers face challenges in creating equal and open working environments that instil a sense of belonging. Take these three steps to boost inclusion:

- Create a level playing field of opportunity. Use analytics to show that the processes for deciding promotions and salaries are transparent and fair. Eradicate bias from performance reviews.
- Promote a culture that allows people to speak up. Discuss issues and provide support. Uphold a strict anti-discrimination policy, and tackle microaggressions.
- Combat bias at the personal level. No one is immune from unconscious bias and it can shape views on ethnicity, religion, age, gender, disability, and more. Unconscious bias training can raise awareness, better aligning words and actions with our conscious values.

Tip

BE HONEST
Research by New York University's Stern School of Business shows that employees who **hear the message** "diversity is good, but also really hard" both **support D&I more** and put in **more effort** to develop it than those who only hear that "diversity is good".

Delegating effectively

Managers are responsible for getting things done through other people. You need to accomplish assigned goals by delegating responsibility and authority to others. Empowering others through delegation is one of the most powerful managerial tools for increasing productivity.

Empowering others

Managers delegate by transferring authority and responsibility for work to employees. Delegation empowers employees to achieve goals by allowing them to make their own decisions about how to do a job. Delegation also helps develop employees for promotion opportunities by expanding their knowledge, job capabilities, and decision-making skills.

Delegating lets you **focus on** key **strategic activities** and can also lead to better decision-making

01

ALLOCATION OF DUTIES
Before a manager can delegate authority, the **tasks** and **activities** that need to be accomplished **must be explained**.

Feeling the benefits

Effective delegation is key for any manager. It will free up your time, allowing you to focus on big-picture strategic activities. It can also lead to better decision-making, because it pushes decisions down the organization, meaning that decision-makers are often closer to the problems. It also helps those you are managing develop their own decision-making skills and prepares them for future promotion opportunities.

02

The four components of delegation

DELEGATION OF AUTHORITY

Delegation is the process of transferring authority to **empower a subordinate** to act for you as a manager.

03

ASSIGNMENT OF RESPONSIBILITY

Managers should assign responsibility to the empowered employee for **performing the job** adequately.

04

CREATION OF ACCOUNTABILITY

Managers should hold empowered employees responsible for properly carrying out their duties. This includes **taking responsibility** for the completion of tasks assigned to them and also **being accountable** to the manager for the satisfactory performance of that work.

Letting go

Managers often have trouble delegating. Some are afraid to give up control, explaining, "I like to do things myself, because then I know they're done right." Others lack confidence in their employees or fear that they may be criticized for others' mistakes. While you may be capable of doing the tasks you delegate better, faster, or with fewer mistakes, it is not possible to do everything yourself. If you often feel that your team isn't taking ownership of projects, it may suggest that you are handing out tasks, rather than delegating responsibility. When you delegate, you should expect, and accept, some mistakes by those you delegate to.

Mistakes are often good learning experiences. You should also put in place adequate mechanisms for feedback so you will know what is happening.

If you do have to intervene, do it with care. While the right help at the right time can be crucial, micromanaging erodes trust. Wait for

How to delegate

CLARIFY THE ASSIGNMENT

Explain **what is being delegated**, the **results** you expect, and the **timeframe**.

SET BOUNDARIES

Ensure that the delegatees **understand precisely** what the parameters are of the **authority** you are bestowing on them.

ENCOURAGE PARTICIPATION

Involve delegatees in **decisions** about what is delegated, how much authority is needed, and **standards** to be attained.

problems to emerge before offering assistance – people are more likely to be receptive to advice once they understand the task themselves. Make it clear that you are there only to help, not to take over, and tailor your approach to fit. Does the situation better suit an intensive burst of help or a series of interventions over a longer term?

20%

of your activity yields
80% of your results;
try to do more of the 20%
and delegate the 80%

INFORM OTHERS

Let everyone who may be affected know **what has been delegated to whom** and how much authority has been granted.

ENCOURAGE DEVELOPMENT

Insist from the beginning that when delegatees come to you with a **problem**, they also bring a possible **solution**.

ESTABLISH CONTROLS

Agree on a specific time for **completion of the task**, and set dates when **progress** will be checked and problems discussed.

Motivating others

Every day, people make decisions about how much effort to put into their work. Managers have many opportunities to influence these decisions and motivate their team by providing challenging work, recognizing outstanding performance, allowing participation in decisions that affect employees, and showing concern for personal issues.

Understanding needs

As a manager, you need to understand what drives your team to do the best that they can. American psychologist Abraham Maslow proposed that each person has a five-level hierarchy of needs that they are driven to attempt to satisfy. Once a lower-level need has been largely satisfied, its impact on behaviour diminishes, and the person may need to be motivated to gain the next highest lev

There are two aspects to what makes a person perform well: ability and motivation. Ability is the product of aptitude, training, and resources, while motivation is the product of desire and commitment. All of these elements are required for high performance levels.

Maslow's hierarchy of needs

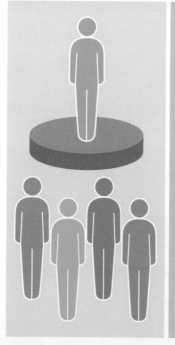

|01 ▶

PHYSIOLOGICAL NEEDS

Our most basic needs are for **physical survival**, such as to satisfy hunger or thirst. At work, this is receiving enough pay to buy food and clothing and pay the rent.

|02 ▶

SAFETY NEEDS

Once physiological needs are satisfied, safety needs are aroused. These can be satisfied at work by having **job security** and **safe working conditions**, and receiving **other benefits**.

40%

of UK employees say a **feeling of satisfaction** would **motivate** them more than their **basic salary**

someone is not performing well, the
rst question you should ask yourself
: "Is this person's poor performance
e result of a lack of ability or a lack
" motivation?" Motivational methods
an often be very effective for
improving performance, but if the
roblem is lack of ability, no amount of
ressure or encouragement will help.
hat the person needs is training,
dditional resources, or a different job.

If you have team members working
remotely, keeping them engaged can
require extra effort. Remote workers
may easily become isolated and lose
motivation, so schedule regular video
chats to hear their views, gauge their
engagement, offer support, and build
trust. Also take time to reward their
contributions – good work by remote
employees can often go unnoticed,
draining enthusiasm.

03 ▶▶

SOCIAL NEEDS

Once you feel
reasonably secure,
social needs begin
to take over. At work,
this means having
good relationships
with co-workers and
participating in company
social functions.

04 ▶▶

ESTEEM NEEDS

Next, we are motivated
by the need for self-
esteem and esteem
from others, such
as **recognition** for
accomplishments
and **promotion**.

05 ▶▶

SELF-ACTUALIZATION NEEDS

The highest level is
to feel that we are
achieving life goals.
At work, this means
being able to **exercise
creativity** and to
develop and fully
utilize our skills.

Using positive reinforcement

Rewarding progress and success and recognizing achievements are powerful ways to motivate your team. By rewarding someone for doing something right, you positively reinforce that behaviour, providing an incentive for doing it again. There are two basic types of reward: extrinsic and intrinsic. Many people depend on and highly value extrinsic rewards that are externally bestowed, such as praise, a promotion, or a pay rise. Others place a high value on intrinsic rewards, which originate from their own personal feelings about how they performed or the satisfaction that they derive from a job well done.

Many depend on **extrinsic rewards** that are externally bestowed, such as praise, promotion, or a pay rise

Case study

PRIORITIZING NEEDS

Theresa, a successful technical writer and a single parent, had been earning a good salary and benefits that enabled her to provide for her family's physical wellbeing: ample food, comfortable housing, and quality clothing. Her company then announced that it was downsizing, and she feared being made redundant. This triggered concerns about her safety needs and meant that she became much less concerned about the higher order needs of belonging to a group or her own self-esteem to perform creative and technically accurate work. Rather, she was motivated to do whatever was necessary to ensure that she kept her job or could find a new one. Once Theresa knew that her job was safe, she changed back to having a higher-order need, energizing her behaviour.

ASK YOURSELF...

Can I draw on my experience? **YES NO**

1 Can you think of a coach, teacher, or manager who motivated you to **enhance your performance** in a particular task? .... ☐ ☐

2 Can you **pinpoint** what this person did to motivate you? .... ☐ ☐

3 Can you remember **how you felt** as a result? .... ☐ ☐

4 Can you **recreate these actions** or use the same approach when trying to motivate your team?.. ☐ ☐

Rewarding success

Try to understand whether each individual you are managing values intrinsic or extrinsic rewards more highly. If you always praise achievements, for example, a motivated person who excels largely for the feelings of intrinsic satisfaction will probably begin to view you as superficial. The professional may think, "I know I did a superb job on this project. Why is my manager being so condescending?"

People also desire different types of extrinsic rewards. Praise may be perfectly acceptable to the person motivated by affiliation and relationship needs, but may do nothing for the person expecting a more tangible reward, like money. Typical extrinsic rewards are favourable assignments, trips to desirable destinations, funding for training/education, pay rises, bonuses, promotions, and office placements.

Motivating your team

STRENGTHENING EFFORT–PERFORMANCE –REWARD EXPECTANCIES

To get the best from your team, emphasize the **anticipated reward value**, whether extrinsic or intrinsic. Make sure that every individual realizes the **link between their performance and the rewards**. Even if your organization does not provide performance-based pay, you can bestow other extrinsic rewards, such as allocating more favourable job assignments.

GIVING PERFORMANCE FEEDBACK

Provide feedback to demonstrate that you know what the members of your team are doing and to **acknowledge improved performance** or a job well done. Especially when individuals are unsure of themselves, you should point out ways in which the person is improving. **Praising specific accomplishments** will help to bolster that person's self-esteem.

CHECKLIST...
Motivating my team   **YES   NO**

1 Do I **set clear goals** and **reward success**? .... ☐ ☐

2 Am I **positively reinforcing** successful behaviour?..................... ☐ ☐

3 Are the rewards I give **salient to each individual** I am managing? .... ☐ ☐

4 Have I considered **linking pay to performance**?............................ ☐ ☐

5 Have I redesigned jobs to **help motivate** the people doing them? .... ☐ ☐

6 Do I make **opportunities to learn** available to my team? .... ☐ ☐

EMPOWERING EMPLOYEES TO ACHIEVE

Empowering the people you are managing, by giving them the **authority**, **information**, and **tools** they need to do their jobs with greater autonomy, can greatly improve their motivation levels.

PROVIDING SALIENT REWARDS

Employees don't all value the same rewards equally, so try to **tailor your rewards** to get the most out of each individual.

REINFORCING THE RIGHT BEHAVIOUR

Quite often what managers say they want, what they reward, and what they get from their team are quite different. If you verbally espouse innovation but reward doing things by the book, you are sending mixed signals and reinforcing the wrong behaviour. **Think carefully about your rewards** and what they mean, and make sure that you reinforce behaviour that you want to see repeated.

Teaching skills

As a manager, an important part of your role is to help those you are managing to develop their skills. If you can encourage the development of skills such as self-awareness, communication, and time management, you will be rewarded with a high-performing team.

Learning by experience

People learn faster and retain more information if they have to exert some kind of active effort. The famous quote, attributed to Confucius: "I hear and I forget. I see and I remember. I do and I understand" is frequently used to support the value of learning through experience. A major implication of this notion is that new skills can be learned only through experimenting with new behaviours, observing the results, and learning from the experience.

Watching, thinking, and doing

The learning of new skills is maximized when learners get the opportunity to combine watching, thinking, and doing. The experiential learning model encompasses four elements: learning new

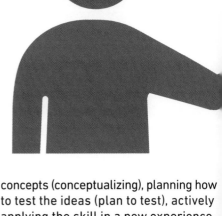

concepts (conceptualizing), planning how to test the ideas (plan to test), actively applying the skill in a new experience (gaining concrete experience), and examining the consequences of the experience (reflective observation). After reflecting on the experience, learners use the lessons they have learned from what happened to create a refined conceptual map of the skill, and the cycle continues.

To use the experiential learning model to teach skills, you need to: ensure that learners understand the skill both conceptually and behaviourally; give them opportunities to practise it; give feedback on how well they are performing the skill; and encourage them to use the skill often enough so that it becomes integrated into their behavioural repertoire.

> **Tip**
>
> **LEARN AT A DISTANCE**
> Employ the experiential learning model remotely by using online materials (videos, articles, blogs, podcasts, tests, presentations...) – create them yourself or get them from a third party. When working one-to-one or giving feedback, use virtual coaching sessions.

How to teach new skills

01 Help learners to form a **conceptual understanding** of a new skill.

02 Plan how they can **test their understanding** of the skill.

03 Get learners to apply the new skill in **concrete experience**.

04 **Observe what happened** and discuss ways in which they can improve.

Encourage others to **use a skill** often enough so that it becomes **integrated into** their behavioural repertoire

Appraising performance

As a manager, you must ensure that objectives are met and also that team members learn how to enhance their performance. Providing feedback through formal performance appraisals can increase productivity and morale, and decrease absenteeism and staff turnover.

Assessing progress

Giving feedback formally in performance appraisal interviews enables you to set goals and monitor achievement, helping to motivate your team. Appraisals allow you to tell how each member is progressing, which can reinforce good behaviour and extinguish bad. But the interview itself is the final step. Appraisal should be a continuous process that starts with establishing and communicating performance standards. Assess how each individual is performing relative to these standards, and then

> Keep your appraisal **goal-oriented**, make sure your feedback is **specific**, and encourage **self-evaluation**

CONDUCTING APPRAISAL INTERVIEWS

Dos	Don'ts
O **Focusing only on feedback that relates to the person's job**	O Sharing your feelings about a person's personality
O **Providing both positive and negative feedback**	O Focusing your comments only on bad performance
O **Sharing first-hand observations as evidence**	O Including rumours and allegations in your appraisal
O **Being unafraid to criticize the person constructively**	O Avoiding offending the other person by sugarcoating your criticism

ASK YOURSELF...

Am I prepared for the appraisal?

		YES	NO
1	Have I **carefully considered** the person's strengths as well as their weaknesses?	☐	☐
2	**Can I substantiate**, with specific examples, all points of praise and criticism?	☐	☐
3	Have I **thought about any problems** that may occur in the appraisal interview?	☐	☐
4	Have I considered **how I will react** to these problems?	☐	☐

...iscuss this in the interview. Take steps to ...mit unconscious bias in the process and ...nsure all employees are judged equally ...y outlining the competences valued in ...ach role and obliging appraisers to give ...vidence to justify their conclusions.

The appraisal interview

...tart by putting the person at ease. ...ost people don't like to hear their ...ork criticized, so be supportive and ...nderstanding and create a constructive ...limate. If you are conducting the ...nterview remotely, there's greater ...oom for miscommunication, so take ...xtra care to talk clearly, listen, and ...e receptive. Begin the interview by ...xplaining what will transpire during ...he appraisal and why. Stay goal-oriented, and make sure your feedback is specific. Where you can, get the person's own perceptions of the problems being addressed – there may be contributing factors you are unaware of. Encourage self-evaluation; people may acknowledge performance problems independently, thus eliminating your need to raise them. They may also offer viable solutions.

Setting action points

At the end of the interview, ask the recipient to rephrase the content of your appraisal. This will indicate if you have communicated your evaluation clearly. Finish by drawing up a step-by-step plan for improvement. Include what needs to be done, by when, and how you will monitor the person's activities.

Leading
others

Leadership is the process of providing direction, influencing and energizing others, and obtaining follower commitment to shared organizational goals. Managers need to lead their team, setting ethical boundaries for them to follow, developing a power base for influencing them to change in positive ways, and helping them improve through coaching and mentoring.

03

Taking an ethical path

Few of us would steal or cheat, but how principled would you be, or should you be, when faced with routine business situations involving ethical choices? As a leader, you need to have a clear understanding of your ethical principles and set a consistent example for your team.

Understanding ethics

Ethics refer to the principles that define good or poor conduct. In the workplace, acting ethically is not just a fanciful idea, it is an everyday occurrence. Consider this dilemma: an employee whose work has been substandard for some time has found another job. You are relieved, but then he asks for a recommendation letter. Do you say no and run the risk that he will not leave? Or do you write it, knowing you are influencing someone else to hire him?

Being responsible

Ethics is important for everyone in an organization, particularly as some unethical acts are also illegal.

Many organizations want employees to behave ethically because such a reputation is good for business, which in turn can mean larger profits. Many employees also want their organizations to behave ethically, citing sustainability and social purpose as increasingly important factors in deciding where to work. Acting ethically is especially crucial for managers. The decisions a manager makes set the standard for those they are managing and help create a tone for the organization. If employees believe all are held to high standards, they are likely to feel better about themselves, their colleagues, and their organization

ASK YOURSELF...
Is what I'm about to do ethical?

		YES	NO
1	Am I **clear** why I'm doing what I'm about to do?	☐	☐
2	Have I acknowledged my **true intentions** in taking this action?	☐	☐
3	Are there any **ulterior motives** behind my action, such as proving myself to my peers or superiors?	☐	☐
4	Will my actions **injure someone**, physically or emotionally?	☐	☐
5	Would I **disclose** to my boss or my family what I plan to do?	☐	☐

Organizations want employees to **behave ethically** as having such a reputation is good for business, which in turn can mean **larger profits**

Developing ethics

The behaviour of managers is under more scrutiny than that of other members of staff, and misdeeds can become quickly and widely known, destroying the reputation of the organization. It is important for managers to develop their own ethical boundaries – lines that they and their employees should not cross. To do this, you need to:

O **Know** and **understand** your organization's **policy** on ethics.

O Anticipate unethical conduct. **Be alert** to situations that may promote unethical behaviour. (Under unusual circumstances, even a normally ethical person may be tempted to act out of character.)

O **Consider all consequences**. Ask yourself questions such as: "What if my actions were described in detail on a local TV news show, or social media? What if I get caught doing something unethical? Am I prepared to deal with the consequences?"

O **Seek opinions** from others. They may have been in a similar situation, or at least can listen and be a sounding board for you.

O Do what you truly believe is right. You have a conscience and are responsible for your behaviour. You need **to be true to your own internal ethical standards**. Ask yourself the simple question: "Can I live with what I have decided to do?"

Ensuring cultural fit

An organization's culture, or personality, refers to the key characteristics that it values and that distinguish it from other organizations. Managers need to be aware of organizational culture because they are expected both to respond to its principles themselves, and to develop an understanding of it in those they are managing.

Analyzing organizational culture

The cultural imperatives of an organization are often not written down or even discussed, but all successful managers must learn what to do and what not to do in their organizations. In fact, the better the match between the manager's personal style and the organization's culture, the more successful the manager is likely to be. Founders create culture in three ways. First, they hire and keep employees who think and feel the way they do. Second, founders indoctrinate and socialize these employees to their way of thinking. Third, founders act as role models, and their personality becomes central to the culture of the organization.

Discerning the culture

Many organizations have given little thought to their culture and do not readily display it. To try to find out more about your organization's culture, you might:

- Observe the surroundings. Look at signs, pictures, dress codes, the degree of openness in offices, and how they are furnished and arranged. Also consider how the firm presents itself on its intranet.
- Listen to the language. For example, do managers use military terms, such as "take no prisoners"? Or do they speak about "intuition", "care", and "our family of customers"?
- Ask different people the same question and compare the answers. How does this firm define success? For what are staff most rewarded? Who is on the fast track and what did they do to get there? Are you happy with your work-life balance?

77%
of people would **consider** a company's **culture** before **applying** for a job there

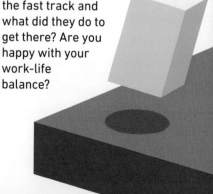

Case study

KEEPING CULTURE CONSISTENT

At coffee retailer Starbucks, all employees go through a set of formal classes during their first few weeks on the job. They are taught the history of the firm, coffee-making techniques, and given coffee-tasting classes. They even receive emotional intelligence training to help them to deliver better customer service. The firm's socialization programme turns out employees who are well versed in the company's culture and can represent Starbucks' obsession with "elevating the coffee experience" for its customers.

ustaining culture

anagers are responsible for sustaining ganizational culture by helping new nployees to learn and adapt. (They may so help hire talent, though this is usually specialist HR task.) A new worker, for ample, must be taught what behaviours e valued by the organization, so that they n learn the "system" and assume the ehaviours appropriate to their role.

> The better the match between your **personal style** as a manager and the **organization's culture**, the more **successful** you are likely to be

Solving problems

Managerial success depends on making the right decisions at the right times. But unless you define a problem and identify its root causes, it is impossible to make appropriate decisions about how to solve it. Effective managers know how to gather and evaluate information that clarifies a problem, develop alternatives, and weigh up the implications of a plan before implementing it. They are able to analyze data and use their teams to develop creative solutions.

Spotting problems

A problem exists when a situation is not what is needed or desired. A major responsibility for all managers is to maintain a constant lookout for existing or potential problems, and to spot them early before they escalate into serious situations – including grievances that have to be dealt with by HR. Managers fulfil this responsibility by keeping channels of communication open, monitoring employees' current performance, and examining deviations from present plans. Four situations can alert managers to possible problems:

- A deviation from past experience
- A deviation from a set plan
- When other people communicate problems to you
- When competitors start to outperform your team or organization

The problem-solving process

Definition is important even if the **solution to the problem** appears to be obvious

01 IDENTIFYING

Being conscious of what is going on around you, so you can spot problems early.

02 DEFINING

Making a careful analysis of the problem to be solved, in order to define it as clearly as possible.

inding solutions

oblem solving involves closing the
p between what is actually taking
ace and a desired outcome. Once you
ve identified a problem that needs to
 addressed, start by analyzing the
oblem and defining it as clearly as you
n. This is a key step: the definition
u generate will have a major impact
 all remaining steps in the process.
you get the definition wrong, all
maining steps will be distorted,
cause you will base them on
sufficient or erroneous information.
finition is important even if the
lution to the problem appears to be
vious – without a full assessment you
ay miss an alternative resolution that
 more advantageous.

   Gather as much information about the
tuation as you can. Try to understand
e goals of all of the parties involved,
d clarify any aspects of the problem
u are unclear about.

Developing an action plan

Once you are satisfied that you have a
full understanding of the issues, develop
courses of action that could provide a
resolution to the problem. There is often
more than one way to solve a problem,
so it is critical to consider all possible
solutions and arrive at several
alternatives from which to choose.

Implementing and monitoring

Your decision will provide you with an
action plan. However, this will be of little
value unless it is implemented effectively.
Defining how, when, and by whom the
action plan is to be implemented and
communicating this to those involved is
what connects the decision with reality.

   Your involvement should not end at
implementation. Establish criteria for
measuring success, then track progress
and take corrective actions when
necessary. Try to develop and maintain
positive attitudes in everyone involved.

03	04	05
MAKING THE DECISION	**IMPLEMENTING**	**FOLLOWING UP**
Evaluating the alternatives and choosing a course of action that will improve the situation in a significant way.	Setting your action plan in motion, by creating a schedule and assigning tasks and responsibilities.	Monitoring progress, to ensure that the desired outcome is achieved.

Building power

Research shows that power is most effective when exercised by those concerned with the interests and needs of others. Learning how to wield your power using social intelligence will help you influence people and develop your career.

Developing power bases

Managerial positions come with the authority to issue directives and allocate rewards and punishments – for example, to assign favourable or unfavourable work tasks, hold performance reviews, and make salary adjustments. But management experts such as Dacher Keltner, author of *The Power Paradox*, argue that true power requires empathy and humility, not forcing or manipulating others into doing your will.

Social intelligence Studies show that socially engaged managers who treat team members with consideratio share power, and create a sense of togetherness win and maintain status.

Modesty Research by University of California, Berkeley professors Dacher Keltner and Cameron Anderson found that modest people were more likely to attain and maintain high status and win respect, while those with inflated egos tended to lose respect.

85%

of midsize firms say it's now more important for managers to **show empathy** than before COVID-19

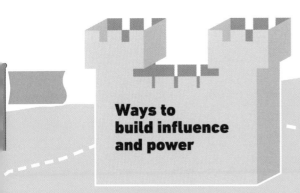

Ways to build influence and power

Being human Artificial Intelligence is taking on many organizational tasks carried out by managers, so emotional intelligence, flexibility, and other more "human" skills are increasingly highly valued and will help boost your status.

Empathy Collectively, we give power to those who serve the interests of the group. Listen and use empathy to see things from the perspective of others so you know how best to collaborate.

Win-win outcomes Research repeatedly shows that it's not manipulative Machiavellian types who rise to power, but individuals who can best understand and advance the interests of others. Power lies with those who can resolve conflicts and mediate tensions in the group.

pression management A socially intelligent e of power brings measurable returns, :luding happier employees who perform tter. In turn this favourably influences w others see, talk about, and evaluate you.

Types of power

Your power within an organization comes from various sources. Use these different types of power in their correct contexts to maximize your effectiveness as a manager.

- **Legitimate power** This derives from your position in the organizational hierarchy and is enhanced by a clear chain of command and corporate structure. In "flat" organizations, which emphasize collective leadership and have few levels of management between staff and the board, this form of power will be limited.
- **Coercive power** The threat of sanction confers power, but should be used

carefully – when the organization is in difficulty or crisis.

- **Referent power** This type derives from being respected and admired by those you manage, and encouraging them to imitate your style. Here, giving staff responsibility for their actions enhances your power. It works best in small workplaces, where you can foster one-to-one relationships.
- **Reward power** This comes from the ability to provide incentives and rewards, such as praise or promotion, to those you manage.

Ways to use managerial power to obtain desired outcomes

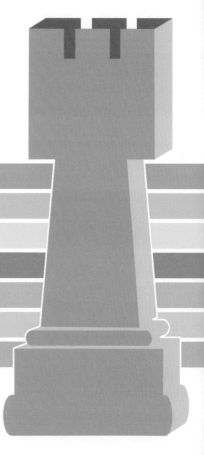

Legitimate power derives from your position in the organizational **hierarchy**, and is enhanced by a clear **chain of command** and corporate structure

HIGHER AUTHORITY

Gain the support of those above you to back your requests. This is only effective in hierarchical bureaucratic organizations where there is great respect for authority.

BARGAINING

Exchange benefits or favours to negotiate outcomes acceptable to both parties. This works best when organizational culture promotes give-and-take cooperation.

ASSERTIVENESS

Be direct and forceful when indicating what you want from others. This strategy is most effective when the balance of power is clearly in your favour.

SANCTIONS

Use organizationally derived rewards and punishments to obtain desired outcomes. This approach is only for influencing those you manage, and may be seen as manipulative.

FRIENDLINESS

Use flattery, create goodwill, act humbly, and be supportive prior to making a request. This works best when you are well liked.

COALITIONS

Develop support in the organization for what you want to happen. This is most effective where final decisions rely on the quantity not the quality of support.

REASONING

Use facts and data to make a logical or rational presentation of ideas. This is most effective when others are trustworthy, open, and logical.

Managing change

Individuals, managers, teams, and organizations that do not adapt to change in timely ways are unlikely to survive in our increasingly turbulent world environment. Managers who anticipate change, learn to adapt to change, and respond flexibly will be the most successful.

Overcoming resistance

Change is the process of moving from a present state to a more desired state in response to internal and external factors. To successfully implement change, you need to possess the skills to convince others of the need for change, identify gaps between the current situation and desired conditions, and create visions for desirable outcomes.

Experienced managers are aware that efforts to change often face resistance. This can be for a variety of reasons, including fear, vested interests, misunderstanding, lack of trust, differing perceptions of a situation, and limited resources. You need to be able to counter this resistance to change through education, participation, and negotiation.

Promoting change

Major change does not happen easily. Effective managers can establish a sense of urgency that the change is needed. If an organization is facing a threat to its survival, this usually gets people's attention. Dramatically declining profits and stock prices are examples, as is the 2020 COVID-19 pandemic, which forced organizations to rethink working practices, supply chains, and delivery mechanisms overnight. But as the world

Tip

TURN TO THE POSITIVE
Try to **use any resistance** to your proposed change **for your benefit**, by making it a stimulus for dialogue and a deeper, more thoughtful analysis of the alternatives.

just to an uncertain, fast-shifting ...st-pandemic world, the ability to ...plement change in the absence of ... obvious crisis is vital for managers. ...ey need to be able to identify potential ...oblems by scanning the external ...vironment, and find ways to convey ...e information broadly and dramatically ... that others understand the need for ...ange. They also have to develop and ...ticulate compelling visions and

strategies to which people will aspire and that will guide the change effort. The vision of the end result should illuminate core principles and values that pull followers together. Lastly, institutionalizing change in the organizational culture refreezes it. New values become instilled in the culture and employees view the changes as normal and integral to operations.

In focus

PHASES OF CHANGE

Planned change progresses through three phases:

Unfreezing This involves helping people see that a change is needed because the existing situation is undesirable. Existing attitudes and behaviours need to be altered during this phase to reduce resistance, by explaining how the change can help increase productivity, for example. Your goal in this phase is to help the participants see the need for change and to increase their willingness to make the change a success.

Changing This involves making the actual change and requires you to help participants let go of old ways of doing things and develop new ones.

Refreezing The final phase involves reinforcing the changes made so that the new ways of behaving become stabilized. If people perceive the change to be working in their favour, positive results will serve as reinforcement, but if not, it may be necessary to use external reinforcements, which can be positive or negative.

Helping others to improve

Helping employees become more competent is an important part of any manager's job. It contributes to a three-way win for the organization, the manager, and the employees themselves. By helping others resolve personal problems and develop skill competencies – and so help them improve their performance – you will motivate your team to achieve better results for themselves and for the organization.

Diagnosing problems

If you can reduce unsatisfactory performance in the people you are managing, you ultimately make your job easier because you will be increasingly able to delegate responsibilities to them. Unsatisfactory performance often has multiple causes. Some causes are within the control of the person experiencing the difficulties, while others are not.

67%

of global employees are not **engaged** with their work, while **18%** are **actively disengaged**

Ways to help others improve

Accept mistakes and use them as **learning opportunities**.

Help **develop action plans** for improvement.

Actively listen to employees and show **genuine interest**.

Recognize and reward even small improvements.

CHECKLIST...

Determining the cause of unsatisfactory performance   **YES**   **NO**

1 Is the person **unaware** that his or her performance is unsatisfactory? If yes, provide feedback .... ☐ ☐

2 Is the person performing poorly through a lack of awareness of **what is expected**? If yes, provide clear expectations .... ☐ ☐

3 Is performance hampered by obstacles **beyond the person's control**? If yes, determine how to remove the obstacles .... ☐ ☐

4 Is the person struggling with not knowing how to **perform a key task**? If yes, provide coaching or training .... ☐ ☐

5 Is **good performance** followed by negative consequences? If yes, determine how to eliminate the negative consequences .. ☐ ☐

6 Is poor performance rewarded by **positive consequences**? If yes, determine how to eliminate the positive reinforcement ... ☐ ☐

Seek to **educate** rather than to assist.	Provide **meaningful feedback** for learning.	Encourage continual **improvement**.
Model the **behaviours** you desire.	Demonstrate **unconditional positive regard** by suspending judgement and evaluation.	Ask questions to **help discover** sources of problems.

Demonstrating positive regard

The relationship between you and the person you are helping is critical to the success of the coaching, mentoring, or counselling you undertake with them. For a helping relationship to be successful it is important to hold the person being helped in "unconditional positive regard". This means that you accept and exhibit warm regard for the person needing help as a person of unconditional self-worth – a person of value no matter what the conditions, problems, or feelings. If you can communicate positive regard, it provides a climate of warmth and safety because the person feels liked and prized as a person. This is a necessary condition for developing the trust that is crucial in a helping relationship.

> The person being helped should be held in "unconditional **positive regard**"

Establish a **non-defensive** climate, characterized by **open communication** and **trust**.

Try to make the person feel **comfortable** and at **ease**.

Start by discussing the purpose of the **helping session**.

Conducting a helping session

Before you speak to someone about how to help them improve their performance, make sure you have **acquired all the facts** about the situation.

Take time to think about **what type of help** the situation requires; consider how the person might react and how they might feel about what you are going to discuss.

Before you discuss the problem you have identified, raise and discuss **positive aspects** of the person's performance.

Mutually define the problem (performance or attitude).

Help the other person **establish an action plan** that includes **specific goals** and dates.

Mutually determine the causes. Do not interpret or psychoanalyze behaviour; instead, **ask questions** such as, "What's causing the lack of motivation you describe?"

After the session, make sure that you **follow up** to see how the person is **progressing**, and modify the action plan if necessary.

Affirm your confidence in the person's ability to make needed changes based on his or her **strengths** or past history.

Summarize what has been agreed upon.

Make sure **expectations** are **clearly understood**.

Counselling others

Counselling is the discussion of emotional problems in order to resolve them or to help the person better cope. Problems that might require counselling include divorce, serious illness, financial problems, interpersonal conflicts, drug and alcohol abuse, and frustration over a lack of career progress. Although most managers are not qualified as psychologists, there are several things managers can do in a counselling role before referring someone to a professional therapist.

Confidentiality is of paramount importance when counselling others. To open up and share the reasons for many personal problems, people must feel that they can trust you and that there is no threat to their self-esteem or their reputation with others. Emphasize that you will treat in confidence everything that the other person says regarding personal matters.

In focus

FIRST-RATE FEEDBACK

People need feedback about the consequences of their actions if they are to learn what works and what doesn't and then change their actions to become more effective. Carefully thought-out feedback can increase performance and positive personal development. Applying feedback in the helping process involves:

- Describing observed behaviours and the results and consequences of those behaviours.
- Assessing the impact of the observed behaviours in terms of organizational vision and goals.
- Predicting the personal consequences for the person involved if no changes take place.
- Recommending changes the person could make to improve their behaviour.

This sequence of actions applies whether the type of help being given to the person is coaching, mentoring, or counselling.

92%

of employees agree that "negative feedback, if appropriately delivered, is **highly effective** at **improving performance**"

Confidentiality is paramount when **counselling others**: people must feel that they can trust you

Tip

BE SUPPORTIVE
Reassure those you are counselling that their **problems have solutions** and that they have the ability to improve the situation.

Dealing with personal problems

Getting a person to recognize that he or she has a problem is often the first step in helping deal with it. You can then follow up by helping gain insights into feelings and behaviours, and by exploring the available options.

Sometimes people just need a sounding board for releasing tension, which can become a prelude to clarifying the problem, identifying possible solutions, and taking corrective action. Talking things through in a counselling session can help people sort out their feelings into more logical and coherent thoughts.

Above all, be supportive and provide reassurance. People need to know that their problems have solutions. If problems are beyond a person's capability to solve, explain how professional treatment can be obtained, through Employee Assistance Programmes, for example, or wellbeing plans.

Coaching and mentoring

Coaching is the process of helping people improve performance. A coach analyzes performance, provides insight on how to improve, and offers the leadership, motivation, and supportive climate to help achieve that improvement. In mentoring relationships, a more experienced person formally pairs up with a less experienced one to help show them "the ropes" and to provide emotional support and encouragement.

Helping others develop

As a coach, a manager's job is to help members of their team develop skills and improve. This involves providing instruction, guidance, advice, and encouragement. Effective coaches first establish a supportive climate that promotes development. It is particularly important that you remain non-judgemental and understanding throughout the process, try to solve problems jointly, and educate those you are coaching about how to solve their own problems in the future. As you learn more about the person you are coaching, try to determine the sources of any problems you discover, and provide meaningful feedback.

Coaching a process

To coach successfully, you will need to follow these steps:
- Explain and then demonstrate the process
- Observe the person practising the process
- Provide immediate, specific feedback
- Express confidence in the person's ability
- Agree on follow-up actions.

The role of a mentor

The goal of a mentor is to help a less experienced person achieve his or her career goals. Mentors perform as both coaches and counsellors as they guide their less experienced associates towards improved performance. Mentoring can help new organization members gain a better understanding of the organization's goals, culture, and advancement criteria. It can also help them become more politically savvy and avoid potential career traps. As a mentor, try to help others reduce the stress caused by uncertainty about how to do things and deal with challenging assignments. Be a source of comfort when newer, less experienced people just need to let off steam or discuss career dilemmas.

55%

of **global companies** run internal coaching programmes

Three key skills for successful coaching

01

FINDING WAYS TO IMPROVE PERFORMANCE

O Help others improve by observing what they do, asking questions, listening, and crafting unique improvement strategies.

02

INFLUENCING OTHERS TO CHANGE THEIR BEHAVIOUR

O Monitor people's progress and development, and recognize and reward even small improvements.

O Involve others in decision-making processes – this helps to encourage people to be responsive to change.

O Break large, complex projects into series of simpler tasks – this can boost confidence as the simpler tasks are achieved.

O Be a role model for the qualities that you expect from others, such as openness and commitment.

03

CREATING A SUPPORTIVE CLIMATE

O Use active listening, empower others to implement appropriate ideas, and be available for assistance, guidance, and advice.

Managing careers

In today's rapidly changing business landscape, managers need to actively manage their careers and provide career guidance to those they are managing. To determine where and how you can best contribute, you need to know yourself, continually develop yourself, and be able to ascertain when and how to change the work you do.

Charting your own career path

Self-assessment is an ongoing process in career management. Successful careers develop when people are prepared for opportunities because they know their strengths, their methods of work, and their values. Self-directed career management is a process by which individuals guide, direct, and influence the course of their careers.

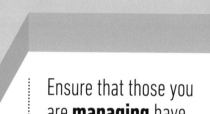

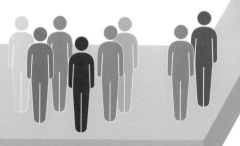

> Ensure that those you are **managing** have **reasonable** workloads

This requires exploration and awareness of not only yourself, but also your environment. Individuals who are proactive and collect relevant information about personal needs, values, interests, talents, and lifestyle preferences are more likely to be satisfied and productive when searching for job opportunities, to develop successful career plans, and to be productive in their jobs and careers.

Driving forward

The first step in self-directed career management is planning. Taking your strengths, limitations, and values into account, start searching the environment for matching opportunities. Use the information you gather to establish realistic career goals and then develop a strategy to achieve them. As you progress through your career plan, regularly undertake performance appraisals to make sure that you are remaining on track and that your goals haven't changed.

irecting others

e most important thing you can do to ntribute to the career development of hers is to instil in them the need to take sponsibility for their own careers. Then u can provide support that will enable

them to add to their skills, abilities, and knowledge, in order to maintain their employability within the organization and avoid obsolescence as a result of technological advances. To help those you are managing develop their careers:

- **Keep your team updated** about the organization's goals and future strategies so that they will know where the organization is headed and be better able to develop a personal career development plan to share in that future.
- **Create growth opportunities** for your team, to give them new, interesting, and professionally challenging work experiences.
- **Offer financial assistance**, such as tuition reimbursement for college courses or skills training.
- **Allow paid time off** from work for off-the-job training, and ensure that those you are managing have reasonable workloads so that they are not precluded from having time to develop new skills, abilities, and knowledge.

In focus

CAREER STAGES

Individuals just beginning their careers are usually more concerned with identifying organizations that have the potential to satisfy their career goals and match their values. After settling into a job, focus shifts to achieving initial successes, gaining credibility, learning to get along with their boss, and managing their image. Managers in the middle of their careers are more concerned with career reappraisal, adding to their skill set, and becoming more of a generalist. In the later stages of their careers, managers focus more on teaching and mentoring others and leaving a contribution before retirement.

Working
remotely

Remote working requires a different approach to operating in a shared space. You need to learn how to organize your days, stay motivated, and achieve a healthy balance between your professional and home life. As a manager, the example you set will inspire other colleagues to excel from afar.

Rethinking the office

Around the world, managers are taking a more flexible approach to how and where their staff work. Tech advances are enabling effective remote collaboration and many leaders are seeing the benefits in terms of better focused and happier employees. Do you still need a shared office at all?

Increasing productivity

While some organizations still need staff to collaborate in person, most are now unlikely to insist on everyone working in the same physical space all the time. Even before the COVID-19 pandemic struck, many businesses embraced the benefits of letting staff work remotely where possible. Adopting home-working days frees up room in work spaces and gives staff time to concentrate on tasks with fewer distractions. It also saves them commuting time, helping to achieve a healthier work/life balance. Any employers sceptical about long-term home working for employees should note that in 2019, 85 per cent of businesses reported increases in productivity after introducing flexible working. So, you can argue that the traditional shared work space is no longer needed in some fields. But whether at home, in a co-working setup, at company premises, or in a combination of locations, staff still need a suitable space with the right technology in place for them to function.

Personal connections

Better meeting technology allows you to stay in "face-to-face" contact with your colleagues. Remote working does not have to be impersonal.

50%

of employees work outside of their main office for at least **two-and-a-half days a week**

THE DAY HOME WORKING WENT VIRAL

Professor Robert Kelly and his family became internet sensations in 2017 when his children burst in on a live TV interview. Sitting in jacket and tie in his home office in Busan, South Korea, the political analyst looked mortified. But he later gave a cheerful interview alongside his family about the realities of working at home. Fast-forward to the 2020 pandemic, and the difficulties faced by workers balancing professional and home lives during lockdown resulted in several similar interviews. Such incidents highlight the demands on today's employees that can disrupt home-working and their ability to stick to the traditional nine-to-five.

Global talent

Remote working gives you the chance to recruit talent anywhere in the world – not just people within commuting distance of your HQ – and to build a global team.

Digital tools

Cloud storage and collaborative software mean you and your employees can access what they need and work effectively as a team, wherever they are.

Clever communications

As a manager, you have many ways to interact with your staff remotely and get everyone collaborating. These include messaging apps, email, video conferencing, and intranets.

Setting goals

When it comes to setting goals, start with your own. Does working remotely change the way you approach them? Armed with a clear plan for yourself, you can work with each member of your team to create goals that challenge and motivate.

Leading by example

Whether you manage staff who work remotely, or it is you who works in a different location from them, set the standard for effective working by deciding a clear structure for your day. Create a weekly list of priority tasks to slot into that structure to help you reach your personal goals. Encourage team members to do the same, bearing in mind their day needn't look exactly like yours. They can still hit their goals when working flexible hours and terms.

> **Clarity is key** when it comes to setting goals. Make sure **everyone understands** exactly what's expected of them

Creating SMART goals when working remotely

To be effective, each goal you set should be SMART: Specific, Measurable, Achievable, Relevant, and Time-bound. When working remotely, you may need to adapt the scope of each SMART goal and be more diligent with progress checks.

S SPECIFIC

M MEASURABLE

A ACHIEVABLE

R RELEVANT

T TIME-BOUND

onitoring progress

port back frequently on your progress
your own manager, highlighting any
oblems you're facing as soon as they
se. Book one-to-one catch-ups with
ose who report directly to you to
view goal progress, and be ready
adapt if you need to.

t goals with specific parameters –
no, what, where, when, and why.
cord everything in an online tool
uch as Workday) that allows team
embers to access relevant
formation wherever they are.

ake your goals measurable by
king them to a quantity – number
sales, for example. With remote
ams, think about **breaking goals
wn** into smaller ones to minimize
e risk of slipping off schedule.

als should challenge, but never set
ople up to fail. Does the person in
estion have all the resources they
ed to achieve this goal remotely?
d extra contingency time for each
e, just in case.

om a distance, people can lose a
nse of where their work fits into the
der business. **Align every goal** with
e strategic goals of the organization,
owing each person how their job is
levant to the company as a whole.

adlines are not only motivating, but
warding once you meet them. **Set
firm end date** and book in regular
eckpoints. Avoid open time frames,
pecially for staff new to working
motely and dealing with lots of change.

Staying positive

Working remotely might leave you
feeling that your efforts are going
unnoticed, and it's the same for your
staff. Maintain good contact with your
team, taking time to celebrate individual
and group successes. This could be via
a quick wrap-up video call to share
positive feedback on achieved goals, or
a reward system (vouchers or a bottle of
wine, for instance). Recognizing people's
efforts inspires goodwill, improves how
people view your management skills,
and helps employees working apart
from colleagues feel less isolated.

In focus

KEEPING FOCUSED

Loss of focus happens
wherever you're working, and
always results in decreased
productivity. When managing
staff remotely, you need to
strike a balance between giving
people space to perform tasks
in peace, while also ensuring
work is completed as required.

- Use meetings efficiently –
plan them well, get to the
point, and make sure
everyone has time to
complete any related tasks.
- Encourage staff to check
emails regularly, but not
obsessively – turning off
notifications for an hour
can boost concentration.
- Keep your written
communications clear and to
the point, helping others to
focus on the task in hand.

Working with others

To be an effective remote manager, you need to understand your staff and colleagues. Get to know people properly, and foster a culture of respect for their individual circumstances, personalities, and working styles.

Collaborating at a distance

When you don't share a work space, you can't pick up on many of the visual cues that people use when communicating – or give them out yourself. This means your interpersonal skills need to come to the fore. Take time to find out about your staff through individual catch-ups, listening carefully, communicating clearly, and showing empathy. This will help you to collaborate successfully, even if you never meet in person.

Communicating well

Stay in regular touch with your team, but bear in mind that video calls can be uncomfortable and anxiety-inducing for some people. Messaging apps such as Slack are good for getting quick answers but a phone call can be more personal if you need to elaborate on an issue or gauge a mood. If you're not sure what's best, ask the individual how they would prefer to talk.

This call is **overrunning** again, but I have to collect my kids

She knows I'm **hard of hearing**, but she won't stop **calling** for updates

I blocked my **lunch hour** in the calendar, but my manager wants a **meeting**

He's forgotten I'm **part-time** and given me an **impossible deadline**

Respecting personal circumstances

Everyone needs a bit of extra support and understanding from their manager at some point. If a staff member reveals they have a health condition, find out what they need to get their work done without cost to their wellbeing. Consider what it might be like for colleagues who live and work alone – do they need additional support from you? Recognize that some people have caring duties for others that put extra pressure on their time. (Note mothers often have the most limited working hours, and workloads don't always shrink to fit.) By working on an individual level, you can come up with flexible solutions to help everyone stay on track.

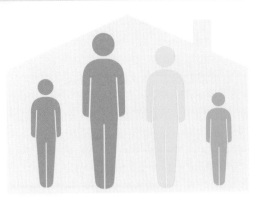

Find out about your staff through **individual** catch-ups, **listening carefully**, communicating clearly, and **showing empathy**

ASK YOURSELF...
Am I an inclusive manager?

		YES	NO
1	Do I use **simple language** that everyone will understand?	☐	☐
2	Do I consider if I'm talking to someone in their second language?	☐	☐
3	Do I take time to find out about **the other person's culture** and any related preferences?	☐	☐
4	Do I offer to **switch to video** so others can **lip read**?	☐	☐
5	Do I take **differing schedules** and personal circumstances into account when I book a meeting?	☐	☐
6	Do I invite **every voice** to be heard?	☐	☐
7	Do I pay attention to **the timing of calls and time zones** when scheduling a meeting with international team members?	☐	☐

Keeping flexible

The best managers are both flexible enough to accommodate differences and capable of adapting to change. In a remote environment, you need to come up with practical solutions to individual scenarios, striking a balance that works for all.

Understanding difference

Your employees don't need to work identically to perform well. Offering flexible working conditions gives you access to a broader range of talents, reflects well on your business, and enhances your reputation as a manager. Once you understand the individual circumstances and requirements of your team members, you can define hours and terms that work for them, without affecting their workload.

Finding time to connect

It can be helpful to overlap as a team for a few hours a day. But if a member is on the other side of the world, or works completely different hours, you will have to come up with other ways to connect. This could be a short bi-weekly virtual meeting or a daily handover email. Occasionally asking someone to join a meeting outside of their agreed hours is fine, but don't make it the norm.

Adapting old habits

THINK BEFORE YOU BOOK

Do you really need that meeting? If you do, does everyone on the team have to be there? Get in the habit of booking shorter slots with carefully considered attendees, minimizing disruption for yourself and others.

BE OPEN TO NEW TECHNOLOGY

Review your existing communication technology and software. Search online and seek recommendations for alternative options that are accessible, simple to use, and affordable.

GIVE PROMPT FEEDBACK

Managers can hold up progress if they don't provide feedback. Respond promptly, so everyone can perfect their projects and move on. If someone has done a particularly good job, tell them – this is especially important for those feeling isolated. When giving negative feedback, be polite, honest, and ready to provide support.

earning to let go

you're new to remote working, you
ay notice a tendency in yourself to
icromanage. This shows a lack of
ust and can cause frustration. When
u're delegating and can't oversee a
sk in person, keep in regular contact
 stay up-to-date, and offer support,
t avoid excessive monitoring.
member that delegating not only
lps you balance your own workload,
t broadens the professional
perience of your staff, priming
em for career progression.

> ## Tip
>
> ### SHARE YOUR SCHEDULE
> **Work calendars** are
> powerful tools for remote
> working. Use one to let
> people know **when you
> are or aren't available**.
> Make sure everyone in
> the team does the same.

Balancing work and life

Working remotely brings many benefits for work-life balance. But it can also erode boundaries between your job and your personal time, compelling you to put in more hours and be on call around the clock. Be firm with yourself and others about maintaining a healthy equilibrium

Setting boundaries

Working more intensely over busy periods is fine, but don't let work stress take over. When you're working remotely, you often feel obliged to do more, especially if you're at home. Set boundaries and share them with your colleagues. Some examples:

- Don't check work messages after hours.
- Respect your own and others' flexible working arrangements.
- Take leave when you need it and encourage others to do the same.
- Put away your work things at the end of the day.
- Move away from your work area when you make personal calls or catch up with a family member.

Tip

FIND YOUR POWER HOUR
Work out **when you're at your best** during the workday and schedule your trickier tasks for that period. You will find you **move through your to-do list** much more efficiently, making it more likely you wrap up on time at the end of each day.

Case study

MAKING BALANCE A PRIORITY

In 2020, Nationwide Building Society brought in a series of new measures to help its remote staff find a healthy work-life balance. The society encouraged employees to use their calendars to re-create some of the structure they had lost after switching from office life to home working. It suggested blocking out virtual commuting time, organizing daily team calls for social catch-ups, and instituted a no-meetings rule over the lunch hour. It also encouraged employees to be more proactive about looking after themselves by providing free company-wide access to Unmind, a mental health platform full of practical information designed to help people monitor and improve their wellbeing.

CHECKLIST...

Achieving balance in your life

	YES	NO
1 Do I often have **time for my hobbies** outside of work?	☐	☐
2 Do I have a **regular exercise routine**?	☐	☐
3 Do I usually get **a good night's sleep**?	☐	☐
4 Do I have **enough energy** to get me through the day?	☐	☐
5 Do I **express my feelings**?	☐	☐
6 Do I have a **clear sense of purpose** in both my personal and work life?	☐	☐
7 Do I make a **real contribution** at work?	☐	☐
8 Do I know **who I am and am I happy** with that?	☐	☐
9 Do I have the chance to **relax properly** after work?	☐	☐

Structuring your time

Working remotely brings new distractions and disruption, so it's important to have a sensible structure for each day. Things run more smoothly when you have a plan. Start when you say you will, give tasks the attention they deserve, remember to take breaks – and finish on time

Planning your day

As a manager, you must be available to your team, but you must also reserve time and energy for yourself. Each day write a list of the tasks you need to achieve, both work-related and personal (team meeting, review Project A, call plumber), and refer to it often. Plan in breaks and stress-busting activities, too. Time-management coach Elizabeth Grace Saunders recommends using what she calls a "time budget". Start out by calculating how many hours you have to "spend" each week in order to get a clea sense of what you can reasonably handl Estimate how long each item on your list will take and note it down – that will sho you how achievable your plan is. If it's to much, simply adjust to fit.

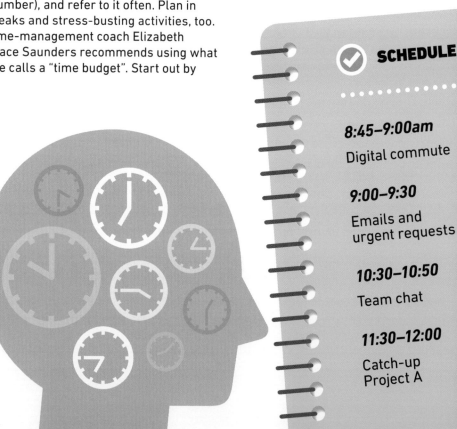

✓ **SCHEDULE**

8:45–9:00am
Digital commute

9:00–9:30
Emails and
urgent requests

10:30–10:50
Team chat

11:30–12:00
Catch-up
Project A

Using your calendar

Your daily task list is just for you, but your online calendar is for everyone you work with. Use it to clearly show when you're available to collaborate. Block out times when you need to work uninterrupted and use the period you would have spent travelling to work to draw a distinct line between personal and work time. Enjoy this "digital commute" however you like: 10 minutes listening to your favourite music, a quick stroll, a five-minute meditation – whatever prepares you for the day and helps you wind down again.

12:00–1:00pm
Lunch

2:00–2:30
1:1 with Rachel

3:00–3:30
School run

3:30–4:30
Prep for coaching session

5:30–5:45
Digital commute

REDUCING STRESS

There are lots of things you can do to lower stress levels while working remotely. Start by muting email notifications when you need to concentrate. Set reminders to take screen breaks, eat your lunch, or simply get out of your chair and stretch. Use your break times to walk, turn on your mindfulness app, or simply take some deep breaths. Now and again, suggest a work social, such as a virtual team meal. Hold this at the end of the day so you can catch up informally over an early dinner. Without a train to catch or traffic to beat, it's easy to let a task drag on past your official hours. Be strict with yourself about wrapping up as planned, turning everything off, and closing the door (literally, if possible) on work.

Learn to **say "no"** when you need to. It shuts down **unreasonable requests** and stops you heading down the path to **burnout**

Understanding personalities

Getting your team working fluidly together is about more than meshing skill sets, it's about managing personalities. The process of understanding people's characters is different when remote working but no less vital. At the same time, be sure not to neglect yourself.

Assessing personality

When asked to describe their characters, people often describe themselves as "introverts" or "extroverts". In a remote setting where people can't interact in person, these traits can be more pronounced: extroverts may become more forceful in their opinions, while introverts may grow more reticent.

Your role isn't to label personalities, but to understand and work with them. When teams meet, personalities affect one other. Quieter members feel intimidated by colleagues who won't stop talking, while those who thrive on thinking out loud get frustrated by those who prefer their own space. Your goal is to get everyone working well together.

Should I say something?

Hmm, I'm not sure that's right

No, I'm sure they've already thought of it

Tip

LEAVE EGOS AT THE DOOR
Every opinion is valid but **"scoring points"** against one another just hurts the team. Professionalism means being able to work with others to achieve a shared goal, so talk to your staff about leaving egos at the door – **your own included**.

IMPOSTOR SYNDROME?

If you've ever felt out of your depth, you're not alone. "Impostor syndrome" was first identified in an influential 1970s study that estimated that up to 70 per cent of people will at some point question their ability to do what's expected of them professionally. In 2018, former US First Lady Michelle Obama told an audience in London that she still experiences impostor syndrome. The syndrome has no clear cause. Theories range from perfectionism, to personality traits such as anxiety, and early formative experiences of "not being good enough". More important is to understand that it's a normal response that can affect anyone, at any level, in any profession. If you think you might be experiencing impostor syndrome, talk to colleagues and friends, and get your fears out in the open. They can help you reframe your thoughts, and focus on your positive qualities. You might even discover they have had similar experiences.

Managing interactions

When your employees are working apart from each other, you need to spend more time making sure everyone is on the same track. That means more time in meetings, where personalities soon become apparent. You may need to rein in more vociferous colleagues, or encourage quieter ones to contribute. You can discuss how individuals like to work in one-on-one chats. You will want to support those who feel uncomfortable speaking up, but be aware that not everyone reacts well to being forced out of their "comfort zone". Let people know they can raise issues privately for you to address with the group later.

That's a really good point, thanks for raising it

Before we go into that, let's hear Asif's take on this

LEADERSHIP

Understanding
leadership

**When you take up a leadership role, you will be expected
to juggle multiple tasks – from meeting goals through to
developing new business opportunities – with multiple
responsibilities. In today's fast-changing world, that
means not only making sure your team follows the same
organizational vision and values, but also managing risk
and building resilience.**

05

Defining the challenge

If you thrive on thinking creatively, inspiring and guiding people, experimenting with different approaches, and making intuitive decisions, you are on the way to being a leader. But truly accomplished leaders also possess sound problem-solving skills, a strong vision, and empathy.

Thinking leadership

Leaders are made rather than born. And while a real desire to lead is a prerequisite for leadership, the key skills you need to lead can be learned. Leadership has many facets: it is the ability to inspire others to overcome challenges, accept continuous change, and achieve goals. It is the capacity to build strong, effective teams, and use your influence to persuade and steer. It is about having a vision and values, and about taking care of the people around you. The old idea of one person at the top issuing orders is on its way out. Leadership now is about creating the conditions for all to rise, and building the structures and cultures that empower any team member to lead when required. In today's dynamic world, we are all potential leaders.

MANAGEMENT

Tip

BE NIMBLE
To be a **good leader,** stay close to your team, and use your **judgement** to move between leadership and management roles as necessary.

BEING A LEADER

Do's	Don'ts
○ Learning quickly what motivates team members	○ Thinking yesterday's result will still count tomorrow
○ Asking your team for their view on the situation	○ Being out of touch with your own emotions
○ Thinking beyond what happens in the short term	○ Not noticing what is going on around you
○ Knowing how to train and develop your team	○ Not asking for feedback on your leadership and ideas
○ Setting standards to build a team you can rely on	○ Not keeping physically fit and thinking positively

LEADERSHIP

A **leader** creates a bold vision and **inspires others** to believe in it, while a **manager** puts the vision into practice by **steering the actions of staff**

Leading and managing

Leadership is a substantially different role from management. A leader is someone who creates a bold vision and inspires others to believe in it, while a manager seeks to put the vision into practice by steering the day-to-day actions and behaviours of her or his employees. You probably aspire to be called a leader rather than a manager but, despite their differences, the two roles remain intrinsically linked. Sound management requires some leadership skills, and great leaders are – or know what it takes to be – good managers.

When you move into a leadership role you won't and can't abandon managing altogether. To be credible as a leader, you need to acknowledge the past and what is currently happening, at the same time as focusing on the future.

Leading from within

The job of a leader is to gift others a sense of purpose and self-worth. This is impossible to do with any conviction if you don't understand your own strengths and weaknesses, or if you are uncertain about the direction in which you want to take your professional and personal life. Improving self-awareness is an essential part of growing into a more effective leader and becoming alert to the effects you are having on others.

Being a frontrunner

People respect leaders who embrace strong values and take responsibility for their own choices in life. To demonstrate this internal strength you need to be seen to be leading by example. Show your team that you have the confidence to take risks, that you can persist through difficult times, and that you are prepare to keep on learning, adapting, and creating new business opportunities, as well as listening to their needs.

Defining thinking styles

STYLE	CHARACTERISTICS	QUESTIONS ASKED
TACTICAL	O Accepts direction O Focuses on how to achieve **a goal** O **Plans** and thinks through any actions **logically**	O How can we achieve the best result in the least time? O How can we organize the actions into a clear plan? O What are the most important things to do or coordinate?
OPERATIONAL	O Sees **opportunities** for action and improvement O Focuses on **practical actions** and implementation in complex situations	O What action can we take? O What needs to be done? O When can we start?
STRATEGIC	O Thinks any problems out from **first principles** O Redefines problems and **confidently** challenges issues upwards	O What if...? O Why have we ruled out these other courses of action? O Why not do this instead? O Who else needs to be involved?

nowing yourself

ople don't all think in the same way.
derstanding your own thinking style
d the styles of others around you
ll give you some valuable leadership
ols. The term "thinking style" does
t refer to your IQ, but how you
ocess information. Broadly, we
n distinguish between three styles:
ctical, operational, and strategic.

Most people tend to get stuck using
st one of the thinking styles. But by
cognizing your own thinking style
u begin to ask different questions
d think about problems in fresh and
citing new ways. By doing this you
ork more effectively with your team
ecause you can understand how they
ink and communicate, and you can
lk to people in their own "language".

We can recognize three
thinking styles: tactical,
operational, and strategic

Leadership styles

Psychologist Daniel Goleman popularized the concept of Emotional Intelligence. He developed the idea that emotions are important in management and identified six leadership styles (see below). Many people use several styles at different times. Goleman found that the visionary style had the most positive impact, but coaching is increasingly key.

When you **embrace the values** by which you live and apply them to your **role as a leader**, people will respect your **sincerity** and sense that you **wish others to succeed**

Leadership styles

COMMANDING

○ Demands that people comply

○ Drive to achieve, self-control

○ **Key phrase:** "Do what I tell you"

○ Negative impact

VISIONARY

○ Leads with a clear vision

○ Self-confidence, empathy

○ **Key phrase:** "Come with me"

○ Most positive impact

AFFILIATIVE

○ Creates harmony, builds bonds

○ Empathy, good relationships, and communication skills

○ **Key phrase:** "People come fir

○ Positive impact

eveloping self-awareness

be effective, you need to lead from
e inside out – what you really think and
lue should emerge in your behaviour.
think as a leader, you should look to
ur self-awareness as well as your
wareness of the outside world.

Leading from within is not just about
eing true to your own principles – it also
rings results. When you embrace the
values by which you live and apply
them to your role as a leader, people
will respect your sincerity, acknowledge
the stake you have in your work and
in your team, and sense that you
wish others to succeed. Growing
self-awareness means analyzing your
thoughts and emotions, seeking as
much feedback from others as possible,
and developing keen listening skills.

EMOCRATIC

Consensus through
participation

Collaboration,
team spirit, and
communication
skills

Key phrase: "What
do you think?"

Positive impact

PACESETTING

O Sets high
performance
standards

O Drive to achieve,
conscientiousness

O **Key phrase:**
"Do as I do"

O Negative impact

COACHING

O Develops skills
in other people

O Developing others,
empathy, self-
awareness

O **Key phrase:**
"Try this"

O Positive impact

O Now increasingly
important

Tip

COMMIT TO CHANGE
Seek out an **experienced** coach to guide you in building **EI**. The **transformation** means you changing your **attitudes** and habits, as well as learning **new skills,** and requires a real **commitment** – in time and resources – from you and from your organization.

Applying self-knowledge

The benefits of self-knowledge in the workplace may not be immediately apparent when set alongside other, more practical and cognitive skills, but its value has been acknowledged by psychologists for decades. The term Emotional Intelligence (EI) was coined to describe an ability to identify, discriminate between, and use one's own and others' feelings to guide your thoughts and actions. The importance of EI cannot be overstated – there are many studies that indicate that EI is a fa better indicator of leadership potential than standard measures of intelligence such as IQ. The emotions that leaders experience affect the culture of an organization, shaping productivity, employee satisfaction, loyalty, and so having a real influence on results.

Using emotional intelligence

RECOGNIZING EMOTIONS

REGULATING EMOTIONS

USING EMOTIONS

EMPATHIZING

NURTURING

The **emotions** that **leaders experience** affect the **culture** of an organization

ssessing the benefits

nderstanding and controlling your
ner self has some real applications
at benefit you and the organization:
Being able to control your temper,
to elevate yourself from boredom,
or to turn dejection into positive
energy are all desirable abilities.
Knowing that sad or negative moods
tend to bring your focus on to details,
while happy moods direct you to new
ideas and solutions, improves your
productivity and time management.

- Confronting and analyzing your
  fears may illuminate a problem
  you are facing, so this may lead
  to a solution and save you time.

Expertise in the key competencies
of Emotional Intelligence opens the
door to more sophisticated ways of
forming and sustaining productive
relationships. What's more, these
competencies can be learned through
training and practice. So you will be
able to change your behaviour
in a genuine, sustained manner.

○ Accurately **identifying and categorizing** your own feelings
and the feelings of others.

○ **Being aware,** moment-by-moment, of what you are feeling.

○ Recognizing that **how you feel influences how you think.**

○ Knowing **which of your moods** are best for different situations.

○ Not letting others **manipulate** your emotions.

○ Using **deliberate strategies** to make your feelings – even
negative ones – work for you.

○ Harnessing emotions so that you can take **positive actions,**
even in the face of difficulty.

○ Recognizing that **emotions provide information** about others.

○ Being able to **see a situation** from another's point-of-view.

○ Genuinely **caring** for others.

○ Showing **real appreciation** for peoples' contributions.

○ Having others' best interests at heart when setting goals.

Leading through vision

As a business leader, you will be expected to set out the values of an organization and provide its stakeholders with an emotionally appealing and achievable vision of the future. You will need clear, thoughtful communication at every level in order to develop this vision and translate it into medium-term strategies and day-to-day action.

Setting out the vision

Leaders focus on developing a vision and overall aims, and inspiring and helping team members as they figure out how to achieve the agreed objectives in a way consistent with the organization's values.

A business vision is a description of your future as a team or organization. It outlines what things will look like when we get to where we want to be. Your leadership role may be to develop the vision and strategic objectives at the top of your organization, or it may be to devise your team plan in alignment with a bigger corporate strategy.

Tip

EXPLAIN WHY

"Why" needs to be **explained** in two ways: "Because of A..." (referring to a past/present reason) and "In order to do B..." (explaining possible **future consequences).**

In focus

JUST REWARDS

Think laterally about the way you reward members of your team. Financial rewards often have less motivational value than your recognition and thanks. If you are respected by your team, your greatest gift is your time. Make time to give full attention to each person in your team at regular intervals. Never over-promise and under-deliver future benefits to your team members.

Developing the vision

Involve your team in developing the vision from the start – if they are shaping it early on, they will be more likely to embrace it. Begin by writing it down. As you move forward, you will need to restate and recreate the vision by communicating with your team through open question and answer sessions, one-to-one reviews and team meetings. Soon each person will learn how to make a meaningful individual contribution towards team goals.

People are motivated by a clear understanding of what they need to do to fulfil the vision, by when, how well, and why. These are key signposts on the journey to their professional development and to the achievement of the team's vision. Your job is to help everyone in your team to plan the route, and to review their progress.

Each person will learn how to make **a contribution** towards **team goals**

Working with teams

Your key tasks as leader are to inspire emotional attachment to the vision developed and to make success visible. This will help team members see that their individual work counts and doing their best really does lead to a better life for all concerned.

1 O **Give everyone a role** to play in implementing the team vision and ask them to report back to you on what has gone exceptionally well and what not so well.

2 O **Ask individuals** to present highlights to the rest of the team so that everyone can learn about doing things in new ways. When you review these practical steps with the team, keep linking them back to the overall vision.

3 O **Remember to say** "thank you" individually and in front of the team to help them keep their momentum and motivation.

4 O **Celebrate team successes** to keep the team moving forwards together. Recognize even small steps in the right direction.

5 O **Explore** with individual team members their unique mix of values, life experiences, knowledge, and skills plus potential abilities. Understand what specifically motivates each person to engage with their work and willingly release the extra they have to give.

Growing with your role

Growth is built into the vision of most organizations; and when an organization grows, its leaders must be prepared to adapt with it. Your role as a leader may become bigger and more strategic with each organizational transition, so anticipating change is a cornerstone of thinking like an effective leader.

Start-up

When an organization starts up, it is entrepreneurial – focused on delivering a new service to new customers. Often, communication is informal, and people are prepared to put in long hours. Customer feedback is quick and the small group of people responds rapidly with enthusiasm and energy.

Leadership at this stage is about keeping close to customers and staff, and encouraging new ideas. As a leader, you may well be involved in frontline activities as well as decisions.

3x

more revenue
is generated by
founder-run large
US companies
over 15 years

Rapid growth

As the organization grows, you may start to see problems with the quality of delivery. Communication with the team may become more formal and some of the initial energy and initiative can be lost. More of your time will be spent on designing and implementing systems, structures, and standards.

At this stage, you need to work hard at remaining accessible to people who seek your advice and resist retreating into a purely management role.

ontinued growth

e next organizational transition occurs
hen you begin to realize that you can no
nger control everything – there are not
ough hours in the day. You may notice
at team members are complaining
out how long it takes for decisions
be made. They may ask for greater
eedom to make their own decisions.

At this point, you should begin to recognize the need to delegate – essential if you are to retain and develop staff. You should be putting increasing amounts of your time and effort into leadership and communication and less into your original expertise – for example, accounting, sales, marketing, engineering, or operations.

> You should be putting **increasing amounts** of your time and effort into **leadership and communication**

Devolution

As the organization continues to grow, you may become part of a high-level core leadership team directing strategy and co-ordination, while a group of managers in business units lead teams on a devolved basis.

You need to become a strong communicator because a significant part of your role is resolving tensions between devolved units and the centre. You need to manage relationships to ensure that all parts of the organization work collaboratively and are fully committed to the overall strategy. Bear in mind the development of future leaders is essential to the long-term survival of the organization and is another one of your new responsibilities.

Taking up your
leadership role

When you are given a leadership position, you need to prepare yourself for intense learning and adaptation. Whether you're a new recruit or moving up internally, there are many challenges in store, from getting your feet under the desk to developing your competences.

06

Preparing to lead

When you become a leader, you need to quickly understand what is expected from you and from your team. Your employer will provide you with guidance, but don't assume that you'll get the complete picture. A lot of the groundwork is going to be up to you.

Giving yourself a headstart

It pays to prepare for your leadership role even before your first day in the post. Do some basic groundwork and research: ask your employer where you fit into their organizational plans; ask when you will be expected to produce objectives for your team; and when and how your performance – and that of your team – will be assessed. If possible, ask to meet the outgoing leader and discuss the demands of the role and the team dynamics. Research your team: request performance figures and personnel files; ask the outgoing leader and your peers what information will be of most use.

Ask your employer where you fit into their **organizational plans**

Managing data

Throughout the first few weeks in your new role, you will be deluged with information. Unfortunately, you won't necessarily know which of this data is of strategic importance, and which is just minor detail. Head off early errors by being systematic; file the information and make a list of everything you have received. Review this list weekly and try to place the relative significance of each piece of information in a broader contex

23%

increase in performance may result from **best management practice**

Managing people

You'll also be introduced to many new people throughout the organization. After each meeting, make a note of the name, position, and distinguishing features of the person you have met, along with anything memorable they said to you. When you meet them next, you'll remember who they are and how they fit into the organization; moreover, you'll be able to pick up your conversation with them.

CHECKLIST...
Exchanging information

	YES	NO

1 Have you had or requested an **induction briefing?** .... ☐ ☐

2 Have you **identified** areas in your **new role** where you need training? .... ☐ ☐

3 Have you studied the company's **organization charts?** .... ☐ ☐

4 If you have been **promoted,** have you told your existing **contacts** in the organization of your new role? .... ☐ ☐

5 Do you know which **meetings** you are expected to attend? .... ☐ ☐

Tip

ASK FOR SUPPORT
If you have been **promoted internally**, people will assume you have a good knowledge of your organization. But you will still need **support** in transferring to your new role – so don't be afraid to **ask for it**.

eing realistic

ur arrival as a team's new leader will
ise expectations of change for the
etter. However, you may discover that
me expectations are less than realistic.
r example, your team's previous leader
ay have provided detailed guidance
n how work should be carried out.
your leadership style is more about
npowering your team to make their
wn decisions, they may initially feel
orly supported and even resentful

of the added responsibility. Early in your
tenure, ask others what assumptions
they have about you and your role.

- Outline what success looks like to you.
  Does their view match yours?
- What expectations do they have of
  how long things will take?
- Have they been made any unrealistic
  promises about what you will deliver?

You can then begin to address any
discrepancies between their expectations
and your reality.

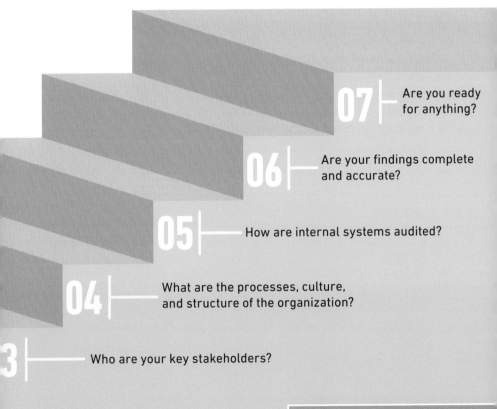

07 ─ Are you ready
for anything?

06 ─ Are your findings complete
and accurate?

05 ─ How are internal systems audited?

04 ─ What are the processes, culture,
and structure of the organization?

3 ─ Who are your key stakeholders?

─ Are there potential problems?

Ask crucial questions

/hat are the aims of your
rganization or team?

Focusing your energy

As a leader, you are likely to be inundated with communications, requests, new tasks, and initiatives. Recognizing – and focusing on – what is really important is critical to your success and that of your team; it is vital that how you spend your time reflects your priorities.

HIGH

URGENCY

LOW

How to prioritize tasks

HIGH URGENCY: LOW IMPORTANCE

Typical activities

O Dealing with messages as they come in

O Dealing with others' priorities not in line with your vision

What happens when you spend time on this

O Lack of clear goals

O Crisis management

O Feeling out of control

O Behaving inconsistently

Action: Delegate it

LOW URGENCY: LOW IMPORTANCE

Typical activities

O Low-level meetings

O Time-wasting

O Unfocused browsing

What happens when you spend time on this

O Failure to take responsibility

O Inability to complete jobs

O Increased dependence on others

O Insecurity

Action: Leave it

LOW **IMPORTANCE**

Managing your time

is easy to get distracted from key
sks by less important, but nonetheless
rgent activities. Prioritizing your actions
something you should schedule in
very day, and approach with discipline.
simple solution is to write a "to do" list
at the end of each day. Scrutinize this
list, assessing each item against your
vision, values, and key objectives; then,
number each item in order of priority.
Alternatively, try categorizing your tasks
more systematically under the four
headings shown below.

HIGH URGENCY: HIGH IMPORTANCE

Typical activities

O Dealing with crises

O Being closely involved with
time-critical projects

O Attending key meetings

**What happens when you spend
time on this**

O Constant crisis management

O Exhaustion and stress

O Burnout over the long-term

Action: Do it now, but review your time planning

LOW URGENCY: HIGH IMPORTANCE

Typical activities

O Planning ahead

O Anticipating problems

O Guiding and training the team

O Delegating

O Building relationships

**What happens when you spend
time on this**

O Overview

O Vision

O Balance

Action: Schedule it

IMPORTANCE   HIGH

WORKING SMART

Do's	Don'ts
O **Improving standards**	O Doing work you could delegate
O **Building networks**	O Never leaving your work space
O **Recording and analyzing how you spend your time**	O Reacting to stimuli as they arrive
O **Being realistic about durations**	O Starting without a clear schedule

Getting back on track

Missed or delayed deadlines and recurring problems that you never seem to get around to fixing are symptoms of faulty time management. If the root cause is not addressed, your work life could soon run out of control, sapping your energy and stifling your creativity. Stop, take some time out, and refocus your thoughts. Plan in some time to address strategic activities, and think what you could do to improve delegation within your team.

Reserve at least **10 per cent** of overall **project time for contingencies**

Tip

MAKE ROOM FOR CONTINGENCIES

You should set aside time with your team to **brainstorm** likely barriers to delivering on time. **Reserve** at least **10 per cent** of overall project time for **contingencies**.

Delegating successfully

Delegation is a critical leadership skill, and one that – when done well – has great benefits for you and your team. It liberates your schedule, makes members of your team feel valued, and develops capabilities in people throughout the organization. Delegating well requires more than just handing a task over to a subordinate; there are many issues you need to consider carefully before you act.

How to delegate

O Choose carefully **who you delegate a task to.** Assess the probability of things going wrong.

O Only delegate tasks that can be **clearly defined**. If you can't specify the desired outcome and timeframe, it is unreasonable to expect someone to succeed.

O Delegate **time-consuming, recurring** tasks.

O Establish and agree on **milestones,** working procedures, resources, and **deadlines.**

O Check that the person to whom you are delegating **shares your understanding** of the task in hand.

O Monitor progress and provide support, but avoid micromanaging. **You cannot abdicate responsibility**, but if you delegate well, you can trust people to do a good job.

O Delegating means allowing people to **find their own solutions:** you must accept that these will not necessarily be the same as your solutions.

O Don't apportion blame if things don't work out: remember it is you who **shoulders responsibility** for ultimate success or failure.

Selecting personnel

To identify the best member of your team to take on a particular task, try using a "Plan to Delegate" table, such as the sample right, to give a degree of objectivity when making a decision. To use the Plan to Delegate table:

- List all members of your team.
- Devise your criteria for choosing someone – those on the sample table are a good starting point.
- Rate each member of your team for all criteria from 1–10.
- Add the scores.
- Add comments on the type of training, development, or support each individual needs. Do they need short-term input, intensive support, or long-term guidance?

When you carry out this exercise, the best fit candidate is not always the most obvious. You may have developed the habit of just asking one experienced and skilled team member to do jobs for you. However, others on the team may have more time to devote to the task, and will benefit from the experience and responsibility.

1/3 more **revenue** is generated by US CEOs who are top **delegators**

Tip

CARRY OUT A DEBRIEF
Once a task is **complete, allow time** for a debrief – discuss what went well, and what did not. How would you **change the process** next time? What was **learned?** Was this a **suitable** task to delegate to the individual?

Plan to delegate

CRITERIA

Current capability and experience

Skills/competences

Development potential

Availability

Motivation/commitment

Task consistent with individual's goals for development

Total score

Other comments, such as training or support needed

Milestones/reviews

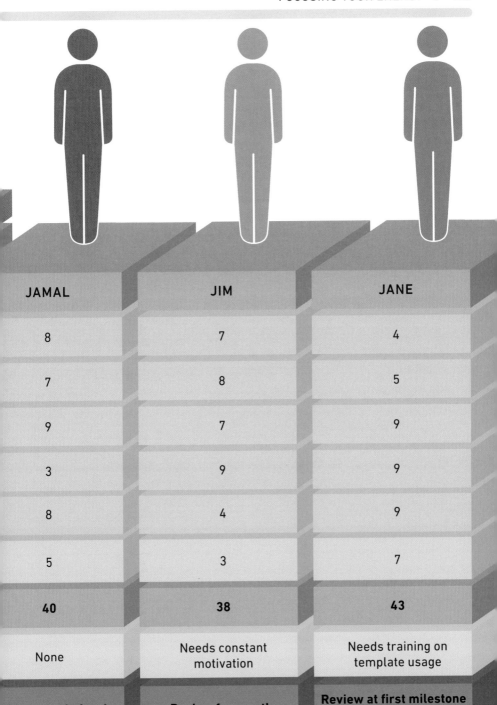

JAMAL	JIM	JANE
8	7	4
7	8	5
9	7	9
3	9	9
8	4	9
5	3	7
40	**38**	**43**
None	Needs constant motivation	Needs training on template usage
view at end of task	**Review frequently**	**Review at first milestone and end only**

Working at relationships

From your earliest days as a leader, you will need to build relationships with your team and a range of stakeholders throughout the organization. The ability to understand and empathize with people is a key skill, and thinking of relationships in terms of "stories" gives you tools to understand what drives others and help productive interpersonal relationships thrive.

Telling stories

We each carry in our heads our own stories – the narratives we have constructed over the years to make sense of our collected experiences, emotions, habits, and thoughts. These stories bias our perspective in all new situations and may push us towards embracing challenges or – conversely – constrain our actions.

Relationships are built by exchanging these stories with other people we meet. As we tell our stories, we disclose more about ourselves, our backgrounds, roles, and beliefs – and create new, emergent stories. Just as individuals have their own stories, so do organizations; these stories encompass the history and values of that organization and describe how they get things done.

85%

of CEOs **agree** a firm's financial performance is tied to **empathy**

Do the stories **convey a strong moral code, judgements,** or beliefs?

Listening to stories

By listening empathetically to a person's story, you may be able to understand why they want to work with you and their likely motivations. It's about grasping what the other person is experiencing from their frame of reference, not yours. Stories also point to ways of negotiating with individuals or organizations, and even indicate if a joint venture will succeed. Leaders who fail to take account of a person's or firm's past thoughts, culture, actions, and aspirations – as well as what they observe in the present – may face an unexpected culture clash. A lack of empathy and sensitivity gets in the way of team performance, innovation, learning, and business success.

Tip

LISTEN TO THE SUBTEXT

Listen for recurrent patterns in **people's stories.** What do they **tell you** about the way they **relate** to others, their modes of thinking, biases, and barriers?

Do the stories **express** themselves in **protective** jargon?

Do the stories claim particular **skills** for the individual?

Are the stories **explorative** and **adventurous,** or conservative, **focused** on maintaining equilibrium?

Do the stories place the individual in a **particular role** – hero, participant, or victim, for example?

Are the stories mostly set in the **past, present, or future?**

Do the stories make or break **connections** between things?

Case study

BOOSTING THE BOTTOM LINE

When Riikka Mattila joined Scandic Hotels in 2012 as its HR director for Finalnd, employee engagement was the lowest of all six countries in which the group operated. Taking an empathetic approach, Riikka focused on bolstering leadership, forging trust, and empowering staff. Each employee was asked to give input on how they did their jobs on the group's online learning platform.

Initially, participation was low, so the firm asked employees what changes might make them use it. Persistence paid off and at the Great Place to Work awards in 2018, Scandic Hotels won best workplace in Finland for the second year running and third best workplace in Europe. The return on investment was lower employee turnover, improved financial performance, and more satisfied customers.

Learning from stories

By listening empathetically to the stories people tell, you gain an insight into what drives them and how they relate to others. This doesn't just build better working relationships, it also gives you a competitive advantage. Empathy filters through into increased customer satisfaction, happier employees, higher revenue, and a stronger brand. Be aware that it takes extra effort to forge relationships with people you don't meet in person. Building trust when you can't pick up on the visual cues we all use when talking requires you to listen more carefully, communicate more clearly, and be even more open and flexible.

Psychologists Daniel Goleman and Paul Ekman identify three facets of empathy:

- **Cognitive empathy** helps in understanding how a person feels and what they are thinking.
- **Emotional empathy** aids identification with another's feelings and deepens relationships.
- **Empathic concern** provides motivation to help others.

Empathy is a skill that can be developed especially if you practise it every day. Park your ego and focus on how your work benefits others; in meetings, ensure you know what would fulfil your colleagues' goals rather than only focusing on what you want. You can then achieve the kind of win-win solutions that keep employees engaged

> Park your **ego** and focus on how your work **benefits others**

Seeing something from another's perspective is key. Empathy doesn't mean getting in the other person's head to manipulate them, but knowing how best to work together. If you feel someone is "being difficult", reframe it by reflecting on their story. People don' usually set out to be difficult, but may have a driver that you don't understand With empathy, you can find out what it i

upporting collaboration

npathetic leadership creates workplaces at, in the words of Harvard Business hool professor Amy Edmondson, are sychologically safe". Her work has own that organizations with higher ychological safety perform better on most every metric, from innovation to venue. The term covers four main areas:

Willingness to help Encouraging people to collaborate, explore better solutions, and build new narratives, so everyone wins.

- **Openness** Making it safe for people to speak up with ideas or questions, without being ignored or put down.
- **Risk/failure** Viewing mistakes as a chance to learn, so people continue to express their ideas, nudge their comfort zones, and take on challenges.
- **Inclusivity** Allowing people to be their authentic selves and valuing them for it.

Psychological safety is not about creating an "anything goes" environment. It's about minimizing anxiety and using empathy and respect, not fear, to motivate.

How psychologically safe is your organization?

COMFORT ZONE

May be comfortable in the short term but business success is an illusion if problems are swept under the carpet and allowed to fester. Psychological safety is not about "being nice".

LEARNING AND HIGH-PERFORMANCE ZONE

The ideal state of inclusivity and openness. Allows safe interpersonal risk-taking, fostering innovation, improvement, resilience, and self-development.

APATHY ZONE

Often characterized by a "dangerous silence", when people have learnt that speaking up, even about serious risks, leads to ridicule or retribution.

ANXIETY ZONE

A blame culture in which failure is stigmatized. Organizations will atrophy and fail to make the most of talent when people are on the defensive.

PSYCHOLOGICAL SAFETY — LOW ... HIGH

LOW   STANDARDS   HIGH

Using competences

How can you define what you need to become an effective leader? You may find some inspiration in the lives of great business, political, and military leaders of the past. But a more reliable way of shaping your objectives is to use competences – descriptions of performance output that characterize leadership in your organization.

Emulating the greats

Bookshops are lined with the biographies of famous leaders, which tell us how they acted and dealt with adversity. A lesson that emerges from their life stories is that you lead from who you are. To lead effectively, you must be comfortable in your own skin and live a life according to your own principles. So much as you admire Gandhi or Che Guevara, you can't copy them – this will give rise to inconsistent behaviours that will be interpreted as indecisiveness or insincerity.

Competences define what **effective performance** as a leader looks like and **help leaders to identify** their development needs

Setting objective targets

A more realistic way to shape your aims as a leader is through competences. These are short descriptions that set out the behaviours we want to see in ourselves as leaders. Competences define what effective performance as a leader looks like and – through self-assessment and feedback – help leaders to identify their development needs. You can refer to and use a standard set of leadership competences to review your current performance and set objectives, or carry out research and consult with others to devise your own.

BIAS-FREE COMPETENCES

When creating leadership competences for your organization, make sure that the behaviours listed are not biased against any particular group. Research by Catalyst, a non-profit that supports women in business, shows that senior leaders tend to promote the stereotypically "masculine" leadership traits they are already comfortable with, such as being results driven, action oriented and problem solving, over stereotypically "feminine" ones, such as being collaborative, consulting, and empathetic. If such unconscious bias goes unchallenged, it creates a vicious cycle where certain groups are disadvantaged and all leaders possess the same limited range of talents. Understand that a diversity of traits is important in leadership and that these can be exhibited by a diversity of people. Consider hiring an expert to review your competences for biased language and diversity.

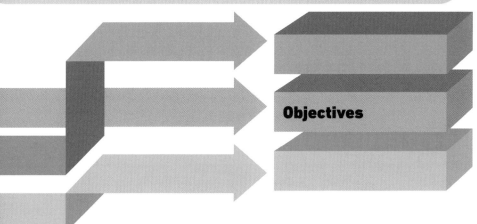

Objectives

Understand that a **diversity of traits** is important and that they can be **exhibited** by a diversity of people

Writing your own competences

Using a set of standard competences, such as the ones on the next pages, to define leadership roles may well be appropriate to you. Alternatively, you can identify and list competences by learning from others' experiences – one of the many benefits of joining a professional body for managers or leaders. But the best option is to develop your own competences – ones that accurately target your company's objectives and values.

Involving others

When writing competences for leaders, involve a cross-section of people in your organization. Start the discussion with them by asking the question, "What does being effective as a leader look like?" Then invite everyone to make their own contributions to the descriptions of the list of competences in terms that mean something to them.

Standard leadership competences

COMPETENCE	DESCRIPTION OF COMPETENCE
Achieving excellent results	Delivers with **energy and determination** on individual, team, and overall objectives that address **core business issues** and contribute to longer-term organizational goals. Behaves in a **professional and ethical** way.
Building relationships	Builds trust, listens to needs, is **open to ideas,** and is sensitive to the perceptions of others. Questions constructively, identifies options, and **develops solutions** by networking with **strategic people**. Is able to work autonomously or in teams, to **adapt to a wide range of situations,** and to appreciate diversity. Remains aware of the needs of others and can **focus on objectives and build relationships,** even under pressure or in the face of personal criticism. Good at **selecting the right people** with complementary strengths to work in teams.
Coaching and communicating	Communicates **a clear vision** of the organization's future. Enthuses and **energizes people,** is accessible to people, and gains ownership of the steps needed to achieve goals. Knows own and team members' strengths and weaknesses and **encourages initiative** and accountability for objectives. Invests in **coaching others,** gives constructive feedback, and knows when to support and challenge. Cultivates **good leadership throughout the organization** so that everyone is heard and can contribute; **brings on** the leaders the business will need going forward.

ollowing best practice

mbine the input from your colleagues
th the latest research on leadership
st practice, and the knowledge you
ve about the future demands on

leaders within the organization. Draft
the competences with one eye always
on their compatibility with the vision,
values, and main strategic objectives
and aims of the organization.

COMPETENCE	DESCRIPTION OF COMPETENCE
Continuous nnovation	Experiments with **new approaches**. Learns from best practice, **responds flexibly to change,** and encourages others to question and review how things are done or could be **continuously improved**.
Focusing on customers	Achieves **mutually beneficial relationships** with customers. **Manages expectations** well in all interactions. Anticipates needs and **responds with empathy**.
Lifetime earning and knowledge-sharing	Keeps up-to-date, **shares knowledge** and information with other people; applies this learning to own work. Encourages others to **learn, develop, and share knowledge**.
Solving problems and aking decisions	Recognizes **problems as opportunities,** explores causes systematically and thoroughly. Generates ideas; **weighs advantages and disadvantages** of options.

Measuring and developing

After you have drafted the competences for a leadership role, you can begin to use them to develop your organization's leaders. The main vehicles for this are formal appraisals and self-assessment:

- Make sure the leader knows and fully understands what the competences are.
- Appoint a "competences advocate" – someone to encourage the leader to use the competences as a development tool.
- Agree the competences to be used in appraisals.
- Train appraisers throughout your organization in the meaning and use of competences.
- Encourage self-assessment against the benchmarks set by the competences.

When being assessed in an appraisal or carrying out self-assessment, it is helpful to recognize four stages of progress towards competence in a given area. So, for example, if you were to assess development in the competence "Solving problems and taking decisions", the results may be as shown below.

Assessing competences: solving problems

STAGE OF DEVELOPMENT	ACTIONS DEMONSTRATED
NOT YET DEMONSTRATED	Has only recently taken up the current role.
DEVELOPING	Finds it difficult to step back from the day-to-day operation and engage with others in **creative problem-solving.**
COMPETENT	Encourages other people to put forward new ideas. **Explores systematically** to understand what is happening and why. **Generates ideas to solve problems** and decides on actions.
ROLE MODEL/ COACH	**Actively encourages** others to think of problems and tensions as **creative opportunities** to improve service and develop products.

It is **helpful** to recognize **four stages of progress** towards **competence** in a given area

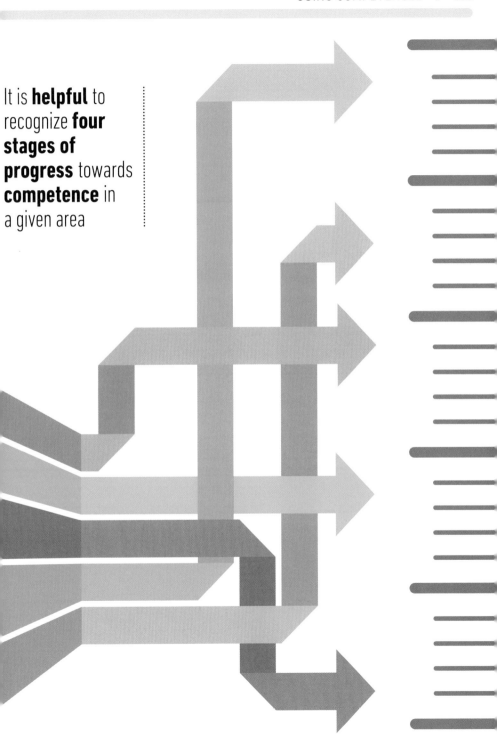

Providing feedback

The ability to both give and receive feedback is an essential leadership skill. Giving feedback encourages development and innovative thinking in your team, while knowing how to receive feedback provides an opportunity to learn more about yourself as a leader and the effect your behaviour has on others.

Opening the dialogue

Giving feedback is not just about telling someone what you think. It is a two-way process that involves listening, asking questions, gaining commitment to change, summarizing what has been covered, and clarifying understanding. Feedback can be given informally in reviews or in quick one-to-one meetings.

Many organizations also provide planned appraisals – regular, formal opportunities for the exchange of feedback, which can include reviews of performance, development, or both. Appraisals happen at least annually and are usually between the line manager

85%

of US professionals believe that **feedback** is important to their **development**

Tip

CONSIDER YOUR FEEDBACK

View a feedback session as a **learning opportunity.** Even if you are being critical, explain your **point of view** and give suggestions for improvement. Unskilled negative feedback will leave the recipient feeling demotivated, with nothing to build on except their feelings of resentment.

and team member although they can include others. Feedback from your boss, your team members, peers, and customers is termed "360° feedback"; when segments are omitted (for example feedback from customers and peers), the term is "180° feedback". Take time to prepare for a feedback session. Book a private room to ensure no interruptions. Always start positively, talk about the recipient's achievements: encourage them to talk about what has gone well. Avoid the tendency to focus more on mistakes they might have made than their strengths; make sure the positive feedback outweighs developmental points you bring up by at least 2:1.

voiding unconscious bias

hen conducting appraisals, it's
nportant to be aware of the damaging
le that unconscious bias can play.
lented employees can be repeatedly
eld back, being forced to prove
emselves time and again, having their
titude or career ambitions questioned,
getting unfairly pigeonholed as a result
appraisers' subconscious beliefs about
eir race, gender, age, class, sexuality,
a disability. Research shows that an
vidence-based performance evaluation
stem – and training staff to effectively
rry it out – can help level the playing
eld. Identify the competences valued
each role and oblige appraisers to
ovide evidence to justify their scores
order to achieve more constructive
edback for all staff members.

eing specific

eedback needs to be specific. Deal with
ne issue at a time rather than trying to
ckle many issues at once. Be clear and
rect in your comments: for example,
The way you gave the information and
rew the diagram was really helpful to
e customer". General comments, such

Tip

LISTEN FROM AFAR
There's even greater room
for misunderstandings when
delivering feedback remotely,
so take extra care to be **clear**
and direct, to **listen**, and to be
open and **receptive**.

as "You were brilliant!" do not give the
recipient any opportunities for learning.

Feedback must also be realistic – only
refer to actions or behaviours that the
person can change. You may have to start
with small steps: for example, "It would
help if you smiled more when you speak."
Gain agreement on small goals, and
praise people for reaching the standards
you have defined. Skilled feedback gives
people information about their behaviour
and a choice about how and if to act on
it – change imposed too heavily invites
resistance. Finally, always ask the
recipient to summarize the actions
they will take as a result of feedback –
this helps you to double-check their
understanding and commitment to change.

CHECKLIST...
Preparing to give feedback

	YES	NO
1 Are you **clear** on what you want to say?	☐	☐
2 Have you prepared a **positive start** and end to the feedback?	☐	☐
3 Can you be **specific** in your developmental feedback?	☐	☐
4 Is this the **best time** to give feedback?	☐	☐

Giving formal appraisals

When giving a formal appraisal, never show boredom or interrupt. If you find that you are talking more than the person being appraised, rethink your tactics. Use open questions – ones that demand more than a "Yes" or "No" answer – to find out what someone is thinking or feeling. The best questions often start with "What...?" because they make the fewest assumptions about the response, so try:

● What went well?
● What have we learned?

Identify activities and training that will develop the individual in their current role and prepare them for the future. Make clear the business case for any investment in development and training – does it help meet business, team, and individual objectives?

The best questions often **start with "What...?"** because they make the **fewest** assumptions about **the response**

Getting SMART – setting realistic objectives

S	**M**	**A**
SPECIFIC	**MEASURABLE**	**AGREED**
Clearly expressed and within the control of the appraisee.	In terms of quantity, percentage, turnover, or some agreed qualitative measure.	Between the two of you rather than imposed.

Setting SMART objectives

Take time to review the individual's achievements since their last appraisal and establish SMART objectives (see below) for the period until the next appraisal. Agree with them how and when you will measure change. There are many measurement tools at your disposal, including: observation; discussion during appraisals; informal one-to-one reviews; team meetings; examination of business results; other key performance indicators; surveys; and assessment against your organization's competences.

Closing the appraisal

At the end of the appraisal, it is your turn as leader to ask for any feedback that might be helpful to your working relationship. Be sure to follow up on any support and training you have offered and review progress against agreed milestones. Throughout the year, examine how realistic the standards and deadlines were that you set at the appraisal.

R

REALISTIC
Challenging but achievable.

T

TIMELY
With schedules specified.

92%

of **organizations** use formal **performance reviews**

Learning from feedback

When you seek out and receive feedback, you develop your character as a leader. The two-way process of disclosing things about yourself and receiving comments on your performance builds trust. This in turn reduces the gap between your public and private faces and increases the authenticity of your leadership.

Seeking the truth

Once you have learned to both give and receive feedback skilfully and constructively, you will be ready to lead your team into greater self-awareness and higher levels of performance.

You can ask for feedback (formally or informally) from any of the people you come into contact with on a daily basis – members of your team, your superiors, clients, or suppliers.

The following questions are a good starting point for discussion with your appraiser, especially if you ask them to back up their answers with real examples:

- What do you see as my strengths?
- What do you think I am blind to?
- What development areas do you think I should be focusing on?

- What should I do less of/more of?
- What potential do you see in me? Or, if you are using competences to set and monitor your targets, try the following phrasing:
- Which competences do I consistently demonstrate? (Enclose a copy of your competences.)
- Which competences do you think I could go on developing further?
- What changes do you foresee in the next 12 months and which competences do you think I should be focusing my development upon?

In focus

RUNNING 360° FEEDBACK
Ideally the 360° process should be managed by an objective external coach to ensure high-quality feedback, a balanced viewpoint, and anonymity for those individuals brave enough to feed back on their boss. However, if your organizational culture is open, and all agree to a no-blame approach, the review could be carried out internally.

ecoming a rounded leader

more formal means of gaining
formation about yourself – or any
dividual in your team – from a
umber of sources is 360° feedback.
sk a selection of four to eight people at
fferent levels in your organization to
mment on the leadership behaviours
ey have seen you displaying over the last
ar. If appropriate, ask them to consider
is against your stated competences.

A questionnaire, set out like a customer satisfaction survey, will help provide a consistent format for the replies.

When you receive feedback from others, compare it with your evaluation of yourself. Which leadership competences are your strengths? Which are your development areas? Which key competences did you find the most challenging last year and which will be even more demanding next year? Note the key development areas and think how you can broaden or deepen your knowledge, skills, or practice – for example reading up on a topic or attending a course. As well as providing valuable insight into others' perceptions of your leadership, 360° feedback is an invaluable tool for helping you prepare for your appraisal discussion with your manager.

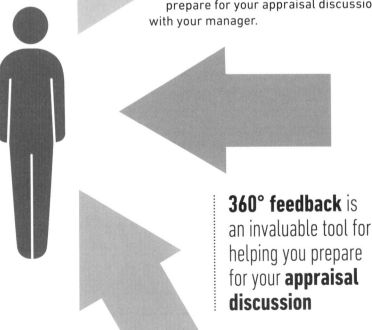

360° feedback is an invaluable tool for helping you prepare for your **appraisal discussion**

Developing yourself

In this action-orientated world, many of us devote insufficient time and energy to our own development. Yet dedicated time for self-development is essential for growing your character and your own individual brand of leadership, as well as the attitudes, skills, and behaviours that will exemplify leadership in others.

Reflecting and reviewing

The best way to accelerate your own development and increase awareness of yourself and of others is through regular review and reflection. Put aside an hour every week for self-analysis and contemplation.

Start by reviewing your current development needs. Ask yourself how much of your activity the preceding week contributed to achieving your stated vision and objectives. Next, look at your future development needs and assess your progress against your stated leadership competences. Finally, consider the ideas you have for the next steps in your career; are you honing the skills now that you know will be needed for your career progress?

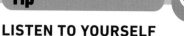

Tip

LISTEN TO YOURSELF

Review your own progress by questioning yourself: are you building on your strengths and minimizing your weaknesses? Are you **training** your team and delegating to them **successfully?** Are you scheduling time to develop **key relationships?**

In focus

YOUR LONG-TERM DEVELOPMENT

As you mature as a leader, you will need to undertake weekly reviews of your own development and achievements. But you should also take time to think about your long-term goals, and your progress towards them. How well are you living up to your life principles? How have you dealt with disappointment and adversity? Do you ever find yourself questioning your ability to do what's expected of you professionally (the so-called "impostor syndrome")? Have you managed to increase your level of performance? Have you fulfilled commitments to yourself and others? Are you happy in your career? What are your next steps?

The more you learn, the more you realize you still have to learn. At this point, you might consider seeking advice from a career counsellor.

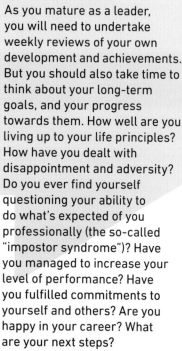

ournalling

eat leaders possess self-awareness
d character – attributes acquired
rough reflection and self-analysis,
t also through dealing regularly with
al-life situations. Using a private
urnal to write down what you have
arned about yourself in your day-to
ay life can be very helpful. Record, for
ample, how you have helped someone
se develop and learn, and how this has
ned your own strengths as a leader.

Use your journal to make personal
servations about how you respond
different conditions – what happens
hen you are tired or stressed? The
urnal can help you record and work
rough relationships that you are
njoying or struggling with, and to reflect
the highs and lows of your moods that
u could not reveal in the workplace.

At first, journalling may seem a chore;
d initially your journal may not contain
any connections or life-lessons. But
ter a number of weeks, you'll find that
urnalling becomes a habit that gives

structure to your review and thinking
time. Looking back over your journal
will reveal how your leadership has
developed, how you can trust yourself,
even in difficult situations, and what
the recurring issues are.

Assess your **progress** against your **leadership competences**

Tip

KEEP YOUR FEET ON THE GROUND

Never become so grand
that you lose touch with
what it feels like to work
with a customer on a project
or to make a sale. Recognize
that your role is now to **help
others enjoy** this too.

ASK YOURSELF...

About your development needs

	YES	NO
1 Are your most time-consuming tasks related to processes? Do you need to **develop time-** or project-management skills, or planning abilities?	☐	☐
2 Are your most time-consuming tasks related to **content?** Do you need to address a lack of knowledge in areas such as marketing, finance, sales, or IT?	☐	☐
3 Are your most time-consuming tasks related to people? Do you need **training** in recruitment, motivation, teambuilding, coaching, or delegating?	☐	☐

Balancing work and life

Most people would say that they want to be healthy, happy, and make a valued contribution at work to a successful organization. Creating and maintaining this sense of wellbeing is an integral part of your role as a leader. It involves taking a measured view of the balance between work and life and having realistic expectations of your team.

Attending to different needs

Good leaders know their team, their capabilities, and what motivates them. The real skill, though, is being able to use this knowledge to balance the needs of the task, the team, and its individual members. Maintaining this equilibrium is not always easy, because emphasis inevitably shifts from one area to another. For example, bursts of intense effort may be needed to meet tight deadlines – fine once in a while, but exhausting on a regular basis. Similarly, switching to remote working brings work-life balance benefits, but can also add pressure to be available at all hours, increasing stress.

> ### Tip
>
> ### ACCENTUATE THE POSITIVE
> Promote a **healthy work–life balance** and you'll not only avoid the pitfalls of stress and burnout in your team, but generate **real benefits** to the business. **Happy** staff deliver better results and empathetic customer service; and staff retention and recruitment then becomes easier.

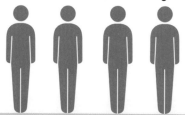

Avoiding burnout

Left unmanaged, chronic work stress leads to burnout, something to avoid as it has no easy fix. Workers who experience burnout – characterized by exhaustion, a cynicism towards work, and a lack of efficacy – often have to change careers, draining your pool of available talent.

CHECKLIST...
Achieving balance in your life

	YES	NO
1 I often buy new books and **have time to read** them	☐	☐
2 People remark on how **open** I am to **new ideas**	☐	☐
3 I have a **regular exercise** routine	☐	☐
4 I usually get a **good night's sleep**	☐	☐
5 I have **enough energy** to see me through each day	☐	☐
6 I **express** my feelings	☐	☐
7 I know who I am and that's **fine**	☐	☐
8 I have a **clear sense of purpose** in my life and make a real contribution at work	☐	☐

Managing stress

Your goal should be to keep your team members stretched and working to their best ability, but not stressed. Ensure everyone has regular and predictable time off. If you have built a strong team during good times, it will withstand short-term pressures, but you may need to invest time in team meetings and calm tensions to maintain balance. Stresses are cumulative: a team member may be able to tolerate stress at work for a while if other aspects of their life are running well. But if work stress is only one of many issues they are dealing with, problems may arise that you should acknowledge.

If you're leading a remote team, set limits on work time and share them with staff to maintain boundaries between your job and personal life. For example, stop checking work messages after hours and respect flexible working arrangements.

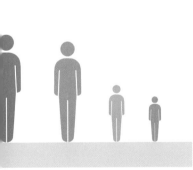

You may need to invest time in **team meetings** and **calm tensions** to **maintain balance**

Inspiring and encouraging

From the way they formulate and express their overarching vision to the thought they put into everyday interactions – the glue of any team relationship – good leaders encourage and inspire others around them at every level of activity.

Setting a good example

One of the basic rules of leadership is that in order to inspire others you must aspire to be a model of excellence yourself. Of course, your personal journey towards excellence will never end, but it will give you two vital qualities – the desire to learn, and, in turn, that will lead to the humility of knowing how much more you have to learn.

Your role is about providing inspiration, and that starts with a clear vision for a better future, which you will need to communicate to your team on a daily basis through your words and actions:

- Make it clear to others that they have the capability and power to make a difference – that their unique attributes can help achieve the vision
- Bring hope for the future to sustain people through change and adversity; if people feel overwhelmed and slow down, bring them back to the vision with simple messages that show the next small steps forwards.
- Point out progress made and signs of success on the way to fill people once again with confidence and the desire to go forwards.
- Praise new ideas and the courage demonstrated in new ventures.
- Keep team members stretched – one step ahead of what they thought they could do.
- Keep positive: explain that most experiments that do not work are not failures – just feedback; turn setback into positive impetus for change.

How to inspire through your vision

Your role is about providing **inspiration**, and that starts with a clear vision for a better **future**

State your vision in **highly positive terms**

BEING POSITIVE

Do's	Don'ts
O **Telling someone you enjoy working with them**	O Complaining to someone that you feel tired or ill
O **Smiling at people – sincerely, with your eyes**	O Being too shy to enjoy life or try new things
O **Thanking others for honest feedback**	O Excusing your falling standards
O **Controlling your emotions**	O Demotivating others just because you feel demotivated

Making opportunities

Think how many opportunities you have in a single day to interact with your team, colleagues, bosses, and other stakeholders. Over 100 contacts a day – by phone, email, face-to-face, etc. – is not unusual for today's busy leaders and managers. Every one of these interactions, however brief, is an opportunity to encourage, inspire, and make your leadership felt. When you make every meeting count, you create thousands of potential advocates for you, your team, your vision, and your organization. Moments add up to real commercial gain.

Tip

ZAP, DON'T SAP
At every meeting, give people a zap – a **quick burst** of **positive energy** – and avoid the sap – anything that leaves them discouraged.

Encourage others to **enrich the vision** by describing success in their own terms

Contextualize the vision – describe when, where, and with whom it will be achieved

Focusing on the now

Inspiring people is less about delivering passioned speeches and having a forceful personality, and more about focus and consistency. Treat everyone you deal with as a valued customer. Place them at the centre of your universe for the duration of any interaction you have.

Give them your full attention whether you are speaking face-to-face or on the phone. Be dependable in your daily interactions: your consistency builds trust and peace of mind in your team members, freeing them to focus on their key tasks rather than worrying about you.

Leading through
challenges

In business, change is a constant. Organizations are forever having to adapt to new realities and create opportunities for growth – something that's truer than ever in today's fast-shifting "new normal". It is your role as a leader to steer the changes, encouraging others to take on new challenges, and project credibility and integrity even in times of uncertainty.

07

Focusing on the future

As a leader, you'll need to make tough decisions, plan a course of action and take your team with you. The best way to achieve this is to involve your team from the start; explain what criteria your judgement is based upon and how plans are connected to other activities in the organization.

Making decisions

Leaders set the agenda in three key areas – by determining the direction in which the organization will move, by shaping how the organization does business, and by setting the pace of change. Decisions you make in any of these three key areas should be based on objective criteria; research shows that an evidence-based approach – in which decisions are made using evidence and critical thinking – is more effective than simply relying on personal experience, conventional wisdom, or anecdote. Test your decision by assessing its strengths, weaknesses, opportunities, and threats (SWOT).

Locating change

Deciding which opportunities to explore, exploit, and reject requires a crystal clear understanding of your organization's purpose and mission. In particular, you must know what gives your business its edge over the competition and use this knowledge to guide your future focus. Competitive advantage is based on what customers value and the organization's strengths relative to the competition. It takes into account external trends that will help or hinder momentum. In a SWOT analysis, internal factors are strengths and weaknesses, while external issues are opportunities and threats.

ASK YOURSELF...
What's our competitive advantage?

		YES	NO
1	Do we know what **business** we are not in?	☐	☐
2	Do we know our **core values**?	☐	☐
3	Do we know what **business** we are in?	☐	☐
4	Do we differentiate ourselves by offering our customers **unique benefits**?	☐	☐
5	Do we differentiate ourselves by offering our customers **better prices**?	☐	☐

Question your decisions using a SWOT analysis

S

STRENGTHS
- O What **advantages** or **unique ideas and proposals** do you have?
- O What do you do differently or **better than anyone else?**
- O What **unusual materials or low-cost resources** do you have sole access to?
- O How can you build **organizational resilience**?

W

WEAKNESSES
- O What challenges or areas should you avoid?
- O Do new products or processes need **further development or investment?**
- O Have market research results been **positive, or is there insufficient demand?**

O

OPPORTUNITIES
- O What emerging opportunities or **trends** can you identify?
- O What interesting **changes in technology** and developing products are you aware of?
- O Are there new **consumer spending patterns** or demand for different services?
- O How can investing in **analytics** help you identify opportunities?

T

THREATS
- O Are stringent **quality requirements** being imposed?
- O Are you in a **financial position** to adapt to change quickly?
- O Would any communication or technological issue **challenge your market position?**
- O How do you **recognize risks** earlier?
- O And how can you be ready for the **risks you can't foresee?**

Keeping objective

A weighted assessment will make clear the criteria you can use to make a decision and give your decision transparency. In the simple example, right, a decision has to be made to adopt one of two projects – A or B; both seem attractive and have similar costs. To carry out the assessment, first engage with your team to make a list of criteria that the projects should satisfy. Not all criteria are of equal importance, so give each one a score from 1 to 10 depending on how valuable the team considers it to be. Check that the criteria are rounded – not all skewed towards finance, for example. Score each option (A and B) out of 10 on each criterion, and multiply each score by its corresponding weighting. Add the scores to see which project fulfils the criteria best.

Not all **criteria** are of equal importance, so give each one **a score from 1 to 10** depending on **how valuable** the team considers it to be

Weighted assessment

CRITERIA

Maximize long-term customer satisfaction

Maximize return on investment

Maximize sustainability

Maximize high quality standards

Maximize long-term profit potential

Maximize staff satisfaction

Maximize added value for customers

Minimize hassle and administrative complexity

Maximize fun and interesting work

TOTAL

EIGHTING	SCORE PLAN A	PLAN A x WEIGHTING	SCORE PLAN B	PLAN B x WEIGHTING
10	6	60	9	90
9	5	45	4	36
8	9	72	4	32
8	6	48	10	80
8	8	64	5	40
7	2	14	10	70
7	6	42	8	56
5	10	50	7	35
4	3	12	8	32
		407		**471**

Setting the pace

When orchestrating strategic change within an organization, you need to give careful consideration to timing. If the rate of change is too slow, the process may simply run out of momentum; if it is too fast, you risk creating stress and burnout.

Aim for a sustainably fast pace at which your major initiatives will have started to produce measurable results within a year – even if the whole process is scheduled to take much longer. Steering significant organizational change is hard work: typically, there is a trough in visible results just at the point where you need the most effort and commitment from all stakeholders. Investors, in particular, may lose heart in this trough period, so need to be reminded regularly of the benefits to come.

Plan in "quick wins" throughout the process of change – achievements that have high visibility but require little effort. Celebrate and publicize these successes, and drip-feed messages about how project milestones and results achieved so far are bringing the vision nearer to reality.

> Aim for **a sustainably fast pace** at which your **major initiatives** will have **started** to produce **measurable results** within a year

Connected organizational plans

Strategic Business Plan

Tip

OPEN CHANNELS
Keep **listening** to everyone you are connected to; **share ideas,** and keep **open channels of communication** that are needed now and may be needed in the future.

96%

f organizations are
ı some **phase of**
ransformation

Integrating change

Everything in an organization is
connected. Processes and systems
in one area impact on others. As a
leader, you should make explicit the
connections between different plans
and explain how each one contributes
to the vision. Understanding the bigger
picture will help your team to recognize
their role and commit to change.
The message can be a complex one,
so communicate little and often, and
check regularly how well people have
understood the connections between
plans, departments, and roles.

**uman Resources and
rganization Development Plan**

**Operations Plan
(products and
services)**

Finance, IT Sourcing, and R & D Plans

Marketing Plan

Enabling change

Opportunities for innovation exist at every level of an organization, and leaders must continuously plan change to move forwards and stay ahead of competitors. Processes, systems, skills, and competences can always be improved, or the whole business can be moved in an entirely new direction. Leading change requires a sense of balance between priorities and keen awareness of responses among all stakeholders.

Balancing priorities

A key leadership skill is keeping a good balance between short-term improvement and long-term innovation. If you are continuously improving at the margins while neglecting strategic innovation, it will lead to organizational myopia and the risk of missing out on the next big trend. Conversely, constant innovation at the core can become counterproductive because people will eventually feel worn out and unwilling to take on yet another new initiative.

Maintaining stability

The leader seeks to progress with both short- and long-term change while maintaining equilibrium. This can be a challenge: while most people will quickly accommodate small steps that visibly improve the way things are done, bold strategic innovation requires the leader to inspire people, sometimes for many years, before seeing a return. Before implementing change, discuss its implications with multiple small groups of stakeholders. People should feel free to ask questions and express their concerns. Help people to see what will remain the same – these things can provide an anchor of stability for those who dislike change.

How to recognize the stages of adaptation to change

Expectation: anticipation and excitement

Standstill: numbness, disorientation, denial

Lack of energy: missing "the old days"

eacting to change

ople react differently to change.
one extreme are the innovators
ho may be so keen on walking
wards a new future that they fail
realize no one has followed them.
 the other end are the stragglers,
ho join in only when everyone else
s moved on. Traditionalists hang
 to the past, viewing change as
threat. Surprisingly, they have one
ing in common with the innovators –
ey respond to the impending change
ith emotion. The remainder – the
utious majority – are likely to
eigh up the arguments put across.

Incompetence: depression,
apathy, resentment

Conflict in the team:
resistance, anger, squabbling

djusting to plans

s leader, you need to use both logic and
motion when explaining your plans. Be
ersistent and emphasize to everyone
e benefits to come when the changes
ave been made.

People take different lengths of
me to adjust to change and you should
repare for the long haul: typically, the
djustment process falls into distinct
hases, which are characterized by
ifferent sets of behaviours. Be aware
at people who adopt change quickly can
how impatience with the slowest; this
an lead to conflict within the team, which
ou may be called upon to help resolve.

Tip

EXPECT DISSENT
When you introduce
high-level change, expect
at least 50 per cent of your
people to hate the idea.

Low output: feelings of
loss, the need to let go,
detachment from others

Increasing energy: gradual
acceptance of the new reality

Problem solving: exploring
the new situation and ideas,
experimenting, hope

Increased effectiveness:
search for new purpose,
commitment to new situation

Productivity:
re-engagement,
commitment, motivation

Energizing the team

When you put together a group of people – whether it's two or several thousand – you don't automatically get a team. For that to happen, the group must be energized, focused, and view success as a collective rather than individual aim. Your job as a leader is to create that transformation.

Choosing your team

Selecting team members who work together well, motivating the group, and dealing with conflict are the essential aspects of team leadership. And as increasing amounts of work are project-based, you need to develop team cohesion and focus quickly despite rapid changes in the mix of the team. This is even harder if you have team members working remotely, so ensuring that everyone can contribute ideas and access data equally is paramount.

Invest time at the start of a project to choose or strengthen the team – your investment will be repaid when the pressure rises. Pick team members with complementary skills that will come into play at different stages of a project. Your team should have a good mix of the thinking styles listed below. If the team is small, members may have to fill more than one role.

The leader – ensures everyone understands the objectives; motivates and communicates.

The creative – an imaginative thinker who has bold concepts at the outset of a project and provides ideas when the team is stuck.

The analyst – the problem-solver who tests the plan at every stage.

The facilitator – has good interpersonal skills, is sensitive to the group dynamic, and acts as the "glue" in a team.

The administrator – pays attention to details and keeps the team on time and focused on the task.

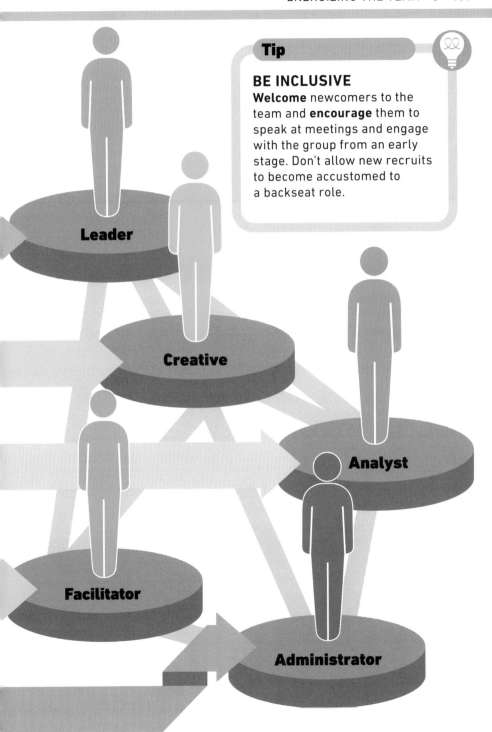

Tip

BE INCLUSIVE
Welcome newcomers to the team and **encourage** them to speak at meetings and engage with the group from an early stage. Don't allow new recruits to become accustomed to a backseat role.

Leader

Creative

Analyst

Facilitator

Administrator

Running your team

Make clear the roles that each individual will play in the team. Devolve decision-making to the group as far as possible, and encourage everyone to participate in decisions – this will share the ownership of goals. Set out shared values, develop ground rules that describe how the team will work together from the start, and watch the way that group dynamics develop. Take action immediately at the first sign of conflict or if an individual starts to act in a way not consistent with the agreed team rules.

When you build and manage your team successfully, **group members** will make one another **accountable** for achieving individual tasks, and begin to **appreciate collective success**

The signs of an energized team

Showing commitment

Listening

Sharing

Getting results

Showing interest

Building trust

Giving recognition

21%

greater **profitability** is shown by **highly engaged teams**

Building trust

Be supportive, give credit for good cooperative work and knowledge shared, and always promote and celebrate team achievements.

When you build and manage your team successfully, group members will start to make one another accountable for achieving individual tasks, and begin to appreciate and share in collective success. Trust will build gradually as each member commits to actions at team meetings and carries them out as promised.

Innovating

Supporting one another

Giving constructive feedback

Being trusting, honest, and open

Taking risks

Collaborating

Managing conflict

Building a successful team depends on cooperation between all members of the group. But what if some people won't play ball? Unproductive confrontations with you as leader or between team members can take up a lot of your time, create a bad atmosphere, and stop you achieving your aims, so finding positive ways to deal with disagreement is a key leadership skill.

Dealing with conflict

Conflict arises when people stop listening and approach a situation from their own point of view. As leader, you must look beyond the confrontation to understand what it is really happening and discover the roots of the hostility.

Begin with yourself: your role means you may be a factor in a team member's dissatisfaction. Differences in outlook, behaviour, and style can lead to tension – which can be used constructively to stimulate creativity and enrich the team or, if left unmanaged, can cause division.

Meeting standards

It is tempting to work round conflict, but this undermines the team and your position as leader. You should explore all courses of action to bring about improvement. But many people find adversarial situations hard and may sabotage their own future if they do not see a way out. If open discussion and support fails to achieve changes, you w need to work within your organization's disciplinary policy and procedures to deal with the situation, and prevent an adverse effect on the rest of the team.

ASK YOURSELF...
Is it me?   YES   NO

1 Have I explained **new initiatives** clearly – could they be causing insecurity or anxiety? .... ☐ ☐

2 Do I come across as **approachable** and **accessible**? .... ☐ ☐

3 Have I made unreasonable demands? .... ☐ ☐

4 Have I been **fair** in my praise or my criticism? .... ☐ ☐

5 Am I portraying the **right image** for a leader? .... ☐ ☐

Why conflict arises

CAUSE	EFFECT	REMEDY
Reaching the limits of current capability	Team member **makes errors** and cannot do the job to the **required standard.** Other team members become impatient.	Offer **support and training** over a reasonable timescale. If there is little improvement, their future in your team is limited.
Becoming disengaged	**Rejection of the job;** withdrawal from involvement with the team. Often caused by frustration when high achievers have been held back over time. Will have **an adverse effect** on the entire team.	Explore causes in a **one-to-one discussion.** If you have inherited this team member, you need to release the burden of all the past broken promises and **build new trust.** Consider counselling.
Getting distracted	**Focus moves elsewhere** reducing effectiveness. The cause is often personal and while colleagues will sympathize initially, they will soon tire of the issue.	Listen sympathetically and **arrange time off** if you think this will help to solve the problem. Make sure that you recognize when the problem goes beyond your ability and ask for further help.
Losing motivation	Too little or too much delegation or challenge in the role can bring about **demotivation and decreased effectiveness.** The team member can quickly have a negative effect on team morale.	Get to know what particularly **motivates each member of the team.** Ask yourself if you are over- or under-delegating to the person. Over-delegation can cause paralyzing fear of failure.

Balancing targets

Results are what it's all about. They are the synthesis of all your thinking, planning, and enabling as a leader. To get what you want from a project, you should clarify standards and objectives from the outset. Your targets need to be realistic, and they also require a means of measuring the performance of all involved.

Getting the right results

The targets you set for your team should stretch everyone but also be realistic, in line with the SMART criteria. Ensure the aims you set are balanced; alongside financial targets, include goals in areas such as speed of response, product and service quality, customer and team satisfaction, and brand development. List the desired results in each of four key areas – customers, operations, people, and finance – so that no one objective takes assumed priority over another. Review results in each area monthly so that you can prove progress to yourself, your team, and your investors.

CUSTOMERS

O Customer service staff motivated
O Customers satisfied
O Customer experience enjoyable
O Lifetime loyalty promoted

140%

more money is likely to be spent by customers who enjoy **positive service experiences**

Setting service-level agreements

Clarify the results you expect from interactions between purchasers and providers or between departments in a service-level agreement. You can then present the obligations in a written forma – minimum or maximum standards and timescales, or other measures of reliabili or availability, for example:

- Our obligations: to provide you with information within four hours of request, etc.
- Your obligations: to respond to service requests within four hours of phone call enquiry, etc.

KEEPING MULTIPLE TARGETS IN PLAY

PEOPLE
- Perception of being a good employer
- Personal development
- Mutual respect fostered
- Interesting work

OPERATIONS
- Stocks delivered to warehouse in time
- Safe working throughout
- Delivery to customer as promised
- Competitive prices

FINANCE
- Profits
- Investment
- Sales
- Cash

List the **desired results** in each of four key areas – **customers, operations, people, and finance**

Improving confidence

Confidence is a cornerstone of good leadership. Especially in times of uncertainty, upheaval, or crisis, believing in yourself and making the right decisions will give you credibility and integrity, which in turn will enhance the organization's reputation and build trust in all stakeholders.

Being prepared

Confidence can come in a number of different ways. It comes from experience as your track record as a leader improves. It comes from having well-formed plans and anticipating challenges, and it comes from the knowledge that you have a strong business built on productive working relationships.

Tip

BOOST YOURSELF
Regularly **affirm** your own **strengths** as a leader by privately listing your **abilities and achievements.** This will give you an instant **confidence boost** and banish that internal critic living in your head.

COMMUNICATING WITH CONFIDENCE

While there are no shortcuts to building confidence, there are ways that you can project confidence to your team and to your stakeholders.

O **Use confident language** to describe your vision. Listen and learn from political leaders, who characteristically employ optimistic language that suggests a future state – words such as "innovative", "special", "original", "latest", "breakthrough", "updated", and "leading-edge". Used regularly, this kind of vocabulary spreads through the organization.

O **Deliver your vision** messages in soundbites no more than 30 seconds long that sum up the benefits of the opportunities you wish to explore.

O **Use the right non-verbal signals – c**ommunication is about more than what you say. Adopting a relaxed posture, using small gestures kept close to your body, speaking at a firm volume, smiling, and making plenty of eye contact all help project confidence and calmness.

CHECKLIST...
Staying calm in adversity **YES NO**

1   Do I know what **triggers** an emotional overreaction in me? .... ☐ ☐

2   Can I **spot** the signs of stress in myself? .... ☐ ☐

3   Am I able to delay my **response** for a few seconds before
    I respond? .... ☐ ☐

Acknowledging ideas
Your inner confidence will grow when you behave in a confident manner and gain the trust of your team and colleagues. An ability and willingness to devolve power and decision-making is one vital characteristic that marks out a confident leader, so take every opportunity to involve others and empower them to act on their ideas. Be open about what is not working for you, your customers, suppliers, or employees; your frankness will be interpreted as an expression of confidence because you approach success and adversity with equal zeal. Encourage people to discover and understand situations for themselves rather than spoon-feeding them issues and answers – remember your power increases as you give it away.

Take every opportunity to **involve others** and empower them to act on their **ideas** – your power **grows** as you give it away

Tip

FACE YOUR FEARS
Confidence comes from **self-knowledge;** understanding your thoughts and actions gives you the ability to control them. A good way to become more **self-assured** is to face your fears – do that presentation, confront your difficult CEO, and reply to that demanding client now.

Being consistent
As a leader, your every word and action is scrutinized by your team and could be given far more significance than you intended. Perceptions of you as a confident leader can be undermined by conscious or unconscious slips, so try to think in a measured way about the kind of signals you are sending out. Consistency and calmness in adversity are characteristics that most people will perceive as confidence.

Learning from entrepreneurs

Entrepreneurs enjoy creating value by taking advantage of opportunitie and solving problems for customers. Leaders in organizations of all sizes – and in all markets – can learn from their bold approach: it is just a question of looking at old problems in new ways and producing innovative solutions.

Finding opportunities

What marks out entrepreneurs is their preparedness to listen to their customers, see new opportunities, and back their ideas with drive and determination. They also have a refreshing attitude to "failure" –

everything is viewed as a useful experience, and trial and error is seen as a legitimate path to success. Entrepreneurs think ahead, don't accept the status quo, and ask questions that begin with "why?", "why not?", and "what if...?".

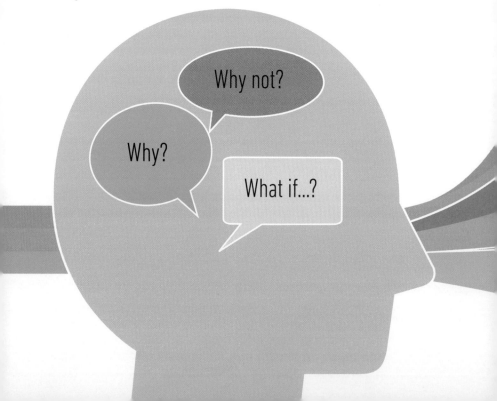

49%

reater productivity is
chieved in firms created
y **serial entrepreneurs**

How can we help you? Celebrate
both **successes and failures** as
signs of entrepreneurship, and be
sure to **reward** the contributions
people make to creating value for the
business, and responding flexibly to
opportunities to solve problems for
customers. Scrutinize your business
for **new opportunities.** Think hard,
and above all, **think creatively.**

Large corporations are increasingly
encouraging their leaders to show
entrepreneurial zeal within the
mature organization – a phenomenon
called **intrapreneurship.**

Looking at your business with
an **entrepreneurial mindset**
will help you generate ideas for
maximizing **opportunities for
growth** that no one else has
seen – either within or outside
the organization.

Embrace **uncertainty** like an
entrepreneur. Don't be afraid
to take **calculated risks**, and
accept your failures as
learning experiences. Doing
nothing is the only approach
destined to eventually fail.

Develop your own
**entrepreneurial
leadership skills** by
asking more questions of
customers and colleagues
– what issues cause you
regular hassle?

Developing entrepreneurial skills

Entrepreneurs exhibit many important traits and crucial skills that you can examine and develop in yourself to benefit your own organization. Most entrepreneurs are risk-takers, goal-focused, and determined – all traits you can learn. When looking for new ideas, examine your own organization first: can you exploit existing assets? In a fast-changing world, is your organization able to adapt quickly? As you search outside your company for emerging trends and products, remember to apply SWOT criteria to test and assess your decisions.

Where to look for entrepreneurial ideas

UNDERUTILIZED INFORMATION OR ASSETS

O Can we sell our **information** externally?

O Can we get **better performance** by outsourcing?

O Can we **lease** our assets?

O Can we repackage our assets using **emerging technology** to create new products?

WAYS TO CHANGE THE BUSINESS MODEL

O Will acquisitions **boost** our **capabilities?**

O Can we cut out the middle-man?

O Should we **support** employee spin-offs?

O Can we replace on-premises solutions with more cost-effective **cloud-based** ones?

Tip

HARNESS TALENT
You may have a **natural entrepreneur** already in your team. Give them the space to **innovate** and put up with their often challenging nature and you will gain a real asset.

35%
of US workers are only given time to think **creatively** a few times a year

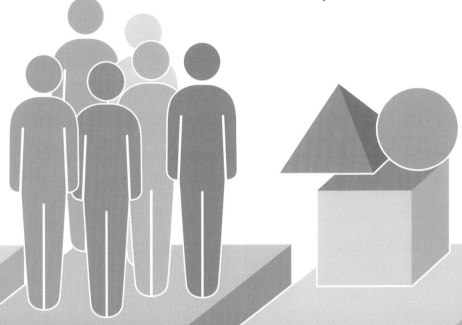

NEW MARKETS, NEW CUSTOMERS

- O Can we **change** our pricing structures?
- O Can we do what we do for our **best customers** for others?
- O How do we **extend** our markets?
- O Can we use **customer data** to increase sales?

NEW PRODUCTS AND SERVICES

- O Can we **sell our products** or services as a system?
- O Can we turn internal services into **sales?**
- O Can we **meet** unmet needs?
- O Can we use reporting and **analytics** to create new products and services?

Developing
leaders

By discovering and developing up-and-coming leadership talent, today's leaders play a vital role in the future of organizations across the world. Doing this effectively requires an inclusive approach and an organizational culture that fosters leadership at all levels and across all employees. Get it right, and the result is a legacy that will live on in generations of future leaders.

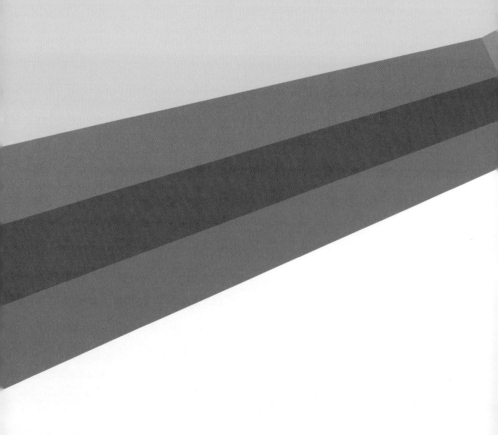

08

Investing in the future

For an organization to expand, it needs to invest in developing the new leaders who will take it forward. Individuals who display leadership potential should be considered important assets who will grow if nurtured, and be lost if not.

Appointing talent

A successful organization needs a ready supply of new leaders. Recruiting all future leaders from outside of your organization simply isn't cost effective: it takes a substantial amount of management time and money to find the right candidates and bring them up to speed. By contrast, leaders who are promoted from within your organization already have a good understanding of its culture and working methods, and will have been nurtured and trained by you to have exactly the suite of skills and knowledge required to take on their new role.

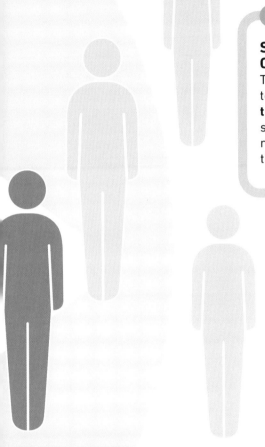

Tip

SPOT THE SIGNS OF CHANGE
Train yourself as a **leader** to recognize the **signs of transition** between different stages of **leadership,** and be ready to support individuals as they push for the **next level.**

30%

of organizations say
they are effectively
developing leaders to
meet evolving challenges

ealizing potential

he of your key goals as a leader is to cognize leadership qualities in others, d to know how to encourage and assist ture leaders so they can realize their ll potential. Take a long-term approach developing talent, rather than filling sitions as they arise, creating ganizational structures and cultures at foster and enable leaders. You might en consider implementing a distributed adership model, empowering any team ember to lead if required. To ensure u are developing talent across the ard, use an evidence-based appraisal stem to combat unconscious bias.

It can be helpful to think of leadership growing as a series of transitions in self-awareness, skill, and responsibility. Recognizing these crucial changes in others, and responding appropriately, will help to accelerate the development of new leaders. Each stage on the path to leadership brings challenges – both in terms of taking on new responsibilities, and leaving behind old behaviours. This can be a stressful time for new leaders, who may feel overwhelmed just when they are expected to shine. They are unlikely to be comfortable raising their concerns with you, their manager, for fear of looking like they are failing.

How to help potential leaders make transitions

Identify the stage of leadership the individual is currently at

Potential leaders start taking on more responsibility and begin **questioning** the ways things are done

Others in the organization start to **recognize their vision**

Help them identify what they needed to let go of to reach this stage

CHECKLIST...

Creating future leaders in your organization

		YES	NO
1	Do you look for **win–win situations** for you/your team/other teams/the organization?	☐	☐
2	Do you demonstrate **good stewardship** of talent for the whole organization's benefit?	☐	☐
3	Do you have a **track record** of unselfishly releasing potential leaders to take up development opportunities?	☐	☐
4	Do you **initiate** the development of potential leaders?	☐	☐
5	Do you **encourage** members of your team to apply for internal promotion or transfers?	☐	☐

ecognizing leadership stages

e first sign of leadership potential
the transition from being self-focused
d performing your individual role to a
gh standard to becoming more aware
, and helpful to, others. Potential
aders then start taking on more
sponsibility and begin questioning
e ways things are done and coming up
th ideas for doing things differently.

As a potential leader develops, others
the organization start to recognize
eir vision and that they have a talent
r spotting important opportunities that
will benefit the team or the organization
as a whole. Potential leaders thrive on
added responsibility, and when they
have a team to manage, they contribute
at a higher level, working well with
their peers, and showing a talent for
developing team members. Other staff
members naturally gravitate towards
them to sound out ideas – a process that
may develop into more formal mentoring
or coaching roles. Ultimately, they start
to develop the skills needed to nurture
the next generation of leaders in
your organization.

Ask them what they do
differently now they are
at this stage

94%

of organizations plan to
increase or maintain
their current spend on
leadership development

Decide between you the
areas you would like to
develop next

When they have a **team to
manage,** they contribute
at **a higher level**

Identify role models who
could help them make the
next transition

Making leadership transitions

STATE OF LEADERSHIP	TAKING UP THE NEW	LETTING GO OF THE OLD
SELF-AWARENESS	O Doing more than the job description O Performing excellently O Accepting more responsibility O Inheriting corporate memory O Becoming a team player O Suggesting improvements	O Doing the job description O Keeping yourself to yourself O Focusing on your own performance O Carrying out everything to the letter O Referring to "I"
OTHER-AWARENESS	O Greater empathy O Helping fellow workers O Being diplomatic O Looking for win–win solutions O Preferring people to procedures O Referring to "we"	O Conforming to previous procedures O Carrying out without challenging O Not questioning the brief O Going your own way O Focusing only on own excellence
GUIDANCE	O Looking for added value opportunities O Accepting responsibility for growth and results O Understanding and promoting vision and purpose O Prioritizing high-value opportunities	O Valuing people based only on technical skills O Using only financial indicators O Focusing on people not results O Going for the easy option O Blaming everyone else for poor performance

STATE OF LEADERSHIP	TAKING UP THE NEW	LETTING GO OF THE OLD
DEVELOPMENT	O Developing talent for the benefit of all O Helping others to perform well O Becoming a mentor O Planning development opportunities O Choosing a team to complement you O Nurturing future leaders	O Prioritizing results above people O Holding on to good people O Failing to delegate enough O Allowing too little time with others O Postponing training if under pressure O Underestimating time for meetings
EMBODIMENT	O Facilitating others to grow O Initiating peer networks O Acting as a leader of leaders O Mentoring/coaching leaders	O Focusing only on the organization O Sacrificing social life O Allowing leader-centric power games

Coaching for success

A good coach can accelerate the development of your future leaders, helping them to manage the transitions they need to make to gain leadership experience and develop the suite of competences required to be a top leader within your organization.

Releasing potential

It isn't easy to find time to invest in coaching your potential leaders, but there will be a considerable return to you, your team, and the organization if you do. The selection of coaches needs to be undertaken with care – the careers of some of the brightest prospects in your organization will be in their hands.

> ### Tip
>
> **COACH VIRTUALLY**
> Distance is no barrier to effective coaching, but **virtual sessions** do need extra focus to connect and build trust. **Think beyond** scheduled video calls: quick email and text-message check-ins can **give support** at crucial moments, while phone chats – without face-to-face contact – can help people **open up** about difficult information.

The right experience

You may choose to coach your potential leaders yourself, or you may prefer to appoint other internal or external coaches. Whoever you choose, they must have the right business and coaching experience or have received training on how to coach effectively.

Successful **coaching** creates an increased **self-appreciation** in your future leaders of their personal **strengths, competences, approach, and actions**

Challenging and supporting

The hallmark of a skilled coach is knowing when to challenge and when to support the individual being coached. Successful coaches work to build self-awareness and release potential, by, for example, unblocking limiting or constricting beliefs or confronting unhelpful behaviours. They encourage the people they are coaching to reflect deeply, think strategically, release their instinctive creativity, and feel good about who they are.

The results of successful coaching should be an increased self-appreciation in your future leaders of their personal strengths, competences, approach, and actions. These newly developed leadership elements, in turn, should align with your organization's stated values and aims.

Tip

MAP OUT THE PROCESS
When providing **coaching,
explain** what the process
is, how long it will take,
and what will be covered.
Encourage the coachee
to journal their progress.

Benefiting the business

Coaching and mentoring – especially of
first line and middle managers – is often
focused on specific issues or to help
people make leadership transitions.
In this case, experienced mentors from
your organization may be most suitable.
Senior managers may benefit from an
external coach with more experience at
board level. With successful coaching
you may find leaders become better at
innovating and developing the overall
capability of their teams. The effects of
coaching flow through the organization
and provide significant business benefits
including those listed here:

etention of key
ecutives

Enhanced working
relationships

Greater alignment of
individual/corporate
objectives

**The benefits
of coaching**

New perspectives
on business issues

The effects of coaching
flow through the
organization

Adapting to a changing landscape

In today's corporate world, the old idea of a job for life has been all but superseded by that of the portfolio career. Leaders now face near-constant transition, and only those who develop the change-management skills to cope will survive. The emphasis has shifted from excelling in a particular corporate position to excelling in one vital project – leading your own life based on consistent principles.

Profiting from change

In business today, leaders need to manage and inspire not just their core teams but groups of freelancers, temporary staff, and outsourcers. Engaging such potentially disparate groups to align them with the vision and values of the organization is the new leadership challenge. Leaders today may be heading up a virtual team – with members based globally – formed around a customer problem that needs solving or an innovative idea rather than a group of people physically working together for the same employer. Leaders with the ability to be agile, to build virtual networks, teams, and alliances quickly, will be the long-term winners.

Leaders are looking less and less to their employers to provide a framework or support system for their life – they need to develop it themselves. As an individual aiming to survive in this rapidly changing environment, you must be excellent at understanding customer needs and have supreme confidence in your ability to deliver, and market, yourself. Thinking creatively and with vision, both about your career and personal mission, should become a life-long process and a central theme in your continued success.

|08 Identify your next direction for development

|07 Refine your brand

|06 Practice ne skills and behaviours

randing yourself

o how do you develop yourself as a ader able to thrive in today's shifting orporate world? One way of answering at is to think of what you can deliver to ur customers as a brand. Your brand gnals your professional, technical, and nctional knowledge and skills, and also

your position in the market. Aim to develop yourself much as you would steer a brand. Shape your product (what you offer) to anticipate customer demand, and develop your identity to make the best fit with desirable clients. For example, should your next client be a small enterprise where you can work closely on your entrepreneurial acumen, or should it be a large corporation where you can refresh process management knowledge? Consider your next step carefully – how will it shape your brand?

How to develop continuously

01 ssess your mpetences d match with stomer needs

02 Take an assignment to stretch you

03 Listen to customers; engage with others; join networks; initiate alliances

Leaders with the ability to be **agile,** to build virtual **networks** and alliances quickly, will be the long-term **winners**

04 Learn from best practice

05 Recognize your potential for development

ACHIEVING HIGH PERFORMANCE

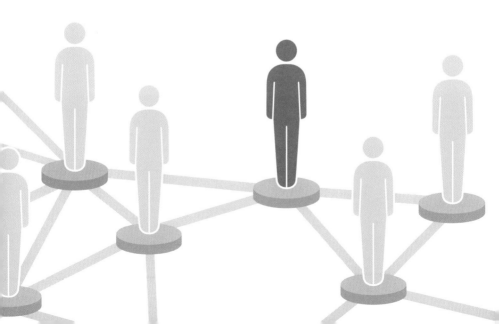

Knowing **yourself**

To prosper in both life and business, you need to understand yourself. What are your talents and flaws, what do you enjoy, and what do you really want to achieve? By reflecting upon and analysing your own characteristics, and how you are perceived by others, you can begin to produce a plan for self-development and ultimate success.

09

Looking in from outside

Other people's perceptions of you may be significantly at odds with your own view of yourself. Finding out what others think of you is an important element of self-exploration, and helps you modify your behaviour in order to be offered the opportunities that you might otherwise have missed.

Seeking new perspectives

You may feel you lack confidence, or that you are too quiet, but others may see you primarily as someone who is trustworthy, honourable, and wise. Conversely, you may describe yourself as assertive and confident, while others see you as aggressive and avoid involving you in their projects. Other people's views are important because they shape the way they behave towards you. That's not to say you should always aim to please others, or change the person you are, but being aware of how others see you will enable you to modify the signals you send out.

70%

of **employers** say **personality** is a top consideration when **hiring** a person

---

In focus

PSYCHOMETRIC TESTING

Psychometric tests, such as the widely used Myers Briggs and offshoots, such as the NERIS Type Explorer Test, offer a psychological approach to self-understanding. These tests look at personality and attempt to give an indication of the type of environment in which an individual is likely to thrive.

Myers-Briggs Type Indicator positions people against four pairs of factors: extroversion and introversion; sensing and intuition; thinking and feeling; and judging and perceiving. There is nothing wrong with any of these personality traits. But if, for example, you are at the extreme end of the scale on "thinking", you may be ignoring people's feelings when you make decisions. If you are a "perceiving" rather than a "judging" person, you may need to set more goals and deadlines for yourself. Several psychometrics tests are available to take online, including the Myers Briggs test at mbtionline.com and the NERIS test at 16personalities.com.

etting answers

e only way to find out what other people nk of you is to ask. Many companies use process called 360-degree feedback, nich is a formal means of eliciting mment from people around you at all vels, from staff and bosses, to clients, d friends. It is often used to develop nior management teams, but you can rry out a similar process yourself on a smaller scale. Approach people who see you in different roles – perhaps your business partner, work colleagues at the same level, your immediate boss, some suppliers and clients, and a couple of friends. Think of the best way to ask the questions: a questionnaire ensures consistency, while structured, face-to-face interviews give respondents the opportunity to elaborate, but may also inhibit honest responses. Apps, such as Spidergap and Sage HR, can help you do this, too. Keep questionnaires short and simple, concentrating on specific questions you want answered, such as:

- How confident do I appear to you?
- Am I approachable?
- Do I communicate clearly?

Tip

MAKE AN IMPRESSION
Lasting judgements can be made, based on subconscious cues, within the **first few seconds** of meeting. Think about any **visual cues** you display and the **tone of voice** you use – these can often be **more significant** than what you actually say.

Using feedback
The feedback process won't give you a definitive view of what you are like in the eyes of others, but it is certain to produce some valuable insights. It's too easy to focus on criticisms when you see them in black and white, so make sure that you value and reflect on the positive points that emerge, and use them in your planning for the future.

Setting goals

Work takes up a large chunk of your life, so job satisfaction is important. Achieving it doesn't necessarily mean changing your position, it could just be a matter of broadening your existing role. Knowing what you enjoy and want to achieve will help ensure you're in the right place. If you like what you do, you're more likely to succeed.

Examining your ambitions

Getting a clear view of your ambitions is not quite as easy as it seems. First, you may have arrived where you are more by chance than by design and it can be hard to avoid being influenced by your current situation. So, if you are working in sales, you may not look beyond a future in which you progress through the ranks to become sales manager and then sales director. Second, you may have family ties or other responsibilities that limit your freedom to follow your dreams. Third, your "ideal" job may change over time as you develop skills and experience.

Think specifically and generate images of **your ideal world**

Looking to the future

There are many ways to systematically look at your career and life goals. Some people prefer to work with a coach – an objective, sympathetic, and experienced person who can help identify directions for progress. Others favour less formal consultation with their colleagues or peers, but it is equally valid to work through the options on your own. Indeed, the question is so central that it is worth applying more than one approach and repeating the analysis from time to time as your circumstances change.

70%

of people in a study who sent **weekly progress reports** to a friend achieved their **goals**

Visualizing the way

Visualization is a technique that can help you clarify your goals. Set aside some time to sit undisturbed and relaxed. Picture yourself at various points in the future, say in three, five, and ten years' time. Think specifically and generate images of your ideal world, asking yourself questions such as:

- Where will I be living?
- What job will I have?
- What type of organization will I be working in?
- Will I own and be running my own business?
- What will I be doing on a daily basis?
- Will I have a team working for me or will I be a specialist?
- Will I be commuting or working from home, perhaps?
- What will my interests be?

te down your thoughts and assess
e picture that emerges against fixed
nstraints, such as other obligations you
ay have, to your family, for example.

Now reflect on the results. How can
u work towards being where you would
e to be? This process is not intended to
ake you dissatisfied with your present
rcumstances, but to open your eyes
new possibilities.

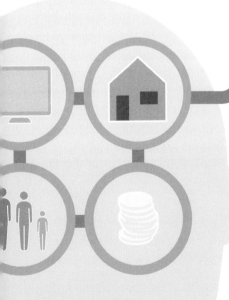

Tip

THINK BIG
Reach for the sky – it is
important to **dream** before
you do a reality check.

How to discover what is important to you

Take five sticky notes.

Write on each sticky note
something you enjoy at
work, for example
"managing my team".

Take another five sticky
notes in a different colour.

Write on each sticky note
something you would like
to do, but currently do not,
for example "travel".

Arrange all of the sticky
notes on the wall in order
of priority. The results will
help focus your efforts.

Analysing your strengths and limitations

To achieve high performance in your job, you need to understand and play to your strengths. You also need to recognize what you are less good at doing, so that you can develop appropriate skills and acquire the necessary knowledge and experience.

Describing your capabilities

When you ask yourself what you are really good at, your answer should encompass three important areas – your basic technical ability, your interpersonal "soft skills", and the knowledge and experience that you have acquired throughout your career.

Most people have a preference for what they like to do. Some people are good at working with numbers, while others excel at languages. These skills are the building blocks of your job – they are sometimes called your basic technical ability.

> ### Tip
>
> **REVIEW YOUR SKILLS**
> Even if you plan to stay in the same job, **look closely** at what's happening around you. Your work environment is in flux and you should **constantly be learning and adapting,** to cope and thrive with the **new circumstances** your role presents to you.

Gaining skills and experience

Soft skills are just as important, perhaps more so, than technical ability. You may be a good listener or a powerful communicator, or have the ability to influence people or negotiate well, or you may command respect, have great presence, and be highly motivated. You need to achieve a certain level of skill in all these areas, but that level will depend on your precise role in the organization.

The third dimension of your personal strong and weak points is your knowledge and experience, both of the sector and the role in which you work. For example, if you work in human resources, do you have sufficient knowledge of employment law? Reflect on your skills and knowledge: they may be good enough for your current role, but will they suffice in the future? Try to identify the role that best fits with your ambitions, and ask yourself what skills you will need to fit that role. Published job descriptions and job advertisements provide a good guide to current industry standards and what employers are looking for. Set about gaining those skills through additional training, or by realigning your role with your current employer.

SWOT analysis for a human resources executive

STRENGTHS

- O Experience in **training**
- O **Presentation** skills
- O Good **communicator**
- O Good **knowledge** of employment law

WEAKNESSES

- O Poor **understanding** of recruitment systems
- O No **experience** of disciplinary meetings
- O Don't like **conflict**

OPPORTUNITIES

- O Set up my own **training business**
- O **Broaden** my role to include recruitment

THREATS

- O Company may **outsource** training
- O Company may want all-round **HR skills** in the future

Carrying out a SWOT analysis

A simple way to assess yourself is to carry out a SWOT analysis. List your strengths and weaknesses, and the opportunities open and threats to you in your current role, as in the example above. This SWOT analysis provides a picture of the development you need in order to excel in your present situation, and the skills, knowledge, and experience you will need to acquire to succeed in your next professional role.

Developing your brand

We have looked at the importance of how other people see you and of understanding yourself, your strengths and limitations, and your ambitions. Developing your brand is about how you bring these factors together, use them to differentiate yourself from other people, and develop your career.

Giving the right impression

A company brand is a unique and consistent set of values that underpins its product or service. Just as a company builds its brand, you need to know what you stand for and what sort of image you want to project to others. You need to make sure the messages you give out are consistent with your personal brand.

This does not mean you should try to be something you aren't. Pretending may work for a short time but it will be impossible to keep up over a long period. Your "brand" has to be something that you are completely comfortable with. It should reflect your values and be uniquely yours.

> Just as a company builds its **brand,** you need to **know** what you **stand for** and what sort of image you **want to project** to others

Creating the right look

There are some aspects of the way you look, sound, and behave that are essential to your brand, wherever you are working. Paying attention to your appearance, whatever your style, being polite, and fulfilling your promises, for

Tip

EXPAND YOUR NETWORK
Boost connections with your company, university, colleagues, and others, both **online and off,** to **build your brand** and open up opportunities.

example, are all "musts". Your brand needs to take into account your "target audience", such as the organization you work for and the customers you work with. If you work for an old-fashioned firm of lawyers, for example, wearing the latest fashion in shorts and flashy jewellery probably won't inspire your clients with confidence, but it may do if you work for a high-fashion retailer.

Being personable

While appearance is one aspect of personal branding, how you behave is often far more important. If you look the part but fail to do what you have been asked or are bad-tempered and difficult then no amount of image makeovers will help you succeed. The key to defining your brand is to pay attention to every element of the image you project, and make sure your actions are consistent and acceptable to your target audience.

What defines your brand?

LOOKING THE PART

- The **clothes, shoes, and jewellery** you wear – style and colours
- The way you **style your hair** – always well groomed
- The appearance of your **hands and nails** – clean at all times; if you wear nail polish, it should be appropriate to your situation
- The way you **move – with a purpose**
- The way you present yourself on **social media** – have a completed up-to-date, well-written profile, with a professional photo

ACTING THE PART

- **Shaking hands** firmly, but not squeezing too hard
- Saying **thank you**
- Returning **calls or emails** within a reasonable time
- **Respecting** other people's views and giving
- Giving other people the **credit due** to them
- Doing what you have **promised** to do
- Behaving **ethically,** treating people **equally,** being **inclusive**
- **Standing your ground** when necessary

SOUNDING THE PART

- The **tone of your voice** – lower-pitched voices carry more weight
- The **pace of your speech** – slow enough to sound purposeful but not hesitant
- The **words you choose** – short, active, and positive, or longer and more descriptive?
- The **expression in your voice** – approachable and friendly

Planning for the future

**There is a saying that "all plans are useless, but planning is vital".
Plans are useless as they quickly become out of date. But without the
process of planning, you won't prepare for the future. You do need to
plan, but don't stick to your plans so rigidly that you miss opportunities**

Knowing where you're going

Life is unpredictable, so why plan? First,
all of the things you want to achieve in
your life require effort and preparation.
So, you need to ensure you acquire the
qualifications and experience that will
allow you to progress in your chosen
career, and to do that, you need a plan.
Having a plan gives you a framework
against which to measure your progress.

Setting objectives

Have you achieved what you set out to d
If not, why not? What can you learn from
your successes and failures? A plan als
provides a reference against which you
can judge new opportunities. How much
will this opportunity contribute to you
achieving your goals? If it doesn't, why
do you want to do it? Is it a distraction
or have your goals and plan changed?

In focus

WHAT'S ON YOUR CV?
One good way to plan the future is to create
a version of your CV three, five, and ten
years in the future. What qualifications
would appear? What job titles would you
have? Which companies would you have
worked for? What experience would you
have gained in each of the roles you have
undertaken? If you don't know what to
put on the CV, why not look online for job
advertisements. They will tell you what
companies are looking for when filling these
roles today. This should give you some idea
about how to construct an outline future CV
to work towards. However, given the pace
of technological change, knowing what
skills will be needed for many careers in
the future – and whether those careers will
even exist – is not easy. You also need to stay
adaptable and on top of developments.

HAVING AN EFFECTIVE FUTURE PLAN

Dos	Don'ts
O **Defining key measurable goals that logically lead to achieving your vision**	O Relying on chance rather than your own efforts
O **Setting goals that are believable and achievable**	O Choosing goals with unattainable qualifiers
O **Always using your plan when making big real-life decisions**	O Reviewing and revising your plan infrequently

A plan provides a **reference** against which you can **judge** new **opportunities**

Creating a plan

A good plan for your future needs to include four key elements:

- A vision statement that describes where you want to be
- A set of objectives that, if achieved, will lead you to the vision
- A "success map" showing how these objectives link together
- An indicator describing what success will look like at each stage (see below).

Think first about your vision of the future: is it all about a single goal, such as becoming president of a multi-national company, or is it about a lifestyle, such as striking a healthy work/life balance? Use some of the exercises described over the previous pages to help you to think about your vision. Next, write your vision down in a vision statement. This should not be longer than a paragraph, but needs to contain all the attributes that are important to you. Spend time on this statement; it is the important first step in planning your future.

Write your vision down in a **vision statement.** This should not be longer than a paragraph, but needs to contain all **the attributes** that are **important** to you

Developing a vision

Once you have a clear idea of your overall vision for the future, break it down into its main constituent parts. Do this by creating a set of top-level objectives you will need to achieve to reach your vision

ASK YOURSELF...

Am I on track to reach my goal?   YES   NO

Create an indicator of success for each of the objectives in your success map by asking yourself:

1 **Do I understand** why this objective is important? .... ☐ ☐

2 Do I know how it links into my **success map**? .... ☐ ☐

3 Can I identify **what is to be achieved** and by when? .... ☐ ☐

4 Can I **measure** this? .... ☐ ☐

5 Do I know how often I should **reflect on progress**? .... ☐ ☐

6 **Do I know what I should do** if the objective is not being met? ...... ☐ ☐

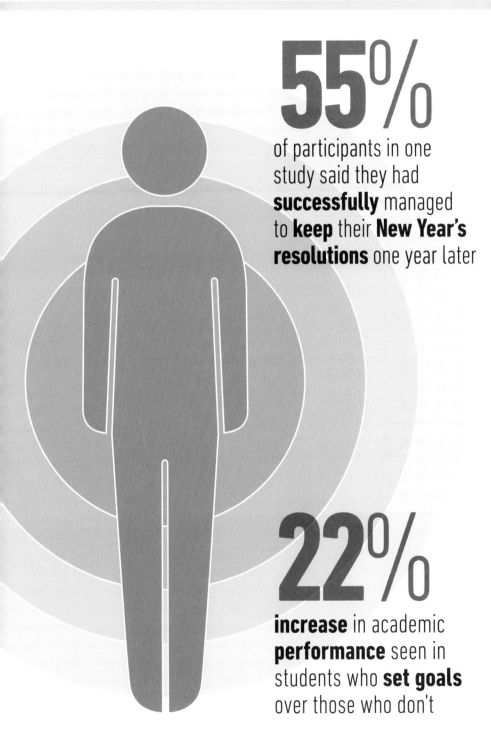

55%
of participants in one study said they had **successfully** managed to **keep** their **New Year's resolutions** one year later

22%
increase in academic **performance** seen in students who **set goals** over those who don't

Creating a success map for your future

A success map is a useful tool for thinking through the key actions you need to take to achieve your goals and for representing these in a single picture.

- To create your success map, start from the top – your ultimate goal. Write this at one edge of your map.
- Think about how you will achieve this goal. For example, imagine your vision is to become sales director for a major pharmaceutical company. To achieve this goal, you will need to have been a regional sales manager for three to five years, to have handled some major clients within your portfolio, and to have gained a professional sales qualification. These objectives become the second-level goals on your success map.
- Next, ask yourself how to achieve these objectives, and fill in the next level of your map.
- At all stages, use lines to connect later objectives that are dependent on you having first achieved the earlier objectives.
- To check that your success map is complete and follows a logical progression, work along from one edge to the other. For each objective, ask "Why am I doing this?" – the answer should be to obtain the objective above.

A **success map** helps you think through the **key actions** you must take to reach your **goals** and to represent them in a picture

Success map for an aspiring sales director

Raise my profile within the company

Spend a secondment in brand marketing

Attend the Sales Management programme

Spead five years as a sales executive

Develop an excellent sales record

Pass the Institute's exams

70%
of people do not
feel any **urgency**
to **achieve**
their goals

Spend **three to five
years** as regional
sales manager

Handle **large
accounts** and have
major clients within
my portfolio

Achieve promotion
to the level of
**national sales
director**

Obtain the relevant
**professional sales
qualification**

43%
of people **set goals** that
are **difficult** or **daring**

Improving
your skills

Think of your portfolio of skills as your toolkit. Once you have acquired your skills, they will stay with you – as long as you maintain them. From time to time, you will need to add new tools to your kit as the requirements of your job change or evolve, and as new ways of doing things emerge.

10

Managing your time

While you can raise additional finance for your business, employ more people, and buy more machinery, there will only ever be 24 hours in a day. Time is one of the few commodities you cannot buy, but there are many techniques to help you use your time more effectively.

How to set up a time log

Planning **encourages you to think** not just about the day ahead, but also the **more distant future**

At the end of the week, analyse how you have spent your time and draw a pie chart to show where your time goes.

Tracking your time

Before you can start actively managing your time, you need to find out how you spend it. Rather than just guessing, record your expenditure of time over a period of at least a week in a time log. Time-tracking apps, such as RescueTime and Toggl, can do much of this for you, but a pen and paper also work (see graphic). When you have completed the analysis, consider if the way you spend time reflects your key objectives. For example, you may find you spend five per cent of your time visiting customers. Is this an activity that delivers key results (because it generates sales)? If it is, consider if you would be more effective by spending more time on it.

As you work, record in the right-hand column the letter of the activity you have completed in the last 15 minutes.

6 mins

the average **time** workers **spend** between **checking emails** and **messages**

Categorize your tasks, e.g. answering emails, writing reports, planning, thinking, visiting clients, travelling.

Assign a code or letter to each of these categories (e.g. emails = E, thinking = T).

Keep a sheet of paper on your desk, divided into two columns.

Split your day into 15-minute segments; enter these periods in the first column.

Making time

Planning encourages you to think not just about the day ahead, but also the more distant future. It's all too easy to put off big but necessary strategic projects, such as arranging training for your staff or creating a database of contacts, because you are immersed in day-to-day activities. Think about the longer-term projects you would like to implement in the next quarter. Break these tasks into manageable chunks, and estimate how much time it will take you to complete each chunk.

Planning your day

Using a time-management app or pen and paper, prepare an action plan setting out your activities for the day ahead. Do this either first thing in the morning, when you feel fresh, or at the end of the day, for tomorrow's activities. Build time into your plan for day-to-day duties and work on longer-term projects. Failing to stick to an over-optimistic plan can be demotivating, so be realistic in your timings, allowing for interruptions and some breaks.

Calculating priority

When writing your plan, prioritize your tasks objectively – it often helps to categorize tasks according to importance and urgency. Give priority to those that are both urgent and important (for example, producing up-to-date figures for the next day's sales meeting). Tasks that are important but not urgent (such as completing segments of your large projects) take second priority. Tasks that are not important but urgent (such as dealing with someone else's request for information) take third priority, and those that are neither important nor urgent should be delegated or not done at all.

Categorize tasks according to **importance and urgency.** Give **priority** to those that are both **urgent and important.** Tasks that are important but not urgent take **second priority**

Tip

BE DISCIPLINED
Try to **deal with documents** only once. Add a marker (such as a colour tag or character) to a file each time you work on it; attempt to minimize the number of markers – **the discipline will slowly work** its way into all your processes.

How to prioritize your tasks

21%

f working hours
re spent looking
t **entertainment,**
ews, and **social media**

Structuring your day

To make the most of every work day, get to know the times of day when you are most effective and creative. If you are a "morning" person, plan to tackle your creative tasks – such as writing proposals or reports – and your challenging tasks, such as talking to a difficult client, in the morning. Take on routine tasks in the afternoon. If you are an "afternoon" person, do your routine tasks first, but make sure that you don't get hooked into doing them all day.

HIGH URGENCY, HIGH IMPORTANCE | 01

LOW URGENCY, HIGH IMPORTANCE | 02

HIGH URGENCY, LOW IMPORTANCE | 03

LOW URGENCY, LOW IMPORTANCE | 04

Working effectively

To help you work quickly and effectively, always keep your desk tidy and ensure frequently used items are readily available to hand. The same goes for information you use regularly. Set up favourites for websites; keep your contacts up to date, and a list of who knows what; and use a notes app or create a folder for storing nuggets of information you refer to often.

Build thinking time into your schedule: travel is often considered to be a time-waster, but it can also provide just the change of pace and scenery you need to do some valuable creative thinking.

Set aside **15 minutes** every so often to **check email and return calls.** Let people know you will be unavailable between certain times

Focusing your actions

40%

of **knowledge workers** never get more than **30 continuous minutes** of **focused time** in an average working day

VOICE AND VIDEO CALLS

O **Prepare everything** you want to say before you call.

O **Talking by voice or video** helps to build relationships, but sometimes emailing instead avoids distraction.

O **If someone calls** you and you're short on time, tell them you will call them back at a specific time. Be sure always to follow up on your promise.

ealing with interruptions

ake sure the working day is under your
ntrol by eliminating interruptions. If
u are working on a report that requires
ncentration, divert your phone or put it
voicemail; set aside 15 minutes every
often to check email and return calls.

Let people know you will be unavailable,
or share your online calender so that
colleagues can check your availability
without bothering you. If someone drops
in to talk to you unexpectedly, tell them
you are working to a deadline and avoid
eye contact – they will get the message.

EMAILS

O **Streamline** your use of email
by checking for new messages
and responding to them only
at certain times of the day.

O **Use colour** to highlight
important or urgent emails.

O **Target emails:** avoid copying
in people you don't need to,
and ask others to do the same.

O **Clear out** your email
inbox regularly.

WORKING QUICKLY

O **Make your decision** and
don't keep thinking about
it afterwards.

O **Balance time** with quality
control; a report may be
excellent, but if it's too late
it may be of no use.

O **Concentrate** on what you're
doing at a particular time, and
don't let your thoughts flit from
one thing to another.

Participating in meetings

Modern technology allows us to attend meetings from anywhere. But whether you're present in person or joining from your kitchen, it is important to approach things in a professional way. Meetings are where decisions are made that affect your future, where relationships are built, and where you can make your views heard, and find out what others thin

Researching well

Preparation is essential to ensure you make the most of your opportunity. Read any material in advance and note down issues you need to clarify and points you want to make. For important and complex discussions, you may want to sound out other people's opinions to help you form your own view and get an idea of who will support your thinking.

Making your mark

When you attend a meeting in person, try to sit near people who are likely to support your views, and ideally in the middle of the group. During any meeting, it is important to find opportunities to speak. If you are nervous about making your own points, get used to hearing your voice by making short remarks in support of others. A clear, firm: "I agree with that point" will get you noticed. Also, ask questions for clarification, which will make you sound interested. Try drafting points to make in advance, and introduce them early on, but be sure to do so in context. Have the first words of what you want to say in your mind; wait for a pause, then say those words clearly. Pause, then carry on with the rest. Be careful, too, that you don't speak too much: it's better to be known as someone who makes good points than who speaks all the time.

Am I participating well in meetings?

Do I **speak clearly** and loudly enough to be heard?

Do I **support** others?

Do I **look at everyone** as I make my point?

Do I **contribute** to the meeting early on?

Do I **listen** to what is being said?

Do I interrupt others only when **it is necessary?**

ecording meetings

ِu should keep a record of all meetings, en if it is just simple notes of who ٫reed to do what. Take minutes, or if it ِ a virtual meeting, you can record the ِl to share later – though be sure to get ٫rmission from all participants before ٫ing this. For regular gatherings, such ِ staff or committee meetings, it can ِ useful if minutes take a formal style, ٫cause this helps to reinforce the ٫portance of the meeting.

٫king minutes

٫ou are the minute-taker, clarify what ٫rm the minutes should take with the ٫airperson beforehand. For some ٫eetings it is important to know who ٫id what. But for most meetings, the ٫y point is to record actions you decide ٫, who is taking them, and when they

must be completed. If the chairperson does not summarize what has been agreed at the end of each agenda item, ask them for clarification. Always aim to produce the minutes as soon as possible afterwards, when the discussion is fresh in your mind. Try to keep them as succinct as possible, without detracting from making a full and accurate record of everything that had been agreed.

٫HECKLIST...

٫etting ready for a virtual meeting   **YES   NO**

1 Have you **prepared for the content** of the meeting? .... ☐ ☐

2 Have you checked what's **visible in your background?** .... ☐ ☐

3 Have you looked in a mirror to ensure you're **presentable?** .... ☐ ☐

4 Have you checked your **internet connection, camera, and microphone** are all working properly? .... ☐ ☐

5 Do you know how to use the required **software?** Can you **share your screen** and turn your microphone on and off? .... ☐ ☐

6 Have you asked those nearby **not to disturb you?** .... ☐ ☐

7 Have you checked attendees are happy for you to **record the call,** or asked someone to **take minutes?** .... ☐ ☐

Chairing a meeting

Chairing a meeting, whether in-person or virtually, is an excellent way to gain visibility. You don't need to have expertise in the subject, but you do need a range of procedural skills. These range from the technical – how to produce an agenda – to the diplomatic, such as how to keep the discussion moving and stop people from speaking for too long

How to run the meeting

Ensure there is someone to take the minutes and let them know the format you want the minutes to follow.

At the end of the meeting, remind everyone what has to be achieved and summarize what has been agreed, to help the minute-taker.

Calling a meeting

People often complain about how many meetings they have to attend. At a time when few of us have time to spare, joining a meeting that results in no action is just a waste of time. So before you call a meeting, whether in-person or remote, ask yourself: is this meeting necessary or can it be done by another means, such as by email or a conference call perhaps?

Inviting the right people

If you do decide that a meeting is necessary, next consider who should attend. This will obviously depend on the purpose of the meeting. If you are briefing employees about changes tha are to be made to your department's structure, for example, then it's essent that everyone attends. If you want view on how the structure should change, o the other hand, you might want to invit just a few key people. Once you have decided who should attend, communi the date and venue, whether physical or virtual, in plenty of time. Give an indication of how long the meeting wi take, to help your invitees plan their t

etting the agenda

n agenda is essential to ensure that
ur meeting has a focus and to enable
articipants to prepare beforehand.
ow you structure it will have a major
npact on the success of the meeting.
ne best plan is to word the agenda
o that the type of treatment necessary
r each item is clear.

> A **successful chairperson** is able to make **everyone feel** that their **opinions have been valued**

Let everyone speak, but move the conversation on to the next person when they have had their say.

If someone is dominating the discussion, politely say "Thank you. That was useful and I think we've understood your point. I see Joe has something to add."

Keep to time, but allow sufficient airing of the issues.

Try to bring quieter people into the conversation. If you think someone may have something to contribute, ask directly if he or she would like to add anything.

reating items

n item labelled "To discuss" on
 agenda, means an open debate
 the issues. The term "To note",
eans there will not be any real
eneral discussion unless there
 a point someone is desperate to
ise. The timings you allot to each
em and where you place items on
e agenda will give participants an
ea of the importance of that subject.
r regular meetings, it is usually
good idea to ask participants in
dvance if there is anything they
ant to add to the agenda, or whether
ere is anything they want to raise
nder "any other business".

Running the meeting

The role of the chairperson is to ensure the meeting achieves its aims. A chair needs to make everyone feel they have been able to air their views, that their opinions have been valued, and that they have achieved something. If you're chairing a video meeting, it's a good idea to get people to mute their microphones when not speaking. In big groups, ask everyone to submit questions via your software's chat function or a shared text document to avoid interruptions.

Dealing with conflict

Conflict can arise with people who are genuinely obstructive or just those who see the world differently from you. In either case, to manage challenging behaviour, you first need to gain an understanding of the person, and then employ a set of tactics to manage the situation.

Planning for resolution

You can't change a person by being conflictive yourself. You have to set a target for the situation or relationship you wish to achieve, and then create a strategy to reach that goal. The approach you take will depend on the situation, the person, and the type of behaviour. One option is to call a private meeting with the individual in question.

Tip

ACT EARLY
Tackle problematic behaviour as soon as it **becomes evident** – the longer you leave it, the harder it becomes to cope with, and it may affect other members of the team.

Discussing the situation

Select a location to meet in a place where you won't be disturbed or noticed by colleagues. Prepare what you want to say and how you will say it. Tell the person how you see the main issues and problem, logically and without emotion. Ask how the individual sees it – don't interrupt, even if you disagree. Ask for solutions and, finally, add some ways in which you think the problems might be resolved.

Facing up to conflict

Truly challenging people affect everyone. Few will fail to notice their behaviour, so it is important to face any conflict rather that allowing it to fester and affect the whole team. It is important to keep in mind that you need to act and not let the conflict affect you deeply. If the other person becomes threatening or abusive, walk away with dignity, saying you will consider the situation and get back to him or her.

CONDUCTING A MEETING

Dos	Don'ts
O **Letting the person speak**	O Interrupting
O **Putting your case calmly**	O Getting over-emotional
O **Standing your ground**	O Becoming argumentative
O **Breathing slowly and deeply**	O Taking it personally

Strategies for conflictive behaviours

TYPE OF BEHAVIOUR	COPING STRATEGY
Negative Complains and disagrees with everything	O **Keep positive** – avoid being dragged down to their level O Point out **earlier instances** where your **suggestion has worked** O Put their **"trouble-spotting" talents** to good use on a project of their own
Unresponsive Uses silence as an offensive weapon	O **Allow silences,** rather than filling gaps in the conversation O Get them to talk by **asking open questions** to which they can't answer just "yes" or "no" O If you can't get them talking, call the meeting to a halt. **Explain** that nothing is being achieved and **propose another meeting** or course of action. Ask them to consider how the situation might be resolved
Overpowering Uses anger as an offensive weapon	O Let them **express** their anger O Try to **empathize** O When they have calmed down, **find the real cause** and possible solutions
Wants to "go it alone" Doesn't see themself as part of the team	O Tell them how they are seen by other **team members** O **Explain** what team membership requires O Point out how their **strengths can help** the team
Shows enthusiasm but few results Underachieves repeatedly	O Without dampening their **enthusiasm,** ask why something hasn't been completed O Help them **understand** how to get things done O Restrict their **workload**

Becoming
more effective

There is a basic set of skills that can help you become more effective at everything you do. Like the oil in a machine, skills such as listening, decision-making, and communicating help everything run more smoothly and boost your success.

11

Reading and remembering

We are bombarded with information all day. The key to success is to be able to identify what is important and then remember it. Recalling an important fact can make the difference between success or failure in the heat of a negotiation or an important meeting.

Reading rapidly

Reading a text book is not the same as reading for pleasure. There is a process for reading a text book. Start by reading the introduction, then read the last chapter. At this point you should know what the book is about and how it's structured; now, you can decide whether it's worth reading the rest. If you think you would benefit from reading the book, begin by looking at the headings and diagrams on each page; you will be surprised by how much you learn. Once you have done your initial review, leave a gap before you read the book as a whole – this greatly reinforces learning.

Scanning the details

The faster you read, the more you can learn. If you practise long enough, you will be able to scan a document and remember enough to hold a conversation about it. Start by reading whole sentences in one go. To do this, focus your eyes on the sentence rather than on each word. Move to looking at paragraphs. Soon you should be able to look at the page towards the top, in the middle, and finally at the bottom before you turn over.

Try scanning the whole document first. Then read it at your **normal pace.** You will **be surprised** how much you pick up

238

words per minute is the average **rate** for **reading silently** in English

earning from documents
'hen you are learning, try scanning
ver the whole document first. Then read
at your normal pace. Just scanning first
ill improve your understanding and
emory. If you are late and unprepared
r a meeting, try scanning some of your
ocuments. You will be surprised how
uch you pick up. Even if it does not
ork, you will be able to find most of the
formation you need much more quickly.

sing mind maps
"mind map" is an effective way to record
formation in a succinct format that you
an easily remember. To create a mind
ap that summarizes the content of a
ook you have read, for example, start
y writing the subject of the book in the
entre of a sheet of paper. Then draw

branches radiating from the subject
that sum up the major themes of the
book. Next, fill in smaller branches
containing the sub-themes, and finally
add detail to these sub-themes in the
outer "twigs" of your mind map.

Remembering the ideas
Use pictures and colour liberally, as they
make your mind map more memorable
and will increase your recall of the
information. If you want to be sure that
you will remember the content of your
map, review it the day after you have
drawn it, one week later, one month
later, and finally one year later.

Being creative

Creativity enables you to solve, or contribute to solving, all kinds of problems. This will get you noticed. Some people appear naturally innovative, but creative problem-solving is a skill that you can learn and hone through practice. Brainstorming, reframing the problem, and benchmarking are some of the techniques available.

Finding creative solutions

Creativity comes from abandoning linear thought and making leaps of the imagination. All your brain needs is the stimulus to make these leaps. Brainstorming is one technique for helping do this. Getting a group of people together to come up with possible solutions without the constraint of evaluating the suggestions creates energy and sparks new ideas. Another technique is asking people to consider the problem from a different perspective such as: "How will our customers see this?" or "What if we turn the question on its head?"

Practise being creative in your private life as well, and it will develop your ability to be creative at work. Stimulate your brain by taking a different route in your work, completing crossword puzzles, learning a new language, taking an activity holiday, or finding a new experience.

> **Tip**
>
> **STIMULATE CREATIVITY**
> If you want to inspire your creativity, **change your scene** – go for a walk, have a coffee and **relax,** or **interact with others.**

Practise being **creative** in your private life, and it will **develop** your **ability** to be **creative at work**

sking the right questions

hen you are faced with a problem,
s often the boundaries or rules that
nstrain your thinking. "We can't do
s because..." is a phrase that stifles
eativity. Instead, asking the question:
/hat if this constraint wasn't there?" will
ow you to consider all the new options
d benefits open to you, and can create
new world in your mind. You will often
d the opportunities open to you when
u remove a constraint are so great
at it is worth the time and effort it
kes to remove it. Did James Dyson
k the question "What if we don't
ve a bag?" when he invented his
volutionary bagless vacuum cleaner?

Tip

USE PRESSURE
A tight deadline can
increase your creativity.
You will often find that with
a short deadline you'll come
up with **more alternatives**
and often a **better solution.**
However, it's also true that if
you have a complex problem,
"sleeping on it" can help you
find the answer.

Using benchmarking
Not every problem has to be solved
again from scratch. Most problems
have been solved before so all you have
to do is find the solution. Benchmarking
is a very useful tool for doing this.

Benchmarking is about comparing
processes. It is about weighing up the
way your organization does something
against the way in which another
organization performs the same
function. Start by making sure that
you understand your own processes.
Who does what, when, how, and why?
Just doing this will create ideas for
improvement, but it also forms the
basis for benchmarking: comparing
your processes with those of your
chosen benchmark subject.

Who should you benchmark yourself
against? Ideally, find an organization
that is really good at the process you
are trying to improve – for example,
if you want to improve your despatch
function, you might benchmark yourself
against a company that is efficient at
dealing with complex orders.

Being confident

Confidence is precious. It enables you to do what you want to do without constant fear of failure, or even despite fear on some occasions, and to maintain your sense of self-worth and not be dependent on what other people think. If you're confident, you can take centre stage when you want – you don't always have to linger in the background.

Thinking positive

The first step in building your confidence is to pay attention to what you're thinking. Concentrate on your positive thoughts. It's very easy to focus on the negative. You probably find that when you have been given feedback, at your appraisal perhaps, you concentrate solely on the one negative comment even though there were five positive comments.

Creating good thoughts

To help overcome this, build a bank of achievements and positive comments that you can contemplate and reflect on whenever you feel uncertain about yourself and your abilities. Take some time to yourself, and answer the following simple questions:

● What have I achieved in the last year and in the last five years?
● What am I most proud of? What did it feel like when I did it?
● What am I good at? Create a list of your talents and skills.
● What compliments have I received from others?

Concentrate solely on the positives of each situation, don't let negative "but" thoughts creep in. Commit the answers to your "achievement bank" and draw on them in moments of doubt.

Pay attention to what you're thinking. **Concentrate** on your **positive thoughts**

What have I **achieved** in the **last year** and in the **last five years?**

73%

of **women** feel they regularly **lack confidence** in the workplace

What am **I good at?**

What **compliments** have I **received from others?**

What am I **most proud of?** What did it **feel like** when I did it?

OVERCONFIDENCE BIAS

Too much confidence can be just as much as a problem as a lack of it. In a meeting with a client, a young executive working in the product team of a mid-sized software firm revealed that he wanted to make some changes to that client's service, but he had yet to okay the changes with his manager. Because they shared a good relationship, he assumed she would welcome them, but other factors of which he was unaware meant this was not the case. As a result, she was angry with him for going over her head and leaving the company in an awkward position with a client. In bypassing his manager, the executive displayed overconfidence bias – a form of unconscious bias that causes people to be more sure in their positions, abilities, or beliefs than they reasonably should be. Unconscious bias are prejudices we all have that affect our attitudes towards different things, people, or social groups that lie outside of our conscious awareness. Consider undertaking unconscious bias training to help make yourself more aware of such blind spots in order to treat people fairly and make better decisions.

Managing thoughts

Most of us have a voice in our heads telling us to be careful and stopping us from doing things that would cause harm to ourselves. The same voice can also prevent us from doing new things and progressing: "If you do this, you'll make a fool of yourself. Let someone else do it." When you hear that voice, ask yourself: "What's the worst that can happen if I do this?", "How likely is that to happen?", and "What's the best that can happen?" In most cases you will find the good outweighs the bad, and you should go ahead. If not, at least you will have evaluated the risk logically and assessed whether it is one you are prepared to take.

Looking confident

It is also important to build confidence on the outside – how you appear to others. Even if you don't feel it, "acting" confident can have an effect on both you and those around you. If you have a confident demeanour you are likely to be treated like a confident person by others. This will reinforce your self-belief and help you to feel more confident in yourself.

All of us get into bad habits, whether it's slumping in our seat, forgetting to acknowledge people when we meet them, or crossing our arms too much. Take a moment to think about the image you portray – is it one of a confident and professional person?

CHECKLIST...
Appearing confident   YES   NO

1   Do I maintain **good posture?** (An upright posture, keeping your shoulders down and your neck relaxed, makes you look and sound confident.) .... ☐ ☐

2   Do I **control my breathing** when I'm nervous? (Fast, shallow breaths make you light-headed and raise the pitch of your voice, betraying your lack of confidence.) .... ☐ ☐

3   Do I avoid closed **body language,** such as crossing my arms, and instead use open gestures and occupy the space around me as if I own it? .... ☐ ☐

4   Do I **sit comfortably** rather than rigidly, avoiding jerky movements and fighting the urge to fidget? .... ☐ ☐

5   Do I always **dress neatly and appropriately** and feel comfortable in what I wear? .... ☐ ☐

"What's the **best** that can **happen?**"

If you have a **confident demeanour** you are likely to be treated like a **confident person** by others

11% to **15%** increase in **life expectancy** is associated with people who **think positively**

Making decisions

The place that you have reached in your career or your personal life is the result of the decisions you have made. Every decision closes off some opportunities and opens others. Life is full of difficult choices and that is why making good decisions is essential.

Defining the process

Making big decisions isn't simply about mulling over a few options. Big decisions require thought, information gathering, and the creation and evaluation of alternatives before the decision is finally taken. Timing is critical: you may sometimes be able to delay a major decision – although think carefully through the consequences if you do – but for many you will have to seize the moment.

Deciding process

When faced with a major decision, use the process described here to give structure to your decision-making. This will work for large personal decisions that you take yourself, but is even more important if you are working with others in making the decision.

Tip

IMAGINE THE WORST

Avoid **procrastinating** over big decisions by imagining the **worst-case scenario** for each option. Thinking about worst outcomes can help you put your fears into perspective and feel more **comfortable** with uncertainty.

Use **the process** described here to give **structure** to your **decision-making**

How to make a decision

01 Establish evaluation criteria

07 Evaluate the outcome

06 Implement the decision

aking group decisions

oup decision-making can be very
werful, as it creates ownership of
e decision. Make sure that all involved
derstand the process you will use, and
e aware of the input that is required at
ch stage. The decision will even be
pported by those who disagree with
e outcome, as long as the process by
ich you have made the decision is seen
be transparent and fair. However, you
ll have to abide by the outcome of the
ocess. If you fail to do so, the decision
ay be seen as arbitrary and the team
ll be reluctant to be involved again.

60%

etter results are
elivered by **decisions**
ade and carried out
/ **diverse teams**

Establishing criteria

There are two reasons to establish early
on the criteria by which you will evaluate
your decision. First, these criteria will
determine what information you need
to collect to make the decision. Second,
they help make the decision process
transparent. Everyone involved knows
what the list of alternatives will be
judged against.

Prioritizing elements

In joint decisions, create and agree
the evaluation criteria in a group. Your
organization will have its own criteria,
so make sure these are included on
the list. If the result is a very long list,
then persuade the group to agree and
prioritize the most important criteria
for making the decision.

In business, the evaluation criteria are
often hard numbers – to do something
for the least cost, for example, or to make
the most profit. In your personal life, the
criteria are usually more subjective –
the relative size of the property you are
buying, or the desirability of its location.
Often you need both types, which is why
you need to use judgement.

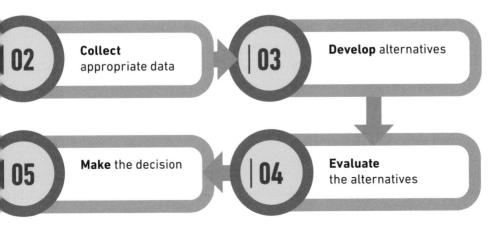

02 **Collect** appropriate data

03 **Develop** alternatives

05 **Make** the decision

04 **Evaluate** the alternatives

Finding alternatives

Decisions are usually choices between alternatives; so successful decision-making depends on identifying the best possible set of alternatives to evaluate. Search widely, but remember you can't evaluate everything. You may need to be creative and on occasions "to think the unthinkable", but don't forget the obvious.

One alternative you should consider is doing nothing. This is not always easy, but may be a real alternative. At the very least it gives you a benchmark against which to compare the other possibilities. In some circumstances you may find it is possible to do two of the alternatives at the same time. This will require greater

levels of evaluation than discussed here but asking the question can sometimes overcome major dilemmas.

95%

correlation between
decision effectiveness
and **company performanc**

Decision chart for choosing between two vans

Van purchase decision

BUY VAN A (ELECTRIC): £40,000 + 15-YEAR LIFETIME

Average price per mile	Annual running cost (10,000 miles)	Running cost over 15-year life	Overall lifetime cost	Overall cost per year
£0.02	£200	£3,000	£43,000	£2,867

sing decision charts

eating a decision diagram or chart
n help you weigh up alternatives. For
ample, imagine you are considering
ying a van for your business and have
und two options: van A, a brand new
ectric van that costs £40,000, and van
a secondhand diesel van that costs
0,000. You are concerned about how
uch each van will cost to run in the long
rm. To compare the two options, first
nsider the average running costs of
ch one: van A costs an average 2p a
ile to run while van B costs 15p a mile.

Now create your decision chart. To
lculate the expected running costs,
ultiply the average price per mile by
e amount of miles you expect the
n to travel each year (10,000) and the
pected lifetime of each van (15 years

for van A; 10 years for van B). This gives
you expected lifetime running costs of
£3,000 for van A and £15,000 for van B.

Next, add these figures to the
original prices of the vans to work out
their overall lifetime cost. Thus, Van A
will cost you £43,000 (£40,000 + £3,000)
to buy and run over 15 years – or £2,867
per year – while van B will cost £35,000
(£20,000 + £15,000) over 10 years – or
£3,500 per year.

Use this information to evaluate your
alternatives, but remember these are
only average expected costs. Averages
rarely happen, so you also need to
assess risk by considering other factors:
how much might price per mile costs
fluctuate according to average speed,
miles travelled, or changes in fuel
prices, for example?

BUY VAN B (DIESEL): £20,000 + 10-YEAR LIFETIME

Average price per mile	Annual running cost (10,000 miles)	Running cost over 15-year life	Overall lifetime cost	Overall cost per year
£0.15	£1,500	£15,000	£35,000	£3,500

Making the decision

By the time you have created the evaluation criteria and evaluated the alternatives, the decision should be all but made for you. Remember, however, that after all of your calculations and analysis, you will have to make the decision based on your judgement of the situation. You will have to decide whether one factor is more important than another, and will choose to value some things above others.

Understanding emotions

There is evidence to suggest that you cannot make decisions without also making emotional choices such as these value judgements. Decision-making is not wholly rational, so be very careful about taking a decision that you are not entirely comfortable with. Your emotions or your subconscious may be telling you something important that the "rational" analysis has missed.

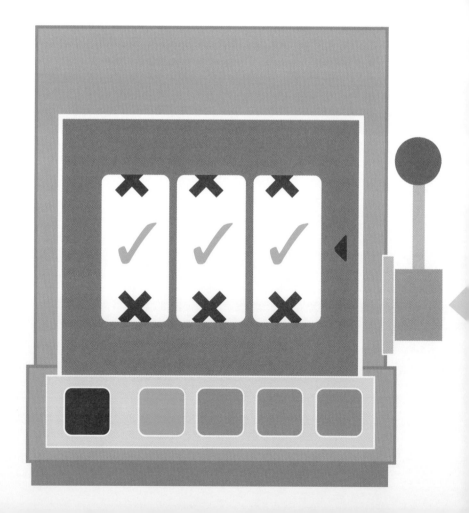

DEALING WITH RISK

All decisions contain risks. To assess the riskiness of your alternatives, ask:
• What is the best outcome I can contemplate?
• What is the most likely outcome?
• What is the worst outcome I can contemplate?
You can then estimate the probability of each outcome occurring
and calculate the likely cost using a decision-tree diagram. However,
regardless of the outcome of these calculations there are two further
questions you need to ask:
• Can the project survive if the worst-case scenario happens?
• Am I prepared to risk that probability of failure?
Your choice may depend on your appetite for risk. Others may have
a different view, so ensure everyone understands the risks involved.

You will have to **decide** whether one factor is more **important** than another

Acting on your choice

Once the decision is made, you will need to communicate it to those who have been involved in the process as well as to those it will affect. Draw up an implementation plan and delegate authority to individuals who will be held responsible for implementing the decision. Appoint a project manager and a project sponsor to oversee the whole project where appropriate.

Evaluating the project

Once the project or task has been completed, evaluate how it went. This isn't about apportioning blame, but an opportunity to learn. Some of the best-performing companies regularly re-evaluate their projects to gain insight and learning for the future. You can even improve your personal decision-making ability by reflecting on what went well and what did not.

Saying "no"

Successful people know what they want and how they are going to get it, and say "no" when what they are being asked to do doesn't fit in with their plans. Being successful is as much about what you decide not to do as what you decide to do.

Maintaining a balance

We all have to keep a balance in our lives. You have to balance what your employer wants from you with what you get from your employer. The latter doesn't only mean money, but also the training you receive, the experience you get, and the opportunities that working for the company opens up for your career.

Assessing work time

You also have to balance your working life and your home life. If you want to get ahead, your employer will expect some commitment and flexibility, but you do not have to be a doormat. Decide how long you are willing to give to them and how much time you will keep for yourself, and then stick to it consistently, even if you work from home. There will be times when intensive effort is required and you may have to put in long hours, but if your employer doesn't reciprocate, you should consider your position.

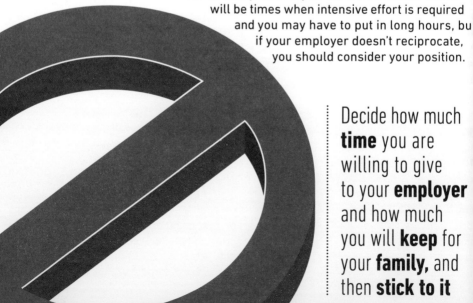

Decide how much **time** you are willing to give to your **employer** and how much you will **keep** for your **family,** and then **stick to it**

ASK YOURSELF...

What's in it for me?

	YES	NO
1 Am I doing this because **I have to**, not because I want to?	☐	☐
2 If I have to do it, will **I get something** in return?	☐	☐
3 If I have to do it, can I make the task **more enjoyable**, or develop the task to align more with my goals?	☐	☐
4 If I have to do it, will I receive **recognition**?	☐	☐
5 If I do this, will it help me **achieve my goals and ambitions**?	☐	☐
6 If I do this, will it give me **an experience** that can go on my CV?	☐	☐
7 If I do it, can I **maximize the benefit**?	☐	☐
8 If I say no, will there be **consequences**?	☐	☐

Getting it right

Use your judgement to assess when and how often you say no. It doesn't look good if you are seen as someone who always says no, or who only says no to the difficult jobs, so make sure that you get the balance right. When saying no is appropriate, do so quickly and politely.

Evaluating the project

You may sometimes find yourself in the situation where colleagues try to offload work on to you because they don't want to do it themselves, and they see you as being accommodating enough to do their work for them. If this happens, think very carefully before you accept. Assess the situation: if there really is a crisis and you can help, then of course you should do so. However, if there are no good

reasons and you feel the other person may make a habit of offloading their work, you should say no. Do this politely but firmly. Do not make complicated excuses, just say something like: "I'm sorry, but I can't help out this time. I have a heavy workload myself."

Tip

THINK IT THROUGH
Think about **the impact** your decision to say no could have. For example, if your boss or a friend is in serious trouble, saying no to helping out could damage your **relationship** with them.

Listening effectively

Many people can talk, but few listen well. If you are good at hearing what others miss, it gives you a distinct advantage. Good listeners are also better at building rapport with others, so listening effectively is a good skill to develop and practise.

Being a good listener

Listening is not the same as hearing. You can hear something but not take it in or respond to it. The words are just flowing over you. When you are truly listening, the person talking to you knows you are listening and will appreciate it. Listening requires concentration, which will not be possible if you are busy thinking about what you are going to say next. Be in the present. If you are really listening you will find your next words come intuitively.

Reading all signs

Listen to what the speaker is saying, not just what you are hearing. Think about what the tone and inflection in the voice tells you about what's behind the words. Are they congruent? If not, what is not being said? Their body language is important, too, and you will probably pick this up subconsciously. Does the speaker's body language match their words?

Confirming your thoughts

As you listen, make sure that you always understand what the speaker is saying. Summarize your understanding and, if necessary, ask the speaker to repeat what he or she said, or ask for further clarification if you are unsure. Never pretend to understand if you don't.

Ending well

Finally, make sure that you end the encounter on the right note. If you need to take further action as a result of your conversation, summarize what you have heard and then discuss the action you are going to take. Make a note of what you have agreed should happen next, ideally in your colleagues' presence. This will emphasize the importance of the matters that have been discussed and decided. Always make a note of important points even if this has to be after the meeting.

> ### Tip
>
> **LISTEN WELL FROM AFAR**
> You can't pick up on vocal subtleties or body language as much when listening remotely. Call from a **quiet place** and be prepared to ask the speaker to **repeat** things. On video calls, **watch the screen** to take everything in.

Giving advice

There will be times when you get the impression that a conversation is actually a request for advice. Be wary of this. It's better to be asked for advice than to offer it unsolicited. If you really feel you have something important to contribute, ask the person whether your advice is welcome, but be prepared to be told "no". Alternatively, give advice by telling a personal story of how you dealt with something similar. Do this carefully, however – no two circumstances are identical.

Empathizing with care

There are some times when there is nothing you can do. The person may be telling you something simply to tell someone. In this case, your role is to listen carefully and empathize, letting him or her know you are always available if you are needed. Above all, when someone tells you something in confidence, keep that confidence.

When you are **truly listening,** the person **talking** to you will realize and **appreciate it**

CHECKLIST...
Listening well   YES   NO

Think about the last real conversation you had:

1   Was I really **listening** to what was being said?............................. ☐ ☐

2   Were **my responses** appropriate while the speaker
    was talking?... ☐ ☐

3   Did my actions **encourage** or interrupt the flow?........................... ☐ ☐

4   Were my questions **well crafted** and appropriate?........................ ☐ ☐

5   Did I close the **discussion** appropriately?..................................... ☐ ☐

6   Was I **helpful**?... ☐ ☐

Becoming
successful

To achieve success in your professional life you need to bring together a coherent set of higher-level skills, from leadership and management to networking and personal development. Regularly monitoring and steering your progress, whether alone or with the help of an experienced mentor, is an integral part of the process.

12

Networking

Networking is about establishing groups of contacts that will add value to your business and career. It is a two-way process in which you must give to receive. Building good relationships will give you a competitive edge, but many find the idea of going out to make contacts artificial. Online networks can make things feel less awkward.

Six degrees of separation

Research carried out by the American social psychologist Stanley Milgram suggested that most people are connected to one another through a chain of just a few acquaintances. Networking gives you access to a wealth of knowledge and expertise; it allows you to gain competitive information, build a good reputation, and even get your next job. And as you progress in your career, who you know becomes increasingly, and sometimes critically, important.

79% of professionals think **networking** is important to **career success**

aluing networks

etworking is about building relationships,
ot selling. Your network should include not
st customers, but others in your profession
trade with whom you can share experience,
well as suppliers, consultants, and others
ith influence. Do not forget about internal
etworks, which may be as important as
ternal contacts in large organizations.

leeting people

usiness contacts are increasingly made online,
rough targeted research or through business
etworking groups, but there is still no substitute
r old-fashioned, face-to-face networking. You
n meet people anywhere. Be open to chance
ntacts, at airports or in elevators for example;
ese unexpected opportunities to meet people
d network can prove invaluable.

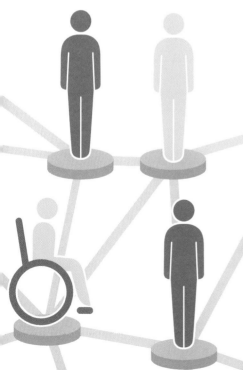

Tip

TARGET YOUR NETWORKING

Make a "hit list" of people
you **want to meet;** keep
your eyes and ears **open
for opportunities** to contact
and help people.

Choosing an event

Conferences, both real-world and virtual, are excellent arenas for networking, because they brir together a group of individuals who have a variety interests in a common subject. At a conference on corporate responsibility, for example, you are like to meet people from other organizations who are in a similar position to you, as well as experts in various aspects of the subject. You may make contacts with suppliers of equipment that could reduce your company's environmental impact, or consultants who could provide advice.

Working a real-world conference

Try not to take too much with you to real-world conferences. If you're loaded with bags, files, a laptop, and stacks of sales brochures, it's hard to appear cool and collected.

In focus

INTRODUCTIONS

At conferences, make an effort to introduce your contacts to other people. The generally accepted rule is to introduce the junior person to the more senior. So, introduce a colleague to a customer or a manager to a director. Try to say something about the person you are introducing that will provide a starting point for conversation. For example: "Leo, I'd like to introduce Halima, who worked on our corporate responsibility programme." Don't hesitate to ask someone to introduce you to one of their contacts if it's difficult for you to do so yourself.

CHECKLIST...
Preparing for meetings

		YES	NO
1	Have I **studied** the attendance list and marked people I want to meet?	☐	☐
2	Have I **researched** those people beforehand?	☐	☐
3	Is there anyone **I know already** on the list?	☐	☐
4	Do I know what the **dress code** is?	☐	☐
5	Do I have my **business cards** with me?	☐	☐

can be daunting to walk into a room full people, but there are ways to appear mposed. Smile as you walk in and look r any existing acquaintances. Talking people you know first can help ease u in, but don't stay with them for more an a few minutes.

Introducing yourself
you don't know anyone, join a group of two or three people who don't appear too ngrossed in conversation. Smile, and ay something like, "Hello, I hope I'm not terrupting your conversation. I'm ...". ve your name and company. In almost l cases they will smile back and invite u to join them.

Where possible, try to enlarge the group you're talking with. This enables u to meet more people and makes easier for you to move on when it appropriate. Do this by noting any eople standing nearby, and turning wards them when you speak. By ddressing your comments to them well as the group, you will bring em into the conversation.

Connecting with delegates
Be attentive to the people in your group, don't scan the room beyond for other prospects – this makes it impossible to create rapport. Ask open questions that will reveal common ground, and be sure to give others in your group an opportunity to speak. Exit conversations politely. If you want to keep in touch, ask to exchange contact information.

Networking virtually
At virtual conferences you don't have the same opportunities to run into people. Before the event, let others know you will be attending by posting on social media, and registering on the list of attendees. Use this list to identify people to connect with. Once the conference is underway, post comments and questions on the event platform and via social media using the event hashtag. Reach out to attendees via private messages, and take part in any ice-breaker or virtual hangout events, too. Afterwards, don't forget to follow up: say thank you, connect online, and find ways to continue the conversation.

Recording your contacts

Networking time will be wasted if you do not record and follow up your contacts. Your record can be very simple – a note of name, company, and contact details, the context of the meeting, a brief account of what was said, and a summary of what you think this person could do for you, or vice versa. Some people find it useful to group their contacts as:

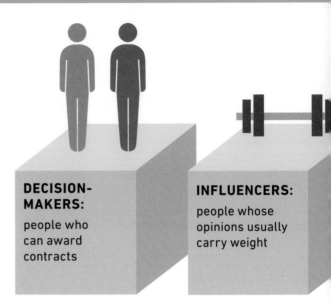

DECISION-MAKERS: people who can award contracts

INFLUENCERS: people whose opinions usually carry weight

Developing your network

You can use an online platform, your phone contacts, or a combination of both to record and manage contacts. But whatever you choose, remember that your network list needs nurturing and maintenance; people will fall off without regular contact. Review your list periodically and identify conspicuous gaps. Remember that when people leave a company they remain as your contacts, so keep in touch – they may go on to bigger and better things and become even more useful to you.

49%

of people find it hard to **stay in touch** with their **network** because they **lack time**

How to follow up contacts

Always send a thank-you email or text after every meeting you have attended.

BRIDGES:
people who can
introduce you
to others

LINKS:
those with
a mutual
connection to
someone you
want to meet

**GATE
KEEPERS:**
people who stand
between you and
the contact you
want to meet

Set up reminder notes
to contact anyone you
haven't spoken to in
the last two months.

Arrange to meet only if
you have a real purpose
for a meeting, otherwise
email or post a snippet of
useful information online.

Bring some new ideas
with you to the meeting
to stimulate thinking.

If you do want a meeting,
make sure the other
person knows why,
and clarify time limits
for the meeting.

Working with a mentor

Finding and using a good mentor can be highly beneficial both to your career and to your personal well-being. A good mentor is impartial, has more experience than you in key areas, and acts as a safe and effective sounding board for your ideas.

Defining the role

Mentors are people who guide others through periods of change towards agreed objectives. They can help you in a number of ways. First, they can enable you to work through your problems in a safe environment. They may not solve your problems for you (you need to learn to do so), but they will ask questions to make you analyse your position and alert you to pitfalls or alternatives. Second, they can give advice. This may be in the form of what to do, or who to approach within the organization to obtain help. They may point you towards training and development programmes, or suggest projects that you should consider being involved with.

Third, they may open up your career. They may have access to interesting job opportunities before they become wide available and may suggest roles that yc would never have considered. If they ar external to your company, they may hav their own networks of contacts, but dor expect this as part of the relationship.

Choosing a mentor

Your organization may run a mentoring service, but if they do not, you will have to set up a more informal mentoring relationship. The person you select as your mentor must, of course, possess the experience you want to access and should also be someone with whom you can build a good working relationship. He or she may not be a technical expert in the field in which you are working. This can be a real advantage because it enables you to work through issues from a fresh perspective.

£195

the average amount that UK mentees say they would **pay every month** to receive the support of their **mentors**

ASK YOURSELF...

What type of mentor do I need?   **YES   NO**

1 Have I decided if I need someone who is **internal or external** to my current organization? .... ☐   ☐

2 Is there a **specific issue** I really want help with? .... ☐   ☐

3 Is this a **short-term need,** not a long-term relationship? .... ☐   ☐

4 Is there an **area of expertise** my mentor should have (psychology, leadership, career guidance)? .... ☐   ☐

Qualities of a good mentor

The attributes of a good mentor depend on your circumstances and your specific role, but he or she should always be:

- Someone you respect and trust, and who won't always just agree with what you say
- Someone you consider to be a role model
- Someone who listens, probing what you say in order to understand you
- Someone who is genuinely interested in you and what you want to do, and who is available when you need help.

Mentoring in-house

Mentors are typically separate from the line-management relationship, but your boss may be the ideal candidate, especially when the difference in age and seniority is large. Some companies establish roles where this is designed to happen – Assistant to the Managing Director, for example.

If you have a very senior manager or director as your mentor, it can open doors to people whom you would not normally meet. Also, it may give you insights into the organization's political process, identify career opportunities, and protect you when things go wrong.

Tip

THINK BEFORE YOU SPEAK
Remember that your boss is part of the organization, so if he or she is your mentor, be cautious about being **completely open** about every aspect of your **ambitions** or personal life.

Moving on

For some, the ideal career is a series of well-timed promotions within one organization, but gaining job satisfaction often necessitates finding a new role in a new company. Each move you make should give you the experience to progress in your career, so you should choose your opportunities carefully. But when is the right time to change and when is it better to stay put?

Achieving promotion

Getting promoted within your organization depends on being seen to be doing a good job and having the capability of doing a bigger job. You will probably need to improve your visibility within the company and cultivate key internal contacts, so become known more widely. Try putting yourself forward as a spokesperson for your team, or devise presentations on aspects of your work that you can deliver to a wider audience. Many large organizations run fast-track schemes, so make sure both your boss and the human resources department know you are interested.

Considering options

A job is not just its title – it is the experience you gain and what you will be able to make of this experience in your later career. If you are in a clerical role, for example, why not volunteer for any career development programmes available, and seek to make your organization more efficient. If people don't see you as management material, develop your leadership skills by volunteering for an external role, perhaps with a charity. Talk to your boss about opportunities open to you. If you are a valued worker, your employer will be interested in your future.

Changing jobs

You may need to leave your current organization to achieve your aims, but don't act without careful consideration. Ask yourself where you want to go to next, rather than focusing on escaping from the present. How will your move look on your CV three or five years from now? Future employers usually look favourably on an internal promotion on your CV. Above all, try very hard never to leave a job on a sour note – you will probably need an excellent reference or testimonial from your current employer to get your next job.

Seeking opportunity

Prospective employers are looking for evidence of five attributes:

01 Appropriate **qualifications**

02 A relevant range of **experience**

03 **Specific skills** required for the post

04 **Previous positions** held

05 How **successful** you have been

At the interview stage employers will also **assess** your **attitude and "fit"** with the organization. Examine any job advert and try to decode it in the context of these attributes.

CHECKLIST...

Deciding if it is time to leave a job

	YES	NO
1 Have I already **gained** all the **experience** I can get from my current role?	☐	☐
2 Have I exhausted all the **development opportunities** open to me?	☐	☐
3 Do I have the appetite for **a change?**	☐	☐
4 Am I concerned about the **future** of my company?	☐	☐
5 Is the new job really **a promotion?**	☐	☐
6 Will the new job provide the **experience and opportunities** I need for my future?	☐	☐

Getting that job

When seeking your next position, make sure that you consider and address each of the five qualities that recruiters are looking for in your application.

Experience is what you gain from **each job** and **each project** you undertake

Key points for successful job applications

01 **Qualifications** These give an indication of your potential and so are particularly important in more junior jobs. Even working towards a qualification signals commitment and ambition to your current, or future, employer. Examine job adverts in your area of expertise and analyze what qualifications employers are seeking; if you don't have them, enrol on a suitable course.

02 **Experience** There is no substitute for experience, but employers are not necessarily looking for candidates who have spent long periods in the same role – two or three years is often adequate. If you have spent less time in a role, and particularly if you have moved several times, you may be seen as someone who lacks commitment. If you have held one job for much longer, you may be perceived to be too set in your ways.

Experience is what you gain from each job and each project you undertake. If you make a mistake, learn from it. Reflect on everything you have done and what you have learnt. Also, use someone to help you through a project so you can learn in real time. A mentor, a good colleague, or even a family member can sometimes fulfil this role.

03 **Skills** Many of the basic skills you will need in any job, such as negotiating, presenting, managing your time, and chairing meetings, have been covered in this book. To hone your skills, identify your preferred learning style and choose development experiences that best suit you:
- Do you learn best from reading books, trade magazines, or online training material?
- Do you prefer learning in the classroom, at conferences, or from colleagues? Short courses give you the opportunity to develop specific skills away from your colleagues, in a safe environment.
- Do you learn best by doing the task? A great way to learn something is by teaching it to someone else.

04 **Position** Grand job titles will look good on your CV and may get you shortlisted for interview, but they are no substitute for experience. Discrepancies are sure to come to light when you are interviewed by your new employer, so be realistic.

When you apply for a new job, check that the content of the advertised role matches the title. Is it really going to offer you the experience you want? For example, the title of Assistant General Manager may sound great, but in reality, will you be deputizing for the General Manager or will you be little more than a clerical assistant?

05 **Success** Most recruiters are looking for success and may not even shortlist you for interview if they don't see evidence of progression on your CV. More astute recruiters will want to examine how you have dealt with difficult and challenging situations. They want to see if you are someone who learns. To address this requirement, present yourself through a success story about your past. For example, compare the two statements below:

- "I was financial controller of a division in Cape Town for three years and every month the books were closed on time."
- "I led a project to replace the accounting system with new software: it was delivered on time and in budget."

The second statement clearly conveys success, where the first simply describes a role. Showing that you have taken up development opportunities and have been successful makes your CV stand out from the crowd.

TAKING YOUR CAREER FORWARD

Dos	Don'ts
O **Working towards qualifications you will need in the future**	O Focusing only on improving your technical skills
O **Demonstrating progression from junior roles to positions of responsibility**	O Expecting to be promoted purely on your impressive qualifications
O **Seeking out new experiences, and actively learning from them**	O Leaving responsibility for your development to your employer
O **Using a mentor to help with your personal development**	O Resenting your lack of promotion

Reviewing your plans

Planning your personal and professional development is essential to achieving high performance, but plans have a habit of being overtaken by events. New opportunities will arise and circumstances change, making it vital to review your progress.

Navigating your success

HOW DO I LOOK TO MY EMPLOYER?

Does my employer:

O **think** I am helpful?

O **value** my contribution?

O **think** I am promotable?

O **trust** and respect me?

O **use** me in projects beyond my role?

Monitoring your progress

At least once a year, you should review your progress against your development plan. Ask yourself questions such as:

- Have I attained the goals I set myself in my plan? If not, why?
- Are my goals unattainable or are they just going to take a bit longer?
- What have I achieved that wasn't in my plan? What new opportunities does this give me?

Reviewing the plan

Review the development plan to see if it still reflects what you want to do with your personal and professional life. Think about whether your development has made your plan unfeasible, whether new opportunities have arisen, or whether your objectives have changed. Do you need to modify your plan or create a new one from scratch?

Development encompasses more than your position and progress in your work. Successful people tend to be well rounded, with a variety of interests and experience, and they measure their success in terms other than how much money they have made and the status they have. Assess and review your own development by asking yourself questions about your current level of success – for example, how well you perform and are developing and learning, how you benefit from work, and how you look to your employer.

Review your own **development** by asking questions about your **current success**

HOW DO I BENEFIT FROM WORK?

Am I satisfied with:

O **my level** of pay?
O **the benefits** I receive?
O **my work–life** balance?
O **the opportunities** this job gives me?
O **my current** role?

HOW AM I DEVELOPING?

Have I:

O **met** the development targets I have set myself?
O **kept** my skills up to date?
O **learnt** something new at work this week?
O **reviewed** my development plan in the last six months?

HOW WELL DO I PERFORM?

Do I:

O **work** in a team that achieves work objectives and targets?
O **consistently** meet my own work objectives and targets?
O **support** my colleagues?
O **have** the experience and skills and the support and tools to do my job well?

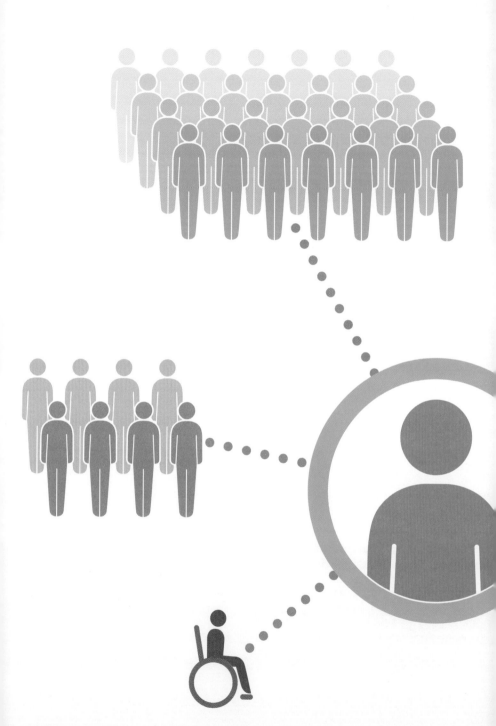

EFFECTIVE COMMUNICATION

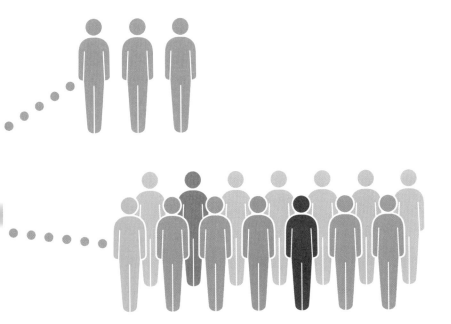

Understanding
communication
skills

Communication is more than just a way to get ideas across or exchange points of view. It is the process by which we interact with others and seek information essential to our daily lives, allowing us to control the circumstances in which we work.

13

Defining communication

Think of communication as a process, involving senders and receivers who encode and decode messages that are transmitted by various med and that may be impeded by "noise". The aim of this process is to creat a shared understanding, in order to generate desired outcomes.

Understanding each other

Humans aren't the only beings who communicate – virtually all forms of life are capable of sending and receiving messages. People, however, are the only living organisms known to communicate not just with signals and signs, but through the use of symbols with agreed-upon meanings. If we think about communication as the transfer of meaning, then for each of us, successful communication means

Defining levels of communication

INTRAPERSONAL

Communication **within ourselves,** sending messages to various parts of our bodies, thinking things over, or working silently on a problem.

INTERPERSONAL

Communication **between** or **among people,** sending messages from one person to another – verbally and nonverbally – with the intention of transferring meaning from one person to another.

ORGANIZATIONAL

Communication in the **context of an organization,** sending and receiving messages through various layers of authority and using various channels to discuss topics of interest to the group we belong to or the company we work for.

MASS OR PUBLIC

Sending messages from one person or source to **many people simultaneously,** through the internet, print media, or television.

at you will understand something
st as I do: we are in agreement about
hat the sender intended and what the
ceiver ultimately understood.

nderstanding the principles

mmunication involves a number of
inciples, which apply across time
d cultures. The process is always:

Dynamic It is constantly undergoing
change.

Continuous Even when you hang up
the telephone, you're communicating
a message that you have nothing
more to say.

- **Circular** Communication is rarely
  entirely one-way. We each take
  in information from the outside
  world, determine what it means,
  and respond.
- **Unrepeatable** Even if we say
  something again in precisely
  the same way, our listeners
  have heard it before, and so
  respond to it differently.
- **Irreversible** We cannot "unsay"
  words: their effect remains even
  if we're asked to disregard them.
- **Complex** We all assign slightly
  different meanings to words.
  This variation is a product of
  our backgrounds, education,
  and experience, and means
  that there is always the potential
  for misunderstanding.

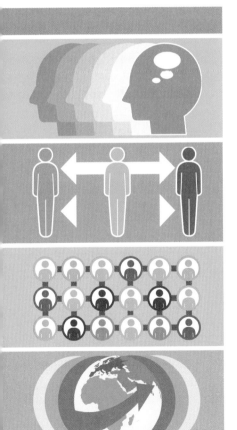

If communication is the
transfer of meaning, then
for successful communication
to occur, you should understand
something just as I do

Overcoming barriers

Why do attempts at communication often fail? Broadly speaking, there are two barriers that keep us from communicating successfully: the operations of our bodies and our minds, and our assumptions that other people understand and react to the world in the same way that we do.

Unblocking your communications

The information we receive about the world comes from our senses. It is possible, however, for our senses to be impaired or for the source of the message to provide inadequate information to be reliably decoded. In sending messages to others, we must be sensitive to the fact that they may not interpret and experience things in the same way we do.

Overcoming barriers to communication

DON'T RUSH TO JUDGE

Never make a judgement **before knowing the facts** about a situation. Acknowledge that you are usually working with incomplete data.

CONSIDER CULTURE

Be aware that different **backgrounds, education,** and **experience** give people different expectations. Your way of seeing the world is not the only one.

WATCH YOUR LANGUAGE

Recognize that language has **different levels of meaning.** People will respond differently to the same words, especially if the words are vague or general.

CONTROL YOUR FEELINGS

Try to present your message with a cool head – you can appeal to people's emotions, but **don't let yours get the better of you.** Accept that other people may have strong feelings about a subject.

~~GHT~~ ~~ΓEREOTYPES~~

~~ɔn~~'t assume that ~~l~~ members of a ~~ɔup~~ share the ~~ɪme~~ characteristics. **~~ɪt~~ aside any ~~ɪreotypical~~ views** ~~ɪu~~ may have; treat ~~ɪch~~ person as ~~ɪ~~ individual.

In sending messages to others, we **must be sensitive** to the fact that they may not interpret or experience things **in the same way** that we do

Ensuring understanding

Communication is more than sending and receiving messages; if the message has been delivered but not understood, no communication has taken place. Everything, from the culture we inhabit to the norms of the groups we belong to, can influence how we perceive the messages, events, and experiences of everyday life. Even individual mindsets, such as unconscious bias, can set up barriers, affecting what we understand and how we react to outside stimuli.

Learn to recognize the barriers likely to block your communications, and how you can overcome them. When speaking to someone, for example, monitor their reactions to confirm you are being understood. Remember that the barrier to understanding may lie in the way you have coded your message. Always take the effort to communicate as clearly as possible.

Communicating at work

Communication is a skill that is central to the human experience. We each know how to do it; we've done it since birth and receive additional practice each day. So why is it so difficult to communicate on the job? As a manager, it is important to understand how the workplace changes the nature of communication for both sender and receiver.

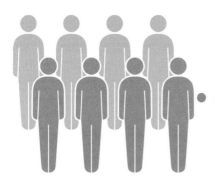

Tailoring your approach

Several factors alter the way we look at communication in the business context. We all have a personal communication style, but within an organization you often have to adapt your approach to accommodate the needs of those you work with and work for. If you put the preferences of your audience – particularly your boss and your clients – above your own, you will often get what you want faster. The way you communicate also depends on your position within the organization. The higher your level of responsibility, the more you have to take into account when communicating. And as you become more accountable, you need to keep better records – a form of communication to yourself that may later be read by others.

Adapting to your environment

Organizations, like the people who work in them, are in constant flux. Businesses change by necessity with the conditions of the marketplace and the lives of the managers who run them. Your communications must adapt to the conditions in which you find yourself. However, this never constitutes a reason for signing your name to a document that is false, or passing along information that you know isn't true.

Matching the culture

All communication must work within an organization's culture. The accepted approach can vary considerably between different organizations: some companies, for example, require every issue to be written in email form and circulated before it can be raised in a team meeting. Other organizations are much more "oral" in nature, offering employees the opportunity to talk things through before writing anything down.

Many companies rely on a particular culture to move day-to-day information through the organization. To succeed in such a business, you must adapt to the existing culture rather than try to change it or ask it to adapt to you.

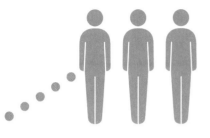

CHECKLIST...

Adapting your style   **YES   NO**

1 Do you understand how the **culture of the organization you
work** for affects the way in which you need to communicate? ..... ☐ ☐

2 Have you adapted your **writing and speaking style** to the
expectations of the culture in which you are working? .... ☐ ☐

3 Have you changed your style to accommodate any changes
in the **structure of the company** or the conditions of
your industry? .... ☐ ☐

4 Have you noted the communication preferences of your
supervisor and **adapted** your **writing, speaking, and listening
styles** accordingly? .... ☐ ☐

Planning your approach

Getting people to listen to what you say, read what you write, or look at what you show them isn't easy. How do you persuade them that paying attention to your message is in their best interest? The key to ensuring that your communication hits the mark is detailed planning.

Choosing your approach

The choices you make, from the content of the message you send to the medium you select, all have a direct impact on the outcome of your communication. Whatever the situation, ask yourself about the following:

47%

higher returns to shareholders are **reported** in companies that are led by **good communicators**

Tip

QUESTION YOUR OWN ROLE

Ask yourself whether you are the **right person** to send the message. Will your signature compel people to action, or might the message be **more effective** coming from your manager, or someone closer to the intended audience?

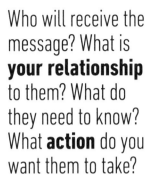

Tip

GET TO KNOW YOUR AUDIENCE
It's all too easy to stereotype an audience, especially when you are working against the clock. Make sure you have **collected all the information** available about your audience, and refer to the **key characteristics** as you prepare your speech or document.

Who will receive the message? What is **your relationship** to them? What do they need to know? What **action** do you want them to take?

MESSAGE

What should your message contain? How should your message **impart the information?** Should your message be broad or detailed?

MEDIUM

What's the best way to send this message? Is one medium **quicker** or **cheaper** than another? Will one offer a **better opportunity** for feedback or carry more detail?

CODE

Will your audience understand the words you've used? Will the **words and images** mean the same thing to the audience as they mean to you? Do these words and images have **multiple meanings** for various audiences?

FEEDBACK

How will you know if you've **communicated successfully?** Will the audience response be delayed? Will it be filtered through another source?

NOISE

How many other senders and messages are out there? Whose **message traffic** are you competing with? Will others try to deflect, distort, or disable your communication attempts?

Understanding your audience

Who are these people you're communicating with? What do you know about them? What do they know about you or your subject? How do they feel about it? When preparing to communicate, ask a few simple questions about the people in your audience. Once you know more about them, you can find ways to motivate them to listen.

Assessing your audience is especially important when planning a big public presentation, or a report that will be seen by many people. But it is also worth doing to help you better understand those with whom you communicate on a regular basis in your team or company. You don't need to conduct a full-blown assessment every time you talk to or email someone, but knowing what makes people tick will help you get your message across more effectively.

Audience backgrounds

When you're assessing your audience, look for any similarities in personal backgrounds. For example, what is the average age of audience members? Consider whether they will be familiar with the concepts you plan to speak about, and the sort of life experiences they may have had. Next, think about the education level of your audience. This will have a significant influence on the content of your talk or document, including its central themes and the vocabulary you employ. The personal beliefs of your audience are an important factor to take into account when planning what you will say. Are they liberal or conservative? What is their political affiliation? Are they committed to a particular religious or social point of view?

ETHNIC AND GENDER TRAITS

The ethnic origin of members of your audience may be worth knowing, but don't overestimate its value. This information can help you know which issues and positions are of greatest concern to them, but you should not stereotype the views of the members of such a group. Sensitivity to ethnic issues and language styles should be sufficient as you prepare. Similarly, knowing that your audience might be predominantly composed of one gender or another is also of limited benefit. Studies show no statistically significant difference in the responses of professional men and women to a range of stimuli. You would be unwise to assume that you must communicate in one way for men and in another for women.

15%

of the average organization's **collective time** is spent in **meetings**

Socioeconomic factors

For certain forms of communication, knowing the economic status and lifestyle of your audience is especially important. Gain as much information as you can about the following:

- **Occupation** Knowing how people earn their living will tell you something about their educational background and routines, as well as their motivations and interests.

- **Income** Knowing how much money an audience earns can give you some idea of what their concerns are. The less they earn, the more they will be driven by basic needs, such as food and housing. American psychologist Abraham Maslow documented the hierarchy of human needs, showing that higher-level needs – such as self-actualization (the ability to become the best version of yourself) – are only relevant to people once their more basic needs have been met.

- **Socioeconomic status** This term describes where your audience is located in the social/economic spectrum. It is, of course, a direct function of other factors, such as income, education, occupation, neighbourhood, friends, family, and more. Think of this as a single descriptor that explains just how much prestige your audience has in the eyes of others in their own society, and use it to target your words to address their problems, hopes, and needs.

Targeting your communication

WORK WITHIN OBJECTIVES

All of your communication should be **consistent** with and **directly supportive** of the strategic objectives of your organization – its mission, values, and beliefs.

ADAPT TO YOUR AUDIENCE

Appeal to the **basic needs** (such as safety, companionship, or social approval) of your intended audience or their **senses** (use motion, colour, and sound). What can you do to hold their attention?

EXPLAIN YOUR POSITION

Use words that your audience will **understand** and concepts they can **relate to.** This means, of course, that you must **know who your audience are,** as well as what they know and how they feel about the subject.

MOTIVATE YOUR AUDIENCE

Encourage your audience to accept and act on your message by **appealing to authorities** that they respect, the social conformity displayed by others they **know or admire,** the **rationality** of your argument, or their desire to behave in **consistent ways.**

KEEP THEM ON SIDE

Try to prevent your audience from being swayed by other points of view by asking if they are willing to make a **tangible, preferably public, commitment,** or reminding them of the benefits to be derived from your approach.

MANAGE EXPECTATIONS

Always let your audience know **what to expect,** and **deliver what you promise,** never less. People are disappointed only if their expectations exceed what they actually receive.

Matching the message

Once you know something about the individuals who make up your audience, begin to think about how to approach them. You'll need a strategy to help devise the right message and to choose the most effective method of communication for its recipients.

Hitting the right knowledge level

A thorough knowledge of what your audience already knows about your subject is useful in a number of ways. First, it tells you where to begin. Don't speak down to the audience by explaining fundamentals they already understand. Second, don't start above their heads. Begin at a point they are comfortable with and move on from there.

Managing emotions

Even more important than what the audience knows about your subject is how they feel about it. What they know about taxation is far less relevant than how they feel about it when they listen to a talk about tax reform. You need to tailor your words carefully to what the emotional response of your audience is likely to be. The greater the degree of ego involvement (or emotional response to a given topic, the narrower the range

Establishing the audience's role

Your message may need to reach only the audience in front of you, or you may be relying on those people to pass on the message to others. Think about everyone who might see or hear your message, including:

PRIMARY AUDIENCE

These are the people who will receive your written or spoken message directly. Make sure that you **understand and address** their needs, interests, and concerns.

SECONDARY AUDIENCE

Others might read or **hear of your message indirectly.** Could the communication be given to a reporter, union organizer, competitor, or go viral on social media?

GETTING YOUR MESSAGE ACROSS

Dos	Don'ts
Knowing as much as you can about who will read or hear your words	Assuming the audience knows all or nothing about your subject
Tailoring your message to the needs and interests of your audience	Acting as if the audience already shares your ideas and interests
Understanding who the key decision-makers are, and their criteria for making decisions	Failing to check who exactly is in your audience, and what they need to know in order to act
Knowing who is respected by your audience and seeking their approval for what you recommend	Assuming your ideas are good enough to stand up on their own, and not discussing them

acceptable positions open to you. other words, people are much ore open-minded on topics they are different about than they are on topics ey care about passionately. If you isjudge an emotional response, ur communication will fail.

Tailor your words carefully to what the **emotional response** of your **audience** is likely to be

GATEKEEPERS

These are the people or platforms you have to **route your message** through, and that might filter, block, leak, distort, or amplify it. Does something stand between you and the audience you hope to reach?

OPINION LEADERS

These are individuals who have **significant influence** over members of the audience. Who do they admire or listen to on this subject? How could they react to your message?

KEY DECISION-MAKERS

These are people with the **power to influence** the outcome of the communication.

Choosing your medium

Most managers make decisions about whether to write or speak to someone based on two criteria: convenience and their own personal preferences. But an effective choice of communication medium or channel depends on much more than what suits you at the time.

Learning to ignore instinct

Many managers choose a form of communication instinctively, and not always for the right reasons. For example, if you need to pass bad news to a colleague but don't want to provoke a confrontation, you might choose to send an email, even though your colleague would prefer to hear from you in person. On another occasion, you might choose to make a phone or video call rather than write a letter, because it seems quicker or easier.

You might make this choice even when the message is complex and would benefit from extensive explanation, detailed description, or visual aids. In fact, just two factors should govern your choice of medium for any message. You should think first about the preferences of the person or audience receiving your message, and second about the characteristics and benefits of speaking versus those of writing.

When to write

Writing produces a **permanent record,** can convey great detail, is often more precise, and can be used for careful wording. If it's important that you say something in an exact way, write it down. Because writing allows you to interpret information in your own time, it can also help reduce miscommunications with those who do not share the same first language as you. And, of course, if your audience likes source material or **lots of detail,** such as large lists, you can provide that as an appendix or attachment.

Keep in mind that you may have to share your message with many people and it may be impractical to speak to each of them. Writing in a **precise, persuasive** way may be the best approach to influence your audience.

In focus

THE PLATINUM RULE

We're all familiar with the old rule: "Do unto others as you would have them do unto you." It's a good rule, but it contains a small flaw. What if others don't want to receive the same treatment as you? What if their preferences are, in fact, significantly different? The Platinum Rule, devised by communication expert Tony Alessandra, who has advised companies such as Apple, Ford, and IBM, is a variation of that age-old maxim: "Do unto others as they want to be done unto." This means treat others as they want to be treated, not how you think they should be treated. Communicate with others in the manner that they prefer and you'll get what you want: their time, attention, and cooperation.

When to speak

Speaking provides a **richer context** – it includes the use of nonverbal cues and allows for more emotion. It is **less rigid,** as it leaves no permanent record, and may also be much quicker.

Speaking to others also **invites their participation.** It may be the best way to elicit ideas, size up other people's feelings, and even discover any possible objections to your message before decisions have been made and formalized in writing. Once something is written down, people tend to feel committed to that course of action, even if the documents can easily be revised. A conversation or discussion, on the other hand, has a more transitory feel to it: it is **flowing and flexible,** and less permanent and formal than written forms of communication.

Tip

TRY MESSAGING

A mix of writing and speech, **instant messaging** is faster than email, but still allows you to be precise, detailed, and chat with multiple people. Use it to **swap documents** or **talk through ideas.**

Speaking
and writing

Two of the most important skills for a manager, and often also the most daunting, are to stand up in front of an audience and deliver a presentation, and to communicate effectively in writing, whether in formal business letters, email correspondence, or detailed reports. For both, clear thinking, preparation, and practice are the keys to success.

14

Planning your speech

Preparing for a business presentation is the most important stage of the process. While it may seem daunting at first, planning your speech becomes much easier once you break the task down into manageable steps, ensuring that you address all the relevant issues at the right tim

Defining substance and style

When it comes to giving a speech, content is king. Substance matters and there is absolutely no substitute for knowing what you're talking about. This means that, whenever possible, you should select a topic that you know and understand, so that you can talk about it with confidence. However, this also depends on your audience; never forget that they are the reason you are giving the speech. Using your knowledge of your audience to tailor the content to meet their expectations is not a guarantee of success, but it is certainly a step in the right direction.

> ## Tip
>
> ### MAKE TIME FOR RESEARCH
> Delivering the speech is the **main goal,** but success only comes through careful preparation. **Remember the 80:20 rule** – spend about 80 per cent of your time on **research and preparation,** and only around 20 per cent on **practice and delivery.**

Identifying your **role** as a speaker and your **importance** to the listeners is essential

Determining your purpose

Before you start to plan the details of your speech, make sure that you know why you are speaking. If you can't come up with a reason for speaking, then don speak. Identifying your role as a speake and your importance to the listeners is especially important. It may be that this audience wants your views on the subje at hand and is keenly interested in your opinions. Alternatively, your purpose may be purely to inform them about a topic, and the demand for your opinions may not be as high as you imagine.

Also find out all you can about the context in which the presentation will take place. You need to know the answers to questions such as: is your audience still in the fact-gathering stage or are they ready to make a decision? What is their reason for listening to you? How urgent is the subject you'll be speaking about? Have recent events, either locally or globally, affected their view of the topic in any way? Are your listeners involved in a process that will require them to take action after hearing what you have to say?

Case study

PREPARING TO SUCCEED

Elizabeth Allen, chief communications officer of the international office supplies firm Staples, Inc., was given the task of drafting a press-conference speech for her CEO, Tom Stemberg, to announce Staples's sponsorship of a new sports arena in Los Angeles. Ms Allen knew that this financial arrangement would be covered by the sports press, not the business press. She also knew that sports figures, civic officials, investors, and reporters would be in the room: "Many people thought the name would be a local, Californian company ... This was a Boston company putting its name on a Los Angeles landmark. There were cultural factors at work here, as well as political and business factors." As she considered how to prepare the speech, she decided three things: she would reduce her thinking to one or two main points; she would include a few examples and anecdotes that the local audience would relate to; and most importantly, she would cite at least one powerful reason why the relationship between her company and the City of Los Angeles would be productive and long-term.

Preparing your speech

Once you have a clear picture in your mind of why you are giving the presentation, who your audience is, and what they want to hear from you, start to make a detailed plan of your speech. This planning stage is vital, so make sure that you don't leave it to the last minute. You need to be completely familiar with the structure and content of your speech by the time you deliver it. There are eight key steps to preparing a successful presentation.

Steps to preparing a speech

01

COMPOSE A THESIS STATEMENT

Write a **one-sentence declaration** of what you want the audience to **know, understand, believe,** or **do.** Make it brief, simple, comprehensive, and as complete as possible.

02

DEVELOP THE MAIN POINTS

Restrict yourself to just **two or three main points,** so that you will have time to explain and support them all. Make sure that all of your **evidence** relates to and is supportive of your principal reason for speaking.

03

GATHER SUPPORTING MATERIALS

Now gather evidence to support your main points. Use your knowledge of the audience to select the kinds of proof that they will find **most convincing.** Make your evidence **compelling, recent,** and fully **transparent** to your listeners.

04

THINK ABOUT STRUCTURE

Consider the order in which you will **deliver the information,** and think about what you will say in your **introduction,** in the **body** of the speech, and in your **conclusion.**

|05

PREPARE YOUR OUTLINE

Write a one-page outline of your speech. Think about the **issues** you plan to raise, the **sequence** in which you will address each of them, and the **evidence** you'll offer your audience in support of those ideas.

You must be **completely familiar** with both the structure and the **content** of your **speech** by the time you **deliver** it

|06

CONSIDER VISUALS

Think about what visuals will best enhance your speech, by helping to **explain, reinforce,** and **clarify your main points.** Sometimes it is easier to show the audience something than to say it.

|07

WRITE THE SPEECH

Now prepare the content of your speech in detail. Some people choose to write in **short bullet points,** others write their **script** out more fully. Choose the way that best suits you, but remember that your audience want to hear you **speak to them,** not read to them.

|08

PREPARE YOUR NOTES

Finally, transfer your speech into the **notes you will use to deliver it.** These may be lines on a PowerPoint presentation, written notes on notecards, or the full manuscript.

Make sure that all of your **evidence relates to** and is **supportive** of your principal **reason for speaking**

Developing visual support

Behavioural scientists have known for many years that visual images can have a powerful effect on the process of learning. In some cases, pictures may reach people who simply don't listen well to the spoken word, or who may not understand what the words mean.

How does visual support help?

Behavioural scientists have found that visual support is important in communication for three main reasons:

- It can help explain, reinforce, and clarify the spoken word during a presentation. If you can't say something easily, you may be able to show it to your audience.
- People tend to recognize ideas most easily when they are presented as a combination of both words and pictures, rather than when presented as either words or pictures alone.
- Some people pay more attention to what they see than what they hear, and can more quickly and easily recall information and concepts with a visual component than those that are just spoken aloud.

89%

of people use Microsoft's
PowerPoint software to
create their **presentations**

Choosing when to use it

Displaying information in a visual manner will enhance
most presentations, but tends to work best:

O When you have new data for your audience

O When the information you hope to convey is complex
or technical in nature

O If your message is coming to the audience in a new context

O For certain types of information – such as numbers, quick
facts, quotes, and lists

O For explaining relationships or comparisons

O For revealing geographical or spatial patterns

Tip

CHOOSE THE RIGHT CHART

Charts and graphs are a useful
way to display data. Be sure to
select the type of chart (such as a
pie chart, bar chart, or line graph)
that **most clearly illustrates**
any comparisons you want to
make, and use colour carefully
to **emphasize your point.**

Visual support can
help to **explain,
reinforce,** and
clarify the spoken
word: try **showing
as well as telling**

Using visuals effectively

Good visuals have a number of characteristics in common. The most important is simplicity. The more complex a visual display becomes, the more difficult it is for an audience to understand. Keep your visuals clear, ordered, and simple when trying to explain an important idea or relationship.

Good visuals use colour to explain and attract. Very few people tend to have exactly the same taste in colours, but almost everyone appreciates occasions when colours are used meaningfully and consistently. Certain traditions, such as using red numbers or bars to indicate a loss and black ones to indicate profit, allow audiences to quickly grasp information. Try using a simple legend to explain colour use on your charts and graphs; it helps the audience and will ensure consistency and simplicity in your visual aids.

> Keep your visuals **clear** and **simple** when trying to explain an **important idea**

Using visuals well

Thinking carefully about the **needs and interests** of your audience as you plan your visual aids

Choosing visuals that **capture the essence** of your main points

Using colour in a consistent, careful manner so that related items are **colour-coded** and **grouped together**

Making sure your visual support is **simple, crisp, clean,** and **uncluttered**

Tip

Although you should respect your company's **brand guidelines,** you don't have to be a slave to corporate PowerPoint or Google Slides templates if they result in dull, predictable visuals. Try experimenting with **novel presentation software,** such as Prezi, or make your own slides using your preferred graphics software and save them in a standard format, such as PDF.

3

seconds is the maximum time it should take to **understand** a **slide**

Limiting the amount of text alongside your visuals to a few key words: this will produce **a more powerful message** than wordy slides

Avoiding generic, or "stock" images, and visuals that are only indirectly related to your main points

Building up a **personal library of images,** symbols, and graphics to enhance your messages

On important occasions, using a **professional graphic designer** to create a polished presentation

Improving your confidence

It's one thing to know your material. It's another matter entirely to believe that you can confidently speak on stage or present remotely to a group of strangers. Understanding your message and having a well-organized speech are important to your success, but so is self-confidence.

Improving your delivery

Rehearsal will help improve your speech and raise your level of self-confidence. Simply knowing that you've been through the contents of your speech more than once builds familiarity and is reassuring. It will also ensure you talk for the correct amount of time. A run-through or two will show whether you have too much, too little, or just enough to say. Rehearsal will also help you to improve your transitions. By practising your speech, you'll be able to identify the rough spots and work on smoothing the transition from one point to another and from one part of the speech to another.

Using notes

The best speakers seem to confidently deliver their speeches extemporaneously, or "from the heart", without notes. Such speeches aren't really memorized word-for-word, but rather are thoroughly researched, well rehearsed, and professionally supported. Many extemporaneous speakers will use

Tip

KEEP NOTES SIMPLE
Losing your place in lengthy notes can give your **confidence** a serious knock, so make sure your notes are **quick and easy to use,** giving you the information you need at a glance.

their visual support – usually digital slides prepared using presentation software – to prompt their memories. Others prefer to use notecards, or the full manuscript. Whichever you choose, make sure that your notes are simple, easy to follow, and allow you to maintain eye contact with the audience.

CHECKLIST...
Being prepared   **YES NO**

1 Have you double-checked the **time and location** for your speech? .... ☐ ☐

2 Are you sure about the **length of time** allotted to the speech? .... ☐ ☐

3 Have you decided how to **arrange the room**? .... ☐ ☐

4 Have you found out whether you are **using a lectern** or are free to walk around the room during the speech? .... ☐ ☐

5 Have you tested the **microphone** and **sound system**? .... ☐ ☐

6 Are you familiar with the **arrangements** and **systems** for visuals? .... ☐ ☐

7 Do you know what **lighting is available,** and have you determined whether it needs to change for **screen visuals** or handouts during your talk? .... ☐ ☐

8 If you are presenting remotely, are you familiar with the platform you are using? .... ☐ ☐

Gaining confidence
The better prepared you are, the more secure you will feel. Think about all aspects of your presentation, from the software and microphone that you will be using, to your video-chat backdrop or the layout of the conference room. The knowledge that you have arranged every detail, and carefully planned and rehearsed your talk, will build your confidence. If you get cold feet, remember that you've been asked to speak because the audience is interested in your expertise and viewpoint. Trust in your ability and intelligence to deliver an effective speech.

Delivering your speech

You've researched the topic thoroughly, written and organized your thoughts, and rehearsed using your visuals. Use the confidence that you've developed in planning and rehearsal to take the next step: get up and speak. You are the medium, or bearer, of the message, and your delivery is critical to the successful communication of your ideas.

Improving your delivery

As you approach the challenge of becoming an accomplished public speaker, keep in mind that no one is born with great public-speaking ability. Language is the habit of a lifetime, and your ability to speak with conviction and sincerity is a function of your willingness to work at it. Your skills will improve with every speech that you make, and as you master the art of presentation, chances are that others in a position of influence will notice and reward you for your effo

> Your ability to speak with **conviction** and **sincerity** is a function of your willingness to **work at it**

In focus

PRESENTING VIRTUALLY

There are a few extra things to consider when delivering a speech virtually. Before you begin, check your camera, microphone, internet connection, and backdrop, and that you are comfortable using your software. Turn off notifications on your device and let anyone nearby know they must not disturb you. Because your audience can't see as many of your gestures as they can in person, it's a good idea to exaggerate your body language a little, and talk more animatedly and slowly; also try bringing your hands into frame. Sit square on to the camera, and feel free to share your screen, but don't forget to switch back to your face in between slides. Asking your audience to turn their own cameras on can help you gauge their interest, and adapt accordingly. Above all, though, smile, sit up straight, and engage.

Ways to keep your audience interested

MAKE A CONNECTION	HELP THEM UNDERSTAND
Prepare yourself: breathe deeply, smile, think positively, and speak	**Blueprint the speech:** tell the audience where your talk is going
Humanize and personalize your speech – share your experiences, values, goals, and fears	**Begin with the familiar,** then move to the unfamiliar
Do your best to be one of them (unless it's clear you are not)	**Talk process first,** then add in the detail
Use humour where appropriate (unless you are not funny)	**Visualize and demonstrate** your ideas where you can
Actively involve the audience as much as you can	**Summarize your key points** as you progress through a speech
Focus on current local events and issues known to the audience	**Give examples** to illustrate your concepts and ideas
	Tell stories, and dramatize your central theme

Use the **confidence** that you've developed in **planning** and **rehearsal** to take the next step: **get up and speak**

Becoming a better writer

Very few people think writing is easy. Good writing – that is, writing with power, grace, dignity, and impact – takes time, careful thought, and revision. Such writing is often the product of many years of training and practice. Even though writing may sometimes seem like hard work, with practice you can learn to do it well.

Organizing your writing

Good business writing is simple, clear, and concise. By not calling attention to itself, good writing is "transparent", helping the reader focus on the idea you are trying to communicate rather than on the words that you are using to describe it.

The key to good business writing is organization. You need to know where you are going before you start, so do your research and identify the key issues you need to cover. Compose a list of the most important points, and use them to create an outline. If your document will include an overview section containing your purpose for writing, write this firs Next, tackle the most important paragraphs, before filling out the detai and any supplementary material.

Have I "translated" any **technical terms?**

Have I explained adequately?

Does my writing **flow in a logical way,** and have I given **complex explanations** in a step-by-step form?

Use **simple, down-to-earth** words, and avoid needless ones and wordy expressions

riting for clarity

hen composing an email, letter, or
port, keep in mind that your reader
en doesn't have much time: senior
anagers, in particular, generally have
ht schedules and too much to read.
ey need your written communication
quickly and clearly give them the
tails they need to know.

Ensure that your writing style is
th precise and concise. Use simple,
wn-to-earth words, and avoid
edless ones and wordy expressions.
mple words and expressions are more
ickly understood and can add power
your ideas. Be direct, and avoid vague

terms such as "very" and "slightly";
this will show that you have confidence
in what you are saying and will add
power to your ideas. Make sure, too, that
everything you write is grammatically
correct – you don't want your busy reader
to have to re-read your sentences to try to
decipher their meaning.

Keep your paragraphs short; they are
more inviting and more likely to get read.
If your document must include numbers,
use them with restraint – a paragraph
filled with numbers can be difficult to
read and follow. Use a few numbers
selectively to make your point, then
put the rest in tables and graphics.

Have I said enough to **answer questions** and **allay fears** without giving too much detail?

Have I used **visuals** to help explain **complex facts?**

Have I cautioned the reader, where necessary, against **common mistakes** and **misreading** of the information?

81%

of **businesspeople** agree that **poorly written** material **wastes** a lot of their **time**

Tip

ALWAYS EDIT
Revising and editing are
critical to good writing.
Putting some time between
writing and editing will help
you be more objective.
Revise your writing with the
intent to **simplify, clarify,**
and **trim excess words.**

Making your writing come alive

To escape from outdated, excessively formal writing styles, try to make your writing more like your speaking, and then "tidy it up". Imagine your reader in front of you – how would you explain things to them? Write your words down, aiming to make them as clear, fresh, and easy to read as possible. You may need to write a first draft for structural purposes, and then go back over your document.

VIGOROUS AND DIRECT

Use **active sentences** and avoid the passive voice. Be **more definite** by limiting the use of the word "not".

Make sure that your writing is:

In focus

THE RIGHT ORDER
A poorly organized document reads like a mystery story. Clue by clue, it unfolds details that make sense only towards the end – if the reader gets that far. Your job is to make it easier for the reader, by explaining each point with an overview, followed by details. To avoid any confusion, always give directions before reasons, requests before justifications, answers before explanations, conclusions before details, and solutions before problems. Try the approach used in many news stories. They start with the most important information and taper off to the least important.

CONNECTING WITH THE READER

Reach out to your reader by occasionally using questions. A request **gains emphasis** when it ends with a question mark. Rather than writing, "Please advise as to whether the meeting is still scheduled for February 21st", simply ask: "Is the meeting still scheduled for February 21st?"

Tip

MAKE IT PERFECT

Eliminate factual errors, typos, misspellings, bad grammar, and incorrect punctuation in your writing. Remember that if **too many details** in an email you have written are recognized to be incorrect, your entire line of thinking may be considered suspect.

MADE UP OF SHORT SENTENCES

This won't guarantee clarity, but short sentences will prevent many of the confusions that can easily occur in longer ones. Try the ear test: **read your writing aloud** and break apart any sentence you can't finish in one breath.

FREE OF CLICHÉS AND JARGON

Tired **words and expressions** make your writing appear superficial.

Imagine your reader in **front** of you – **think** how you would **explain** things to them and **write** your words down

Meeting your reader's needs

Before you write, find out what the reader expects, wants, and needs. If you later discover that you must deviate from these guidelines, let the reader know why. When composing your document, don't include material that you don't need: you may be accused of missing the point. Make sure, too, that you always separate facts from opinions in your writing. The reader should never be in doubt as to what you know to be true, and what you think may be the case. Always apply a consistent approach to avoid misunderstandings.

Capturing and keeping your readers' attention

USE CONTRACTIONS

Make your writing softer and more accessible by occasionally using the contractions that we naturally speak with, such as "I'm", "we're", "you'd", "they've", "can't", "don't", and "let's".

ALLOW SENTENCES TO END WITH A PREPOSITION

Don't reword a sentence just to move a preposition (e.g. "after", "at", "by", "from", "of", "to", or "up") from the end. You are likely to lengthen, tangle, and stiffen the sentence.

WRITE WITH PERSONAL PRONOUNS

Use "we", "us", and "our" when speaking for the company. Use "I", "me", and "my" when speaking for yourself. Either way, be generous with the use of the word "you".

USE THE PRESENT TENSE WHENEVER POSSIBLE

This adds immediacy to your writing. Be careful, however, not to slip from the present to the past tense and back again, as this will make your writing confusing. Select one tense and stick to it.

Find out what your reader **expects, wants,** and **needs:** if you deviate from this in your writing, **let the reader know why**

USE SHORT TRANSITIONS

Use "but" more than "however", and "more than" rather than "in addition to". Use more formal transitions only for variety. Don't be afraid to start a sentence with words like "but", "so", "yet", "and", or "or".

Writing a business letter

Business letters are primarily external documents, although managers will occasionally use letters to correspond with subordinates and executives within their organization. Good letters are crisp, concise, and organized so that readers can follow and understand the content with little effort.

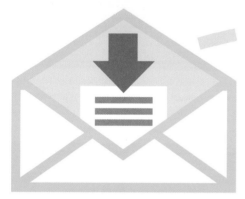

Writing successful letters

Although most business correspondence is conducted by email and messaging these days, physical letters still have their place in the workplace (unless your company runs a paperless office). Often seen as carrying more weight than electronic messages, business letters are good for communicating formal, especially legal matters, where it is important that your recipient gets a hard copy of your correspondence. These include contractual issues and policy changes, disciplinary proceedings and commendations, and resignations, but business letters can be used to convey almost any important issue.

Your success as a business writer depends, in large measure, on your ability to convince others that what you have written is worth their attention. This is more likely if your letter meets three criteria: it should be concise, it should be clear, and it absolutely must organized. Be careful, however. Brevity desirable, but you can overdo it. Avoid being too brief or curt, and make sure that your reader has enough information to understand the subject. Include each issue relevant to the subject, and explain the process, the outcome, or the decision to the satisfaction of the reader. If you were receiving the letter would the information be sufficient? Would you be satisfied that the writer had taken you seriously?

howing interest

hen responding to a letter you have
received, aim to show that you are
enuinely interested. The sender thought
e issue was important enough to write
bout; you should think so, too. Show by
ur words and actions that you care
bout them and the contents of the letter.
  Give everyone the benefit of the doubt.
something in a letter jars, try to put
urself in the writer's shoes. Maybe they

wrote it because they have different
information, or simply made a mistake.
Never write and quickly send off an
angry letter. Venting your spleen may
make you feel good, but it's almost
never a good idea to post a hostile
reply. Take your time and cool down
before you compose an angry letter.
Then wait until the following day to
re-read it. Chances are, you'll think
twice before posting.

Hitting the right tone

If you have to deliver bad news by letter,
say you are sorry. Use phrases such as,
"I am sorry to say that..." or "I regret to
say that we'll be unable to [do something]
because..." to soften the blow. If your
reader thinks you don't care, you may
spark an unwanted reaction. If you have
good news, say you are glad: "I am
delighted to tell you that...". Alternatively,
use a phrase such as: "You will be
pleased to learn that...".

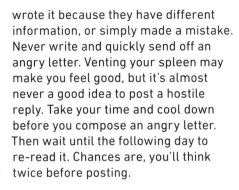

A letter should
be **clear** and
organized. Brevity
is desirable, but you
can overdo it: make
absolutely sure that
your reader has
enough information
to **understand
the subject**

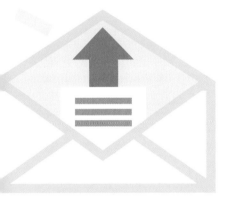

In focus

FORM LETTERS

Form letters are standardized letters on
regularly occurring topics designed to
be sent to multiple recipients. While such
a "one-size-fits-all" approach may be
tempting, it is usually a recipe for disaster.
A letter must answer all of the questions
its audience is likely to have, responding
to their fears, doubts, and concerns. In
situations in which it is absolutely necessary
to use a form letter, test market your efforts
by showing them to several present or past
members of the audience, and asking for
suggestions for improvement.

Using email and instant messaging effectively

Email is now the key means of staying in touch, passing data and graphics, and managing the flow of information needed to run a business. Text, or SMS, messaging, when properly managed, can also be become a productivity booster, a direct, interactive link to customers, and an essential tool to communicate with other staff.

Reducing your emailing time

Email is a tool; don't let it become your master. Limit the time you spend on email by following these tips:

- **Send less, get less** Think carefully about whether you really need to draft new messages or respond to those you've already received.
- **Escape the endless reply loop** Silence in response to an email message may feel rude, but is acceptable. If you wish to reassure someone that no reply is necessary, finish a message with "no reply needed," or a request with "Thanks in advance." Avoid asking any questions for which you don't really want or need answers.
- **Think twice about the "cc" box** If you copy in a large number of people to your emails and they all respond with a reply that needs an answer, you may create unnecessary traffic.

Sending better emails

1 Pick the subject line of the email carefully: make it informative and brief so the recipient can easily find and act on it.

4 Be careful with criticism: be sure to provide enough context and background to avoid a misunderstanding.

5 Keep it short. If you need more than a few paragraphs, send as an attachment, or consider if the matter could be better addressed over the phone.

CHECKLIST...
Knowing when email is inappropriate **YES NO**

1 Do I need to **convey or discern emotion?** .... ☐ ☐

2 Do I need to **cut through** the communication clutter? .... ☐ ☐

3 Do I need to **move quickly?** .... ☐ ☐

4 Do I want a remote communication **to be secure?** .... ☐ ☐

5 Am I trying to **reach someone** who doesn't have
access to (or check) email? .... ☐ ☐

6 Do I want to **engage people** and get an **immediate response?** ..... ☐ ☐

Be sparing in your use of email: think very carefully
about whether you really need to **draft new messages**
or respond to those you've **already received**

2

Now **write the main body**
of the email, using correct
grammar, punctuation,
and capitalization.

3

**Avoid abbreviations and
cyberjargon:** most business
professionals dislike them.
WIDLTO (when in doubt, leave
them out).

6

Use a signature to conclude your
email, but keep it simple: don't
be tempted to add humorous
or "inspiring" quotes.

7

Before you send the email,
check your attachments. Send
only those that your recipient
needs or wants to see.

Developing good email habits

Don't check your email constantly. Check it at regular intervals – hourly or even just three times a day if your work is less deadline-driven. Be disciplined about email management. Aim to handle each message just once. If it's unimportant or irrelevant, hit the delete key. If you spend more than three hours a week sorting through irrelevant mail, you have a problem. If a message is something you'll need to respond to, decide whether to do it now or later, when you will have the time and information you need. Don't put pressure on others by sending emails out of hours. Wait until the next day, or make it clear that you don't expect an answer right away.

Consider if you are posting to the right people on the right channel – if they don't need to be in chat, don't add the

Ask yourself if instant messaging is the right medium for your message – don't use it for formal matters

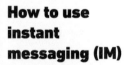

How to use instant messaging (IM)

In focus

INTRANETS

Intranets (private company networks) are great for facilitating two-way communication between staff and management, and among employees. They can also provide access to company knowledge, such as statistics and best practice documents, and enhance collaboration. Many integrate with third-party apps and incorporate social media-style features, too.

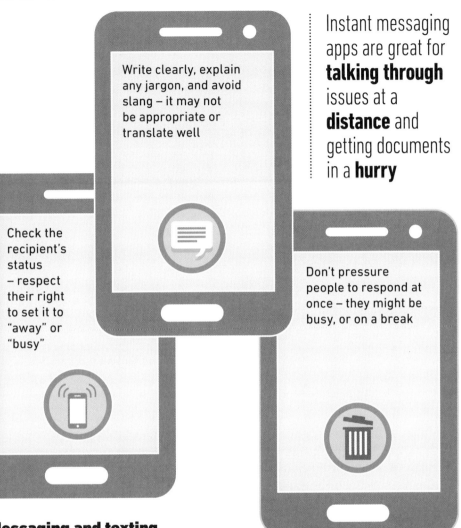

Write clearly, explain any jargon, and avoid slang – it may not be appropriate or translate well

Instant messaging apps are great for **talking through** issues at a **distance** and getting documents in a **hurry**

Check the recipient's status – respect their right to set it to "away" or "busy"

Don't pressure people to respond at once – they might be busy, or on a break

Messaging and texting

Instant messaging has become a popular workplace tool, allowing groups of two, three, or even hundreds of people to connect and receive responses instantly. Apps, such as Slack and Microsoft Teams, are great for talking through issues at a distance, and getting documents in a hurry. But such immediacy also requires new considerations regarding etiquette and expectations (see graphic). Set your status to "away" or "busy" to reduce distractions.

Using text messages to reach out to customers is established practice in many businesses, but few firms use texts for other types of communications. However, they are an ideal medium for alerts, such as notifications of downtime of computer servers, and for simple company announcements, such as motivational messages and new employee introductions.

Writing reports

Reports are longer and more comprehensive than most documents, and are written for the purpose of documenting actions, describing projects and events, and capturing information on complex issues. They are often written by more than one person for audiences with multiple needs and interests.

Planning your report

There are three main questions to consider when compiling a report:

- **Who is in your audience?** Think about their level of interest in the content, and their familiarity with the issues, ideas, and vocabulary you plan to use.
- **What is the ideal format?** Consider how your readers will use the document – will they start from the beginning and read through page by page, or will they skip to sections that interest them most?
- **Is the document properly organized?** Consider using a bold typeface for headings and sub-headings to help organize the information and make it retrievable.

> Busy business leaders may only read the **executive summary** of a report, so it must tell them all they need to know in order for them to **understand** your recommendations

Tip

INCLUDE A COVER LETTER

As a courtesy to your reader, always include a cover letter or email to accompany the report explaining **what the document covers and why.** Where appropriate, include the report's most **important recommendations** or **findings.**

Writing the report

Reports are divided into three sections: front matter (including title page, abstract, table of contents, and list of figures and tables), the main body of the report, and end matter (bibliography, appendices, glossary, and index). Begin the main body with an executive summary, detailing the report's key points and recommendations. Busy executives may only read this section, so it must tell them all they need to know in order for them to agree with your recommendations.

Dividing your report into sections

SECTION	CONTENT
TITLE PAGE	A single page containing the full title of the report, the names of the authors, the date of issue, and the name of the organization to which the report is submitted.
ABSTRACT	A paragraph that summarizes the major points. It enables a reader to decide whether to read the entire work.
TABLE OF CONTENTS	A list of all of the headings within the report in the order of their appearance, along with a page number for each.
LIST OF FIGURES AND TABLES	Reports with more than five figures or tables should include a page listing each one with its page number.
FOREWORD (OPTIONAL)	An introductory statement usually written by an authority figure. It provides background information and places the report in the context of other works in the field.
PREFACE (OPTIONAL)	This describes the purpose, background, or scope of the report.
EXECUTIVE SUMMARY	This provides more information than the abstract, and enables readers to scan the report's primary points. These summaries are usually restricted to a few pages.
MAIN TEXT	This forms the main body of the report, and explains your work and its findings.
CONCLUSION	This contains not only concluding remarks but also any recommended actions for the readers.
BIBLIOGRAPHY	A listing of all the sources consulted to prepare the report; it may also suggest additional reading and resources.
APPENDICES	Information that supplements the main report as evidence, such as lists, tables of figures, and charts and graphs.
GLOSSARY	An alphabetical list of definitions of unusual terms used.
INDEX	An alphabetical list of topics with page numbers.

Communicating
with your team

A team is only as good as its communication; misunderstandings can cause a huge amount of extra work and lost time. When managing a team, focus on giving constructive feedback, briefing thoroughly, and dealing effectively with conflict.

15

Listening effectively

Good communication is not just about getting your point across. It's also about staying quiet and listening to what others have to say. As a manager, listening actively and understanding your colleagues is at the heart of creating a team that performs to the best of its ability.

Learning when to listen

Listening is a skill you acquire naturally, but can improve upon if you're motivated to do so. The first step towards becoming a better listener is, surprisingly, to stop: you need to stop talking, stop trying to carry on more than one conversation, and stop interrupting. Let the other person speak. As others are talking, allow yourself to respond cognitively and emotionally, taking in the factual information and the tone of their remarks, without responding. Then ask carefully thought-out questions that will clarify what they have said and reassure you of its basis in fact.

Tip

LISTENING REMOTELY
Because you can't pick up on as many nonverbal cues, actively listening when working remotely requires more focus. Listen in a **quiet place** and tell others not to disturb you. On video calls, **mute your mic** when not speaking and **watch the screen** to ensure you're taking everything in.

25%

of **corporate leaders** have a **listening deficit,** according to **feedback** from their colleagues

etting the message

art by trying to see things from
e speaker's point of view, and let your
tions demonstrate this. Show interest
th your body language: look the
eaker in the eyes and maintain an
en and non-threatening posture.
ve the speaker physical signs of your

undivided attention: close the door,
hold your calls, and put aside whatever
you're working on.

Listen carefully to how something
is said: look out for hints of sarcasm,
cynicism, or irony in what you hear. Try
to tune in to the speaker's mood and
intention. Communication is a shared
responsibility, so it is up to you to ensure
that you understand the message.

Once you have listened to what a
person has to say and clarified anything
you're not sure of, evaluate the facts and
evidence. Ask yourself if the evidence is
recent, reliable, accurate, and relevant.

Tip

WATCH WHAT YOU HEAR
Just because you want to hear
something, doesn't mean it is
what the speaker is **really
saying.** Avoid falling into the
trap of **selective hearing.**

LISTENING ACTIVELY

Dos	Don'ts
O **Listening regularly to difficult material to hone your listening ability**	O Assuming that everything interesting should be provided in written form
O **Giving your full and undivided attention to the speaker**	O Pretending to listen while actually doing something else
O **Listening to the argument in the speaker's terms, and in the order he or she wishes to follow**	O Criticizing the speaker's delivery and interrupting the flow of what they are saying to ask questions
O **Focusing on the reasons for the speaker's approach and discussion**	O Assuming you already know what the issue is and how to resolve it

Understanding nonverbal communication

Most of the meaning transferred from one person to another in a personal conversation comes not from the words that are spoken, but from nonverbal signals. Learning to read, understand, and use these wordless messages isn't easy, but is essential for effective communicatio

Reading nonverbal signals

The movement, positioning, and use of the human body in various communication settings serves a number of functions:

- To highlight or emphasize some part of a verbal message
- To regulate the flow, pace, and back-and-forth nature of verbal messages
- To reinforce the general tone or attitude of a message
- To repeat what the verbal messages convey (holding up three fingers to indicate the number three, for example)
- To substitute for, or take the place of, verbal messages (such as giving a "thumbs up" gesture).

Nonverbal cues are often difficult to read, especially because there are few body movements or gestures that have universally agreed-upon meanings. A colleague who looks tired or overworked to one person may appear disinterested or

Body language can contradict the **verbal messages** being sent

Using nonverbal signals

different to another. While
oking for meaning in a particular
ovement, position, or gesture, be
reful not to miss more important
gnals that reveal the true feelings
a speaker. Body language can
metimes contradict the verbal
essages being sent. Tears in a
rson's eyes, for example, might
voluntarily contradict a message
lling you that the speaker is fine.

60%

to **65%** of **meaning** in social situations is conveyed **nonverbally**

'ATCH YOUR APPEARANCE
ake sure that your clothing and grooming are appropriate to your
dience, your reasons for communicating, and the occasion.

ESTRAIN YOUR MOVEMENTS
nall gestures, close to your body, will convey an image of
nfidence and authority. Keep your voice low but audible
d your posture relaxed.

AKE CARE WITH TOUCH
ne rules on touching others in a business context vary from
lture to culture. Make sure you know and respect local customs.

'ATCH YOUR EYE CONTACT
ve contact usually reinforces trust; however, in some Asian
ltures, looking a superior in the eye as you speak can be
nsidered disrespectful.

SE VOCAL DYNAMICS
ne, volume, rate, pitch, forcefulness, and enunciation all
nvey meaning about a subject, and how you feel about the
ople in the room.

Running briefings and meetings

Briefings and meetings are an inescapable part of business life. They are a means of sharing information, initiating strategies, perpetuating a culture, and building consensus around business goals. Done well, they're good for both business and morale, whether conducted in person or remotely.

Organizing a meeting

Be clear about the purpose of any meeting before you start planning. Invite only those people who are directly related to your goals, and make sure you include all the key decision-makers. Once you've arranged a time, place, and date that is convenient to everyone, send them all an agenda, making clear the meeting's theme and goals. In putting together the agenda, consider the following questions: What do we need to do in this meeting? What conversations will be important to those who attend? What information will we need to begin?

Prioritize the most important items so they will be discussed early on in the meeting, and assign a certain amount of time for each agenda item.

Giving a briefing

Briefing is a process by which you provide information to those who need it. As with any form of communication, think about your audience, your purpose, and the occasion. Find out all you can about the audience, and what they hope to take away from the session. State your purpose clearly and simply at the beginning of the meeting: "The purpose

ASK YOURSELF...
Do I need to call a meeting?

	YES	NO
1 Do I need to **motivate people**, giving them a "jumpstart" to get going?	☐	☐
2 Do I need to **share** general company or market **information** with people to help them do their jobs?	☐	☐
3 Do I need to **initiate a new programme** or project?	☐	☐
4 Do I wish to **introduce people** to one another, so they can benefit from each other's experiences?	☐	☐

Case study

A COMPETITIVE ADVANTAGE
As CEO of the international retail giant Walmart, David Glass knew the company would have to be quick off the mark with merchandising strategies, particularly in response to moves made by competitors. Each Saturday morning, when sales results for the week were transmitted to the corporate headquarters, Glass would gather key subordinates to share information from people in the field. They would tell the sales team what their competitors were doing; the senior team would then focus on corrective actions they wanted to take. By noon, regional managers would call district managers, and they would discuss and agree the changes they would implement in the next week. "By noon on Saturday," Glass said, "we had all our corrections in place. Our competitors, for the most part, got their sales results on Monday for the week prior."

this briefing is to look at budget ojections for the next 90 days." t them know why you're calling e meeting now.

elivering a brief

hen giving a briefing meeting, choose e delivery that best suits your speaking yle and the needs of the audience. ere are three forms to choose from:

Memorized presentations These are delivered verbatim, just as you wrote them. This gives you total control over the material, but unless you're a trained actor, there's a risk that you'll sound wooden and the material contrived. Worse yet, you may forget where you are and have to start again or refer to notes.

Scripted briefings These are more common, but they can also sound stilted. The problem with reading is that you risk losing eye contact by lowering your chin and it also compresses your vocal pitch. If you do use a script, rehearse carefully and look up frequently, making regular eye contact with your audience.

- **Extemporaneous briefings** These are delivered either without notes or with visual aids to prompt your memory. They are the most effective choice, looking more spontaneous, while actually being thoroughly researched, tightly organized, and well rehearsed.

Tip

ANTICIPATE QUESTIONS
Do your best to address audience concerns, questions, doubts, and fears in advance. **Plan the content** of your briefing around the needs of those in the audience.

Communicating to persuade

Whether your are trying to sell a product, convince your superiors to release more resources, convince an investor, or win a promotion, you need a clear strategy to persuade your audience. Removing the barriers to people saying "yes" is a two-way process.

Understanding the audience

Before you can expect your request to be understood and considered, you first need to understand your audience. What are their interests, their motivators, and their possible objections to your proposal? Most successful attempts at persuasion involve four separate, yet related, steps. Following these steps won't guarantee success with any particular audience, but they will set the stage for the attitudes you're trying to shape in your team and the behaviour you hope will follow.

GETTING THEIR ATTENTION

If you want to motivate people to do something, you first have to catch their attention. Research shows that we **selectively choose** what to pay attention to, both as a defence mechanism against sensory overload, and because we **seek out messages with particular value** for us. We ignore virtually everything else. There are two ways to capture attention:

- Use **physical stimuli,** such as bright lights, sound, motion, or colour.
- Present stimuli that **relate directly to the needs** or goals of those you want to persuade.

PROVIDING A MOTIVATION

Next, you need to **provide a reason** for people to act. A persuasive writer or speaker is one who can **lead others to believe** in what he or she is advocating, and then encourage some form of behaviour in line with that belief. This amounts to giving good reasons for what you believe. These are not reasons you think are good, but reasons your team thinks are good.

Identify the needs and interests of your team and connect them to your message. Which of their needs are you fulfilling? **Appeal to their sense of rationality** – show why it makes sense to act on your message. Or **call on their sense of conformity,** by showing how well others will view them if they act on your message.

When to use one- or two-sided arguments

ONE-SIDED ARGUMENT	TWO-SIDED ARGUMENT
The audience initially agrees with you and your aim is simply to intensify support.	You suspect or know that the audience initially disagrees with your position.
The audience will not be exposed to any form of counter-persuasion.	You know the audience will be exposed to subsequent counter-persuasion.
The audience is not well informed or may become easily confused by an opponent's argument or evidence.	You hope to produce a more enduring result with a knowledgeable audience.

MOVING OTHERS TO ACT

Once you have captured the attention of those you want to persuade and have given them good cause to believe the message, you must provide them with a **clear channel for action.**

First, however, take time to **reassure them**: show them that there is a high probability that **you can deliver** on the promised reward. Your team needs to know that what you've promised will actually come true.

Next, **recommend a specific proposal or action.** Tell your team exactly what you want them to do, describe how you would like them to go about it and set out a realistic timescale. Make sure that everyone on your team knows how and when **progress will be measured** and identify the end point and the rewards for achievement that lie ahead.

KEEPING THEM ON SIDE

The arguments that you use to persuade others can be one-sided, presenting your case alone, or two-sided, presenting your case as well as dealing with real and potential counter-arguments. **Choose your approach** based on the knowledge and preconceptions of your audience. If you decide to use a two-sided argument, you should:

- **Warn your team** that others may try to change their minds.
- **State some opposing arguments** and then refute them. If you are aware of an opposing message, consider previewing at least part of it to the audience and then explaining why it is flawed.
- **Encourage commitment** in some tangible or visible way. It's more difficult for people to back away from positions for which they've publicly proclaimed their support.

Managing conflict

Conflict can arise from a variety of sources, but many experts see it as a function of such workplace issues as personality, personal and professional relationships, cultural differences, working environments, demands of the marketplace, and of course, competition. As organizations increasingly use teamwork, differences among team members can lead to conflict.

LIMITED RESOURCES

Everything from office space to budgets may put people in competition with one another. Allocate scarce resources fairly to avoid this.

VALUES, GOALS, AND PRIORITIES

Confrontation can occur when people in an organization don't agree on strategic direction or basic priorities. Agreement on goals, large and small, can help to avoid this.

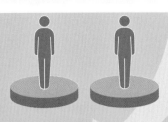

Identifying the sources of conflict

Not all conflict within an organization is unhealthy, but conflict between and among people within an organization can quickly become counter-productive, divisive, and destructive if not properly managed. Conflict may develop over any number of issues or factors, but these five appear regularly:

HUMAN DRIVE FOR SUCCESS

Conflicts can arise as a result of the natural sense of goal orientation that every human experiences. Some organizations actively foster a sense of competition among their members, creating many competitors and few rewards.

CHANGE

Many changes, including those to annual budgets, organizational priorities, lines of authority, or limits of responsibility, as well as restructuring, mergers, divestitures, and lay-offs, can create anxiety, uncertainty, and conflict in an organization.

POORLY DEFINED RESPONSIBILITIES

Conflict may result from differences between formal job descriptions and the daily expectations of the role. Review and agree who is responsible for what (and to whom).

Conflict resolution techniques

Resolving conflicts between team members is an important function of an effective manager. To begin the process, you should first ensure that both parties acknowledge that the conflict exists and the effects that it is having on team performance and morale. It may be that one party sees the problem as trivial, or is ignoring the issue. Next, encourage the parties to set aside time to address the problem – schedule the first meeting, and offer to participate in the process.

Get people to **agree on the small stuff** first: when this happens, the big issues become **easier to address**

LISTEN CAREFULLY

Find out what's on people's minds, and ask them what they're thinking and how they feel.

FOCUS ON INTERESTS

Don't focus on a person's demands, but on their interests – the reasons behind their demands.

RECOGNIZE FEELINGS

Accept feelings in others, and work to communicate empathy. Keep your own emotions in check, to ensure that you act professionally.

SEPARATE PEOPLE FROM PROBLEMS

Rather than saying "I can't support you", say "I'm not in favour of that solution."

KEEP COMMUNICATING

Keep the lines of communication open and speak as frankly and honestly as possible.

START SMALL

Get people to agree on the small stuff first. Once they start to agree on a few things, the big issues won't be as difficult.

Reconciling two sides

SUMMARIZE THE AGREEMENT

Review all the details with everyone involved. Make sure all are in agreement.

DEVISE OPTIONS

Find alternatives for mutual gain. By working together on the options, you can shift the dynamic from competition to cooperation.

CUT YOUR LOSSES

Sometimes the conflict has simply gone too far, and you must decide to make personnel changes.

FIND THE SOURCE

Track the conflict to its source. Don't accept the first answers you find; employees may have underlying concerns.

Communicating
externally

In today's global economy, you may find yourself
communicating across companies, countries, and
cultures, through a variety of media, including the
internet. Focus on your company's core goals and
identity to ensure consistent messaging.

16

Selling

Selling is both a form of persuasion and a process of relationship building. Most people don't want to feel as if they're being sold something; they would prefer to believe that they're buying it. This involves a balance of thoughtful questions, active listening, and a well-prepared presentation.

Prospecting and presenting

Selling involves actively looking for prospects who have the money, the authority, and a desire to buy. Before you contact a prospect, make sure that they fulfil these criteria, and that you know both what you want to achieve, and how. Develop a presentation that you can deliver confidently. This may be entirely memorized, formulaic (allowing some buyer–seller interaction), or entirely flexible and interactive. If you're offering a solution to a specific problem, base your proposal around a detailed analysis of the buyer's situation. Before you contact a prospect, always:

- Determine your call objectives. Are they specific, measurable, achievable, realistic, and well-timed?
- Develop a customer profile. What do you know about the person who is making the buying decision?
- Familiarize yourself with all the customer benefits.
- Develop a sales presentation.

Closing the sale

First ask the prospect's opinion about the benefits you're offering, using a question such as: "How does this sound to you?" If this throws up any objections, handle them as they arise. Don't repeat negative statements or concerns; focus on positive outcomes. There are various ways to close a sale, so choose the one that is most appropriate to your situation.

Ways to close a sale

USE THE MINOR POINTS CLOSE

Ask the prospect to make **low-risk decisions** on minor, low-cost elements. Then ask for the order.

Develop a presentation that you can deliver **confidently.** It may be **memorized, formulaic,** or entirely flexible and **interactive**

Tip

MAKE A POSITIVE FIRST IMPRESSION

Be positive: smile, be enthusiastic, and open conversation with a **thoughtful compliment** or a **prediction** related to your product.

USE THE ASSUMPTIVE CLOSE

When the prospect is **close to a decision,** say: "I'll call your order in tonight."

GIVE AN ALTERNATIVE CHOICE

Give **two options,** and then ask: "Which of these do you prefer?"

SUMMARIZE THE BENEFITS

Present the main **features, advantages,** and **benefits,** then ask for the order.

USE THE SCARCITY CLOSE

If true, tell the prospect that these items are **so popular,** there may not be many of them left.

USE THE CONTINUOUS "YES" CLOSE

Develop a **set of questions** the prospect will answer "yes" to, then ask for the order.

Communicating across countries and cultures

Advances in remote communications technology have brought unprecedented change across the globe. Video chat, instant messagin email, and other tools are allowing people living far apart to connect and collaborate efficiently and effectively. But even as the world come closer together, each of us has retained something essential to our identity as humans: our culture.

Defining culture

Culture is everything that people have, think, and do as members of their society. Culture affects and is a central part of our economy and the organizations that employ us. It is composed of material objects, ideas, values, and attitudes, as well as expected patterns of behaviour. Whatever your business, you're likely to encounter people of different ethnicity, citizenship, and cultural origin. Dealing with people of different cultures, conducting business over international borders, travelling safely, and communicating effectively are not always easy, but are essential for success in today's business world.

Culture is composed of material **objects, ideas, values,** and **attitudes**

CULTURE IS INGRAINED

Few of us would give a moment thought to learning how to be a part of the culture we have grov up in. Our first culture is so clos defined for each of us that we'r barely aware that we have one. Learning a second culture, thoug takes a **purposeful effort**.

Understanding culture

When you're communicating with a culture other than your own, you need to **be sensitive** about the particular beliefs and values of that culture, and how they differ from your own.

ecognizing change

e culture of any country is constantly
dergoing change. The clothing people
ar, the transportation they use, the
oks they read, the topics they talk
out, and so on, all change over time.
s is due to the internal forces of
covery, invention, and innovation; and
ternal forces, including the diffusion of
as from other cultures. Some cultures
ange fast, while others evolve more
wly, either by preference or because
ey are more physically isolated.
anges in culture are often reflected
changes in the way people speak
d write; make sure that your own
mmunications reflect these changes.

Tip

INVESTIGATE THE SUBCULTURES
Virtually all large,
complex cultures contain
subcultures. These are
small groups of people with
separate and **specialized
interests** – essentially, they
are niche markets.

CULTURE IS UNIVERSAL
All societies have an interest in passing along values
and norms to their children, thereby creating and
defining a culture. No matter where you travel, you'll
find people with cultures that differ from the one in
which you grew up; noticing these differences will
strengthen your communications.

CULTURES ALLOCATE VALUES
Some cultures **engage in behaviours**
that others might consider reprehensible.
Be careful never to cause offence when
communicating by inadvertently breaking
taboos or talking about matters that are
considered "off limits".

Communicating internationally

On a personal level, communicating across international borders means becoming more aware of the ways in which your thinking or actions are culturally biased.

Start by recognizing that your own education, background, and beliefs may be considered fine, or even laudable in your own culture, but they may not count for so much to someone from a different country. Take a non-judgemental position towards those from other cultures, and you are likely to find that they will extend the same hospitable tolerance towards you. If you find yourself making personal judgements, keep them to yourself. When you're writing or speaking to people from another culture, try to understand life

Tip

LEARN TO RECOGNIZE "NO"

Some cultures consider it rude to say "no". If you are met with vague answers to requests, such as **"I'll try"** or **"yes, but it may be difficult"** in these cultures, it may be safer to assume that your request has been refused.

from their perspective. Learn to communicate respect for other people's ways, their country, and their values.

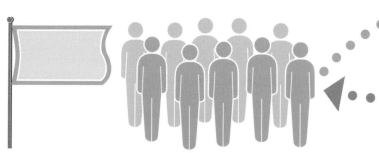

In focus

ETHNOCENTRISM

All cultures, to one degree or another, display ethnocentrism: the tendency to evaluate a foreigner's behaviour by the standards of one's own culture, and to believe that one's culture is superior to all others. We tend to take our own culture for granted. We're born into it, and we live with its rules and

assumptions day in and day out. We quickly come to believe that the way we live is simply "the way things should be". As a result, we often see our behaviour as correct. However, culture is not value-neutral. We have good reasons for believing and behaving as we do, but that doesn't necessarily mean that others are "wrong".

dopting the right attitude

u don't have to adopt the local culture
d begin doing things the way they do.
st be aware and respect that they
things differently. "Your way" of
mmunicating might work brilliantly
your own culture, but less well in
other. Try to adopt an open-minded
proach, focusing on:

- **Developing a tolerance for ambiguity** Accept the fact that you'll never understand everything about another culture. However, you can still appreciate and function within that culture satisfactorily.
- **Becoming more flexible** Things won't always go the way you want. A small measure of flexibility will prove enormously helpful.
- **Practising a little humility** Acknowledge what you do not know or understand. Because you weren't raised in another's culture (or may not even speak the language well), you'll never fully understand all aspects of it. Displaying humility and acceptance will win friends, influence people, and make life easier. Communication consists of the transfer of meaning, so do everything you can to make sure that your messages are not misunderstood.

ASK YOURSELF...

Do I understand the culture?   **YES   NO**

1 Do I understand the **basic business etiquette** of introductions and meetings in this new culture? .... ☐ ☐

2 Do I know how to recognize the **key decision-makers** within a group? .... ☐ ☐

3 Am I familiar with the culture's **business dress code**? .... ☐ ☐

4 Do I know how many **languages are spoken**, and which is the **official language**? .... ☐ ☐

5 Have I learned the preferred **forms of negotiation**? .... ☐ ☐

6 Do I know which **forms of media** are popular among which **demographic groups**? .... ☐ ☐

Writing for the web

The way that people read a website is different to the way in which they read other information. You must take this into account when developing web content. It is not sufficient to simply repurpose content written for print; you need to write specifically for the internet, thinking carefully about what your audience needs and what you want them to know.

Engaging your readers

Why is writing for the internet different? First, people rarely read websites word-for-word. Instead, they scan the page, picking out individual words and sentences. Rather than starting at the beginning of a page and reading from start to finish, internet readers will scan a site looking for relevant items and then if they find something useful, save it for later reference. Guide your reader by highlighting the most important or useful points in your document using headings, lists, and eye-catching typography.

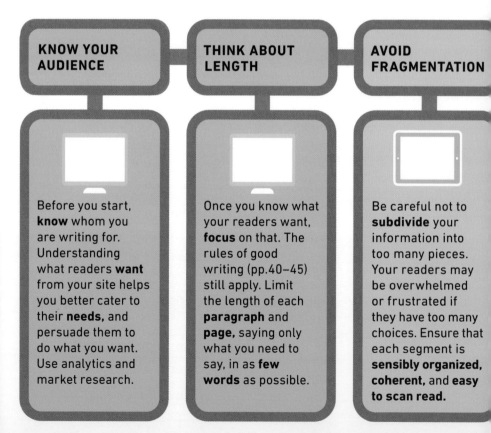

KNOW YOUR AUDIENCE

Before you start, **know** whom you are writing for. Understanding what readers **want** from your site helps you better cater to their **needs,** and persuade them to do what you want. Use analytics and market research.

THINK ABOUT LENGTH

Once you know what your readers want, **focus** on that. The rules of good writing (pp.40–45) still apply. Limit the length of each **paragraph** and **page,** saying only what you need to say, in as **few words** as possible.

AVOID FRAGMENTATION

Be careful not to **subdivide** your information into too many pieces. Your readers may be overwhelmed or frustrated if they have too many choices. Ensure that each segment is **sensibly organized, coherent,** and **easy to scan read.**

16%

f users read a web page **ord-for-word;** most people ͻly **scan** the text, picking out **ighlighted words,** bold or ͻloured **section headings,** ͻd bulleted points

Navigation aids

Web readers generally do not read pages in sequence. Instead, they jump around on a website looking for content that interests them, navigating back and forth across images, ideas, and words. Providing information in precise segments or "chunks" will allow readers to quickly find what they're looking for. A well-constructed chunk provides readers with a comprehensive account, as well as links to related or supporting pages. When your content lends itself to such treatment, use lists rather than paragraphs. Readers can pick out information more easily from a list than from a fully developed paragraph.

ENSURE EASY NAVIGATION	BE ACCESSIBLE	MAKE IT EASY TO FIND

Your main goal is to **provide access** to the information people are most likely to want. Provide **easy-to-follow clues** that lead to chunks of useful information. Include brief but **comprehensive summaries** of longer documents.

Make your content accessible. Help visually impaired readers by ensuring your pages are screen-reader friendly, with clear headings, links, and image descriptions. Want to attract international visitors? Consider translating pages.

Make it easy for readers to find and save information. Research keywords and craft metadata (page descriptions) to make pages more visible on search engines. If aspects of your content are lengthy, try **linking to a** downloadable **PDF** file.

Communicating through social media

Social media channels on the internet – such as Facebook, Twitter, Instagram, TikTok, YouTube, and LinkedIn – have transformed the way people do business. A social media presence is no longer an option, but an essential – people of all ages are influenced in their buying decisions by a brand's presence on social media. So how do you maximize the impact of your social media output?

Devise a strategy

Social media can be used in many different ways – from increasing awareness of your company's brand, increasing traffic to your website, and forging new business contacts at home and abroad, to boosting sales or attracting customers. So, the first decision you should make is to set the purpose of your social media interaction. Be specific in your goals, and list them in order of importance.

Next, carry out some research – formal or informal – into the internet habits of your customers or target audience: who are they? Which social media channels do they use? What do they expect from these channels? You will have far more success if you tune in to the needs of your customers.

Also bear in mind that reaching a sizeable social media audience nowadays involves more than simply posting content. You will likely need to invest in paid-for advertising, as paying the social media platform to show your posts to a wider audience will give them a better chance of generating the impact you want.

Focus on success

Always consider how your social media activities will translate into business growth – there is little point in maintaining a costly presence on social channels if it doesn't affect the bottom line. Think about how you can measure the effectiveness of your activities. Having a large number of followers on Facebook or Twitter, for example, may be impressive, but may be of little value if it fails to translate into improved business performance. Similarly, building up many connections on LinkedIn may be of little use if you fail to leverage these connections to create

73%

of marketers say acquiring **new customers** is their biggest **social media** goal

Three major uses of social media

	CREATIVE BRANDING	BUILDING A COMMUNITY	CUSTOMER SERVICE
ACTIVITIES	O Posting entertaining content in a variety of media. O Creating compelling stories. O Using humour helps boost engagement.	O Creating a space where people with a common interest can interact. O Providing useful information and resources for your community.	O Engaging with customer queries and solving their problems. O Measuring customers' sentiments towards your business.
REMEMBER TO	O Keep your brand message, tone of voice, and writing style consistent across all platforms and interactions.	O Keep your content lively, current, and varied. Just giving links to other web sites will not encourage repeat visits from others.	O Set up a separate account for this purpose and ensure that your responses are quick and authoritative.

w business. Always consider how u'll gauge the value of the effort you vest in social media.

Remember too what social media – social. Too many companies use it a one-way form of communication, e a corporate website, and fail to vite user comment or contribution. e more dialogue you can build with ur customers, the more effective ur use of social channels will be.

gaging with your audience

ow you communicate through social edia channels depends on your als. However, you should always:

- Post regularly: a media stream to which you contribute sporadically will soon dry up.
- Post different types of content: the written word is not enough to engage your audience. Post high-quality images and videos, too.
- Post interesting comments: try to encourage debate, comments, or likes, rather than making passive statements.
- Vary contributors for differing perspectives.
- Always respond to posts from users within a reasonable time frame.

Running a video meeting

Improvements in technology have made video conferencing an essential tool for many businesses. While video-chat apps, such as Skype and Zoom, are easy to use, it is vital to plan carefully to avoid technical hitches, and make the experience rewarding and successful for those involved.

Preparing a video meeting

With more people working remotely, online meetings are increasingly common, allowing dispersed colleagues to connect face-to-face, and encouraging a sense of unity. Running a productive video meeting depends largely on the time you spend preparing for it. Start by deciding what you want your meeting to achieve, and devise a plan accordingly, taking into account issues such as technical requirements, group size, timings, and materials.

Plan your video meeting

Choose your technology and make sure you and your participants are comfortable using it. For conference-style sessions, consider using a specific webinar tool.

Identify the purpose of the video meeting: explain to people what they will be doing and why.

Plan the agenda; don't just try to "wing it" as you go along. Place easily accomplished items first on the list.

Identify a chairperson who will be responsible for starting, stopping, and running the meeting.

CHAIRING A VIDEO MEETING

Dos	Don'ts
O **Asking people to give their names, titles, and locations**	O Introducing some of the participants, but ignoring others
O **Keeping to the agenda and staying on time**	O Introducing new items not agreed to in advance
O **Taking control and providing people with opportunities to speak**	O Allowing people to talk with one another in side conversations
O **Making notes of what is being said and by whom**	O Failing to capture what's been said and agreed to

Video meetings are increasingly common, allowing dispersed colleagues to connect **face-to-face,** and encouraging a sense of **unity**

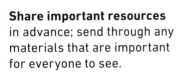

Share important resources in advance; send through any materials that are important for everyone to see.

Confirm the meeting with all participants and send a reminder just before it is due to take place.

Distribute the agenda so other people know what will be discussed and will have time to gather necessary information.

Schedule the meeting for a time and date that suits everyone.

Looking presentable

On the day, dress conservatively: avoid busy patterns, thin stripes, and small prints that draw attention. Act always as if people are watching you, and refrain from quirky mannerisms – these may go unnoticed in a meeting but are magnified in a video call. Sit up straight, pay attention, and project a professional image. Make sure you know where the camera lens is before you start the call, as it is not always above the screen. Make sure to look directly at the camera lens when you are speaking. You'll enhance your credibility dramatically if you focus squarely on the camera; others will think you're speaking directly to them.

Ensure the room from which you are calling is **tidy** and that there's nothing distracting in the **background.**

Pay particular attention to the lighting in the room, making sure that **your face is well lit;** try placing a large sheet of white paper flat on the desk in front of you to **reduce any harsh shadows** on your face.

Succeeding with video calls

Today's computer-based video-conferencing systems, such as Zoom, Microsoft Teams, and Skype, put the power to run virtual meetings in the hands of anyone with a laptop and an internet connection. However, with that power comes the responsibility for looking after every aspect of the call. Follow a few simple technical and presentation tips to make your online meetings more professional and productive.

Try moving your computer's video camera closer to you so that your **head and upper shoulders** occupy the whole screen – any smaller and it becomes difficult to see and read your facial expressions.

Add another light behind you to illuminate the room and provide a sense of place.

Consider **recording the meeting** (but ask permission first).

Close other programs on your computer – especially if they make a noise (email clients, for example).

Check what the other person **can see** before you call.

Look into the camera, not at your picture on the screen.

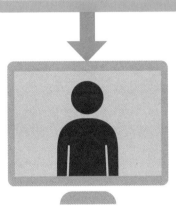

Take some time to **get to know the platform's controls,** so that you can, for example, mute the microphone or share you screen if necessary.

> Use gestures and expressions to **emphasize** your words

Sounding good

Once you are connected, avoid unguarded comments – assume someone may be watching and listening. Speak a bit more slowly than usual, to ensure that everyone understands you, and use gestures and facial expressions to emphasize your words. Don't read a speech, but keep summarizing key issues as you move along. Refer to the agenda and remind people of elapsed time as you move from point to point. In larger meetings, get participants to submit questions via the video app's chat function or a shared document to avoid interruptions. At the end, summarize the issues discussed and agreed to. After the event, prepare and distribute minutes within a few days.

Switch off any potential distractions, such as the telephone, and set your status to "**Do not disturb**" so that you won't get interrupted by other incoming calls.

Communicating in a crisis

There is a huge difference between business problems and crises. Problems are commonplace in business. A crisis, on the other hand, is a major, unpredictable event. Without careful communication, crises have the potential to damage an organization's reputation and financial standing, together with those of its employees, shareholders, products, and services.

Identifying the crisis

Some business crises can be prepared for (to a certain extent), while others require an immediate and creative response. There are two main types:

- **Internal crises** These arise within the company, such as accounting scandals, or labour strikes.
- **External crises** These are caused by an external factor, such as the COVID-19 pandemic, a natural or technological disaster, or external threats by special-interest groups.

It is important to recognize the type of crisis you are facing, as this will help you pinpoint the groups of people you will need to communicate with, and give you an idea of how fast and how far the effects of the crisis could potentially spread.

> Assemble an effective **team** and isolate its members from other **day-to-day concerns**

Case study

L'ORÉAL

French cosmetics company L'Oréal had spent several years expanding its digital operations before the COVID-19 pandemic. But when the crisis hit in 2020 it decided to go all in. Whereas some rivals reacted to the downturn in the beauty market by stripping back marketing, L'Oréal kept communications open online, investing 77 per cent of its media budget into digital. As well as letting people know about its efforts to donate hand sanitizer and financial aid, the company also sought to forge stronger relationships with customers, encouraging them to ask questions and order online. "Social distancing? Yes. Social media distancing? No," as one of its online posts put it. The results were clear: a 62 per cent growth in e-commerce in 2020. "We did in eight weeks what it took three years to do, doubling e-commerce from 18 per cent of our business to 34 per cent at the peak in April," said then chief digital officer, Lubomira Rochet.

ealing with a crisis

mmunicating in a crisis is different m managing a business problem. u are likely to be unprepared, have sufficient information, and be under he pressure. Crisis communication often offers few precedents to work from and intense scrutiny from outside the organization. This can lead to a loss of control and a sense of panic, so it is important to keep your head, and address the crisis systematically.

Addressing a crisis

WHAT TO DO	HOW TO DO IT
01 **Get information**	O Deal from an informed position and separate fact from rumour. Document what you know and don't know for sure. Become the source of reliable information, and keep the information flowing. O Determine the real problem in the short term and the long term. Check whether this is really your problem.
02 **Put people in place**	O Put someone in charge. Give them responsibility, authority, and the resources to get the job done. Tell people who it is. O Assemble an effective but nimble team. Staff it with the expertise needed, and provide resources. Isolate team members from other day-to-day concerns.
03 **Draw up a plan**	O Develop a strategy, which should include ways to resolve the problem, deal with affected parties, and communicate both today and in the long term. O Establish goals. Define your objectives for the short term, mid-term, and long term. Measure relentlessly and don't be discouraged by critics, negative press, or short-term failures.
04 **Start communicating**	O Centralize communications. Incoming communication provides intelligence, while outgoing communication gives a measure of control over what is being said about the situation. O Rely on a strictly limited number of spokespersons who are knowledgeable, authoritative, responsive, patient, and good humoured.

Dealing with the media

Being the subject of a news media interview is never easy, and can be stressful and risky. You might say the wrong thing or forget to say what's most important about the subject of the interview, or your comments might be taken out context when they're aired. However, by following a few basic rules, you can limit risk and use the interview to your advantage.

Capitalizing on opportunity

Learn to see media interviews as an opportunity to reach a large audience. They represent a chance to tell your story and to inform the public of your business or expertise. They also offer an opportunity to address public concerns and set the record straight, if you're the subject of misinformation in the press. They can be a forum in which to apologize if you've done something wrong, and a chance to reinforce the credibility of your organization and its leadership. Don't feel bullied into giving an interview if you're not ready: you can say "no" or delegate to another staff member who is more accustomed to dealing with the media.

Never feel bullied into **giving an interview** if you're not ready: you can say "no" or **delegate** the task

Preparing for an interview

The best way to **ensure a good interview** is thorough preparation.

Gather all the **information** you will need. Make sure you know the latest **facts and figures.**

Research the reporter; deal only with **established,** professional journalists.

CHECKLIST...

Succeeding in media interviews   **YES   NO**

1 Are you clear about **what you hope to achieve**
from the interview? .... ☐   ☐

2 Do you know **which items of information** you can share,
and which are confidential? .... ☐   ☐

3 Have you decided on a method for **avoiding arguments**
if the reporter goads you? .... ☐   ☐

4 Do you know **how to respond** to false allegations, without
repeating the phrases the reporter uses? .... ☐   ☐

5 Are you focused on remaining **professional and likeable**,
no matter what happens in the interview? .... ☐   ☐

Gather all the information
you will need: make sure
that you have the latest
facts and figures

Tip

**GET YOUR POINT
IN EARLY**
A reporter may not ask the
one question you're most
hoping to talk about. **Raise
the issue** yourself, **get your
points in,** and **repeat them
frequently.** Use the free
air time or print space to
your benefit.

Ask your
Public Affairs
or Corporate
Communication
office for **help**
and **guidance.**

Find out the
**subject and
background** of
the story and
ask who else is
participating.

Double-check
the **time, date,**
and **location** of
the interview.

Building brands

Communicating the essence of a brand is more than simply using words and visuals to convey an image. This is because a brand is both a process and a product. It's a living, breathing organism that must be nurtured and protected if it is to survive and thrive.

Winning hearts and minds

A brand is, first of all, a promise of an experience. It is what a product, service, or company stands for in the minds of customers and prospects. At its very core, a brand is a perception or a feeling. It's the feeling evoked when we think about a product or the company that delivers it. And, of course, a brand is the basis for differentiation in the marketplace – a way to separate yourself from all other competitors in the hearts and minds of your customers.

Defining the brand

The most crucial characteristics of a brand are content and consistency. To succeed, a brand must make a clear and unambiguous promise to its stakeholders (customers, employees, investors, suppliers, creditors, and others) and then deliver on that promise.

The Starbucks brand, for example, is clearly aligned with the customer experience. When regulars in Starbucks coffee shops began to complain about the smell of hot breakfast sandwiches, former CEO Howard Schultz decided to focus on the core experiences (and aromas) of freshly ground coffee, and a relaxing environment. Electronics giant Samsung's brand promise is "Do what you can't". It encapsulates the firm's desire to be at the forefront of technology, enabling people to do things that have only just become possible.

Communicating brand image

VISION

Be certain that one consistent, strategic **vision** drives your goals for the brand. Prioritize your plan to **deliver** on the promise (what is most important and why?). Align all stakeholders behind the vision.

CULTURE

Empower your entire organization to **get behind the brand.** Give them the authority, responsibility, resources, and training to **satisfy customer expectations.**

BRAND VALUE

Brands that have a clear sense of themselves and have worked diligently to deliver on their promises are often quite durable, withstanding economic downturns, changes in customer preferences, and game-changing innovations in their product category. The value of developing brands is highlighted in a quote by John Stuart, former CEO of Quaker Oats Company: "If this company were split up, I would gladly give you the property, plant, and equipment, and I would take the brands and trademarks… and I would fare better than you." Swedish furniture giant Ikea has taken this idea of brand–infrastructure separation to heart, building it into its corporate structure. While its stores and operations are owned by one group, INGKA Holding, its brand and trademarks are owned by another, Inter IKEA Holding.

ACTION

Specify and communicate those actions that are **essential to brand success** to those within the organization who must deliver on the promise.

VALUE

Consistently and continually **measure results.** Show your investors, associates, and business partners what you've accomplished and what improvements you have yet to make.

INNOVATION

You cannot stand still; you must **continually innovate** to stay ahead of the demands of the marketplace and the shifts in everything from demographics to target-group tastes and preferences. Demonstrate that you are both innovative and protective of the brand experience.

A **brand** helps to separate you from your competitors in the **hearts and minds** of your customers

PRESENTING

Planning to **present**

A presentation is a way of informing, inspiring, and motivating other people. Whether your audience is a group of receptive colleagues, demanding clients, or strict regulators, your job is to influence the way they think and feel about your message. No matter how charismatic you may be, success depends on careful planning of your content and delivery.

17

Putting the audience first

Presenting successfully means stepping back from your own knowledge of your subject. Examine what you want to say and how you convey that information from the perspective of the audience. Their priorities will almost always be different to yours.

Identifying the need

A presentation serves a very different purpose to a written report – it is far more than just another vehicle for information. A presentation allows an audience to gain knowledge by watching, listening, and being inspired by you. Audiences come not to learn everything you know about a subject, but to gain your perspective – they are likely to remember only the big themes even a short time afterwards. Good presenters understand that audiences are looking for information in context, not in full detail, so ask yourself what you can add through your presentation of the subject.

> **Audiences** are likely to **remember** only the **big themes** even a short time afterwards

Researching the audience

Get to know your audience, even before you plan your presentation. Talk to the organizer of the event about their expectations, and if possible, engage with those attending ahead of time; ask them about their existing level of knowledge, and what they hope to hear about. Work out if they need persuading, informing, educating, motivating, or a mixture of all these. The more you understand your audience's expectation, the better you'll be able to meet them.

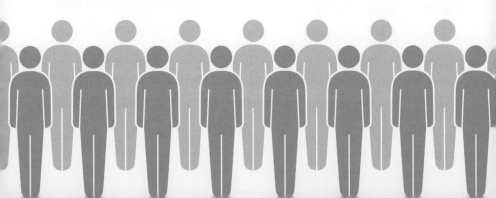

ASK YOURSELF...

Who is my audience?   **YES   NO**

1 Do I know who will be **listening?** .... ☐   ☐

2 Do I know how much they already know? Is there a **common understanding** to build on? .... ☐   ☐

3 Do I know their **expectations?** Will they hold any **preconceived notions** about the subject? .... ☐   ☐

4 Do I know what I want them to **learn?** What do I expect them to do with that **knowledge?** .... ☐   ☐

5 Do I know what I will say to **accomplish my goals?** .... ☐   ☐

Focusing your message

Identify the essential information you want your audience to understand and remember – no more than three such core messages. Build your presentation around these points and add supporting details – but remember that less is more when it comes to presentation. Make your key points emphatically and repeatedly; don't try to be too subtle or clever. Look for the overlap between what you want to say and what your audience wants to hear.

Tip

MATCH THINKING STYLES

Is your audience made up of **creative** thinkers or analysts? Bear in mind that you'll need to tailor your presentation's **content** and your **delivery** to match their thinking style.

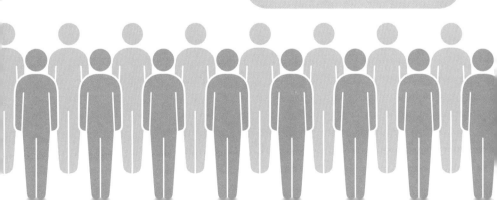

Presenting and selling

Presentations serve a variety of purposes. They can be used to inspire and motivate people or they can be designed to convey information formally (as in a lecture) or informally (as in a team briefing). But most often, they are used to promote a product, service, or idea, or to persuade stakeholders about a particular course of action. In other terms – whether overtly or covertly – most presentations aim to sell.

Pitching your ideas

The better you can meet the needs of your audience, the more successful your presentation will be. So when selling anything, from an idea to a product, your presentation should focus on how it will help your audience, how it will solve their problems. Whenever you talk about your idea, product, or service, don't just list its features – express them as benefits.

Throughout your presentation, your audience will be constantly assessing both your trustworthiness and the strength of your "sell". You need to be able to "read" their reactions so that you can address their concerns. Successful presenters do this by inviting many questions from the audience and encouraging them to interrupt; the questions and comments from the audience provide vital feedback.

> Your presentation should **focus on** how it will **help your audience**

Selling successfully in your presentation

SELL BENEFITS, NOT FEATURES

The presentation must centre on **what matters most** to the buyer – general discussion won't do. Talk about **specific benefits.** How does the product or service help to solve a problem or improve a situation?

BELIEVE WHAT YOU ARE SAYING

An **animated, enthusiastic** presentation is a must. Buyers do not want to buy from someone who doesn't appear **fully committed** to the product, even if it is relevant to their needs.

EXPECT TO CLOSE

If the presentation is **effective,** the decision to buy, or buy in, is a natural next step. Be prepared to ask for some kind of **commitment** and agree to take **immediate action,** even if it is only setting up a further meeting.

SHOW, DON'T TELL

Visual representations and physical demonstrations bring sales presentations to life. People **remember** what they **see and do** for themselves, so be **creative.**

KNOW YOUR STUFF

To establish your **credibility,** you need to know a great deal about your product or service. As well as handling general, predictable queries, be prepared to demonstrate your **knowledge in every respect.**

THE TWO-MINUTE PRESENTATION

We often meet people casually – between engagements or in quick conversations at conferences. It pays to develop a focused two-minute pitch to introduce yourself, your business, and the unique value you can offer. The pitch should be very easy to understand, describe the solutions you offer, and reflect your passion about what you do. A good two-minute pitch will get you a surprising number of follow-up meetings.

Tip

GET TO THE POINT

Engage your audience by addressing what they want to know as quickly as possible. Avoid **opening** your presentation with background about you or your company – when it was founded, where it's located, and so on.

Presenting formally

In many presentations, you are in control of what you say and how you say it. But be aware that some types of presentation are much more formal, following rules, requirements, timescales, or formats dictated by the audience or by a third party. They include presentations to boards, regulatory bodies, and examination and assessment panels, all of which require high levels of planning and rigorous attention to detail.

Keeping focused

When you are asked to make a formal presentation, always request guidance about what is expected from you – what is the desired length, content, and context of your material? Play safe – don't attempt to be too innovative with the structure, but stick with a tried and tested formula.

Introduce the topic, the argument you are about to make, and the conclusion that you will reach.

How to structure a formal presentation

Preparing to succeed

Before a formal presentation, seek out people who know the members of the board. Find out everything you can about their backgrounds, concerns, and predispositions. Use what you have learned to prepare your arguments carefully; if appropriate, try to gain advance support for your position with members of the board.

Confidence is another key success factor. You will be expected to take a strong stand and support all your arguments with compelling evidence. Handle challenges with calm assurance and keep in mind that it is your position, rather than your personality, that is under attack. Finally, if you are presenting with colleagues, make sure you "get your story straight" – that all of your materials are consistent.

Presenting to a board

Keep your presentation concise and limit the detail that you include. If presenting to a board of directors, for example, bear in mind that they don't get involved in day-to-day management and have many demands on their time. Focus on what they really need to know, but ensure you don't withhold anything important – choose your words very carefully to ensure that you cannot be misinterpreted or judged misleading.

eing a panellist

anel presentations are often a feature
conferences. If you are asked to be
panellist, make sure you understand
e specific areas or questions you
ive been invited to address. Find out
ho is talking before and after you,
id what they are focusing on to avoid
peating their content.

Build flexibility into your
esentation, since time slots often
nift to accommodate delays. Make
ire you have time to present your
ey points. If you feel the topic is too
omplex for the time frame, suggest
n alternative.

> You will be expected to **take a strong stand** and support it with **compelling evidence**

Following protocol

Some expert panels are very formally
structured, with individual members
asked to present on a topic in turn
before fielding questions from other
panellists or the audience. Others
are much looser, with any panellist
permitted to interject, add remarks, or
pose questions at any time. If the format
of your panel is unstructured, always be
attentive while others are speaking, don't
interrupt others too often, and don't speak
for too long. No matter how informal the
structure, always take the time to develop
your key messages in advance.

Develop your arguments
clearly and persuasively,
justifying what you say.

Make a conclusion:
summarize your main
arguments and explain the
relevance of the conclusion
made; explain why you are
confident of your conclusion.

Tip

EXPECT TOUGH QUESTIONS

Formal presentations to
boards and panels may
be met with adversarial
questions – boards may
view harsh questioning
as perfectly acceptable,
so come **prepared** with
robust answers.

**Facilitate discussion of your
presentation;** check that
everyone has understood
exactly how you have arrived
at your conclusion.

Planning the structure

There are many ways to organize your ideas to create an effective and convincing presentation. Sometimes, the content you need to convey will fall more naturally into one type of structure rather than another. There may also be an element of personal preference – you may simply feel more comfortable with one type of structure than another. But however you choose to organize, the end result must achieve your communication aim. In other words, content always dictates form, not vice versa.

Setting out the basics

All presentation structures share three high-level elements: the introduction or opening, the body or main content, and the conclusion or close. Most of your time will be spent delivering the body, but don't underestimate the importance of opening with an introduction that captures the audience's attention, and tying everything together at the close.

Quick and easy storyboarding

Sticky notes are a useful tool when storyboarding your presentation. Use a different coloured note for each type of element: for example, blue for a key message, pink for each proof point that backs up a message, and orange for a visual aid. Reposition the notes to experiment with running order, the balance between "showing" and "telling", and to identify weak sections. Storyboarding is a method of sequencing your ideas that can help you decide how to represent them in a logical and compelling order when planning your presentation. It adds a physical dimension that is especially useful for organizing and understanding the impact of a presentation using visual aids.

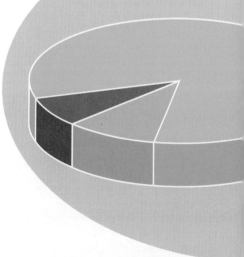

75%

of the presentation should be content, **10%** should be **introduction,** and **15%** should be **conclusion**

THE INTRODUCTION
Think of your opening as a promise to the audience. It should tell them what they are going to hear, and **why it is important.** This section needs to get their **attention** and give them a reason to keep **listening.**

THE BODY
This is where you **deliver on the promise** you made in your introduction. Here you deliver the facts, analysis, explanation, and comment to fill out your message. **Sustain interest** by keeping the opening promise in mind, and making sure every element advances that **goal.**

THE CONCLUSION
Your close is the "so what?" of your presentation. Remind the audience of your **key points** and clearly articulate where they lead, or conclusions that can be drawn. An effective close demonstrates your **conviction** about the action you are suggesting or the position you hold. While you should spend no more than **15 per cent** of your presentation time on the close, remember that it will probably be the section that your audience remembers most clearly. Whatever you want them to remember, say it now.

Tip

KEEP IT BALANCED
Your structured content should fall roughly into these proportions: **10 per cent** introduction, **75 per cent** body, and **15 per cent** conclusion. Let each section fulfil its function: don't overload the introduction or bring in new ideas in the conclusion.

Selecting a framework

To structure your presentation for maximum impact, choose a framework sympathetic to its content. For example, if your material is data-driven, use a numbered list; if you are selling a concept, employ case studies. Described here is a selection of useful structural alternatives.

70%

of people who present often agree that **presentation skills** are **critical** to career **success**

NUMBERED LIST
Use this model to present **modular information** such as the top competitors in your market. Often **quantitative information** helps your audience to understand the relationship between a list of items.

PROBLEMS AND SOLUTIONS

Outline a problem, then reveal how to **fix it.** This structure is excellent when discussing change. It can **help** to position you as someone who can **read a situation** clearly, **explain it,** and offer **a way forward.**

FEATURES AND BENEFITS

Work through the **elements** of a product or proposal and explain the **positive outcomes** each one can generate. This method works well for more **persuasive sales presentations.**

DEDUCTIVE OR INDUCTIVE?

Deductive reasoning moves from general principles to the specifics ("our market is growing, we should do well"); **inductive reasoning** moves from specifics to **principles** ("we've **done well,** our market is growing").

3 4

MESSAGING

Tell them you are **going to tell** them, **tell them,** and then **tell them you have told them.** This simple structure **works well** provided the messages are clear and backed up with proof.

STORIES AND CASE STUDIES

Present your idea or **argument through a good narrative.** People love **hearing stories,** making this a compelling and forceful presentation method. Keep your story simple and explain the "moral".

5 / 6 / 7

> **Tell them** you are **going to** tell them, **tell them,** and then **tell** them you have **told them**

●MPARE AND ●NTRAST

t your material **context** by mparing it :h something ;e. Ensure it similarities d differences e **clear.**

OPTIONS AND OUTCOMES

List some choices and the **pros and cons** of each. Make sure the options are different, not refinements of one idea. If you are going to suggest the best way forward, be prepared to **back it up** with data.

8

TIMELINE

A **chronological structure** is useful for showing **progressive** developments. Its linear structure is intuitive and easy to understand. To avoid seeming one-dimensional, ensure your material has both **purpose and pace.**

9

Taking
centre stage

As your presentation approaches, all the preparation you have put into your material and delivery may be overshadowed by the prospect of having to perform. Don't worry. There are plenty of techniques that will give you a real advantage on the day of your presentation, boost your confidence, and help you deal with nerves or mishaps.

18

Creating a good first impression

The first thing your audience will notice is how you look, and this first impression is hard to shift. Give plenty of thought to the message you want to send through your attire, grooming, and posture. Study yourself in a mirror, and ask colleagues for their opinion on your appearance.

Connecting with the audience

Appearance alone won't win over your audience, but it plays an important role in setting out your intent and credibility. When choosing what to wear, consider which outfit will have the greatest influence on the people you would like to impress the most.

For example, if the audience consists mostly of your casually dressed peers, but also includes two suited directors, dress up not down. And if you are the manager of a factory addressing the shop floor, think how differently your message will be perceived if you are wearing a suit or clean corporate overalls.

Tip

STAY SMART
Dressing correctly is just as important when you are presenting **remotely,** even if only your head and shoulders are **visible.** The right clothes will help you feel more **professional** and convey **confidence.**

ASK YOURSELF...

s my appearance appropriate?   **YES**   **NO**

1   Is my **hair clean,** neatly styled, and away from my face? .... ☐   ☐

2   Are my **fingernails** clean and trimmed? .... ☐   ☐

3   Have I **checked** my make-up? .... ☐   ☐

4   Have I **trimmed** my beard and moustache? .... ☐   ☐

5   Are any potentially offensive **tattoos** visible? .... ☐   ☐

6   Have I **applied** antiperspirant? Is my **perfume/cologne** overpowering? Many people find scent unappealing .... ☐   ☐

ressing to impress

ere are no fixed rules about dress and pearance, but if unsure, veer towards nart, professional, and conservative ther than trying to reassure your dience by "blending in" with their yle. You are dressing to create an air authority and confidence rather than please yourself, so steer clear of sual clothes like jeans and trainers, ather, shiny fabrics, and anything with ominent emblems or designer labels. oid distracting blocks of bright colour, ough colour can be used to provide an cent. Make sure your shoes are clean, lished, but comfortable – if it is painful stand in them for the length of the esentation, change them.

   Minimize jewellery – you don't ant your accessories to be the most emorable part of your presentation – d always pay attention to details, even you won't get that close to the audience.

Tip

KEEP IT REAL
It's important to feel at ease while presenting. While you shouldn't forsake **style** for comfort, avoid wearing clothes so **formal** that they make you feel self-conscious and false.

You can bet that they'll notice if your clothes are wrinkled or your cuffs are frayed. Remove bulging keys, change, and other loose items from all your pockets, and check that your lapels are free from any name tags.

   Whatever your dress, always take the time to groom yourself – your audience will not forgive an unkempt appearance or poor personal hygiene.

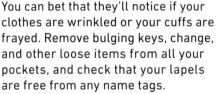

Looking confident

The audience is on your side – they want you to succeed; they want to learn and be inspired by you. But to win their attention and trust, and to exert your influence, you need to impose your presence and demonstrate confidence in yourself and in your presentation material.

Growing self-belief

Inner confidence comes from a combination of self-belief and real enthusiasm for your message. When you are confident, you behave naturally, and in the full expectation of a positive outcome; your self-assurance is genuine and your audience buys into your message.

You can build your confidence over time through exercises in which you visualize success and, of course, through experience. Looking confident and feeling confident may seem two very different things to you, but to your audience, they are one and the same. Employing techniques that make you appear more confident will bring positive feedback from your audience, which will boost inner confidence.

Tip

ACCENTUATE THE POSITIVE
Avoid **crossing** your arms or leaning backwards, away from the **audience;** these **actions** send out very strong negative signals.

When you are **confident**, you **behave naturally**, and in the **full expectation** of a **positive outcome**

stablishing your presence

u can win the respect of an audience
fore you begin simply through your
sture, and how you occupy the space
ound you. When presenting in-person,
en if you cannot rearrange the seating,
u should become familiar with the
om, your position, and the lines of
ght – "owning" the space will make you
el more confident. Give yourself room
move, and ensure the audience can see
ur hands; don't trap yourself behind
e lectern – your position may look
fensive. When presenting remotely,
ake sure you are positioned square to
e camera and fill most of the screen.

Tip

USE PROPS
If nerves deter you from
moving your body, **hold a
prop** – such as a pen or
wireless remote – in one
hand until you find your
comfort level and **confidence**.

0.1

of a **second** is all it takes for
people to **assess** each other

ASK YOURSELF...

o I appear confident?

		YES	NO
1	Is my **eye contact** strong?	☐	☐
2	Am I projecting my **voice**?	☐	☐
3	Am I maintaining **good posture**?	☐	☐
4	Are my **hand gestures** natural?	☐	☐
5	Is my **language** conversational?	☐	☐
6	Are my **movements** purposeful?	☐	☐
7	Do I appear **calm** and in control?	☐	☐

Using body language

If your content is irrelevant or your delivery dull, you shouldn't be surprised if your audience switches off. But they will also disengage if the non-verbal messages that you send out are consistent with your words. Your stance, gestures, and eye contact must support what you say; in the event of any conflicting information, the audience will tend to believe what your body language appears to be saying.

Start your presentation with a neutral but authoritative posture. Maintain a balanced stance, with your feet slightly apart and your weight spread evenly between them. Keep upright, facing the front, with shoulders straight, not hunched, and your arms loosely and comfortably at your sides. Don't lean on a chair or perch on furniture for support.

Timing your movement

For the first 30 seconds of your presentation, try not to move your feet. This "anchoring" will help establish your authority with your audience. As you build rapport, you can relax your posture – this will help win you trust and make the audience feel much more comfortable – leaning forward sends a positive, friendly message.

In focus

TINY EXAGGERATIONS
Pay extra attention to your body language when presenting remotely – it's easy to forget you're "live" when viewing a screen. Your audience can likely only see your head and shoulders, so can't pick up on as many of your gestures as they would in person. For that reason, it's a good idea to exaggerate your body language a little. Smile, sit up straight, and engage.

Your **stance, gestures, and eye contact** must support what you say, **the audience** will believe your **body language**

Tip

SPRING-CLEAN YOUR BAD HABITS
Rid your **performance** of any visible signs of discomfort you may be **feeling.** Avoid nervous mannerisms such as putting your hands stiffly behind your back, looking down at the floor, playing with jewellery or hair, or fiddling with your sleeves or buttons.

30
econds at the **start** of your presentation should be spent standing in a **balanced stance**

Moving for effect

Human attention is drawn to movement – it is programmed into our genes – so one of the most powerful ways to hold on to your audience, and to make viewers focus on you, when presenting in person is to move.

Always use movement purposefully and intentionally – if you merely walk back and forth it will be interpreted as nervous pacing and will distract the audience. However, using movement in tandem with your words will boost impact. Listed below are a few examples where actions will reinforce the message during physical presentations:

When you want to refer your audience to **a projected slide,** take a step back towards it, and sweep your arm to **guide the viewer's eyes** up towards the slide: be careful not to turn your back on your audience as you move.

Move to a different spot on the stage area when **moving from point to point** – this can help the audience to separate out your **key messages.**

Coordinate your movements to **emphasize an important point** – for example, walk across the room, and turn quickly to coincide with the conclusion of a point.

Your movements need not be too theatrical – your aim is to **hold the attention of the audience** rather than to entertain them.

> You may need to **"amplify" small movements** to take into **account the scale** of a room

Using gestures

When presenting in-person, use gestures to reinforce points, just as you would in casual conversation; you may need to "amplify" small movements to take into account the scale of a room: for example, a hand gesture may need to become a movement of the whole forearm if it is to be seen from the back. You may need to practise to make such gestures appear "natural". Avoid at all costs any intimidatir gestures, such as pointing fingers at your audience or forcefully banging your hand or fist on the table or lectern.

Making eye contact

Many presenters deliberately avoid making eye contact with the audience. But if you can keep your nerve, engaging with the audience in this way creates trust and intimacy, and is one of the most effective means of keeping attention, especially throughout longer physical presentations.

80%

of survey respondents admitte their **attention shifted** from th speaker in the last talk they sav

SHAKING HANDS CONFIDENTLY

Dos	Don'ts
O **Bending your elbow and extending your right arm**	O Offering just the fingers of your hand
O **Pumping your hand two or three times before releasing**	O Holding on to the other person's hand too long or too lightly
O **Making and keeping eye contact with the person you are greeting**	O Looking around the room while shaking someone's hand

Keeping a connection

Unless you are presenting to a very large group, attempt to make eye contact with every member of the audience at least once. Maintain contact for no more than three seconds – longer contact may be seen as hostile. If you find this unnerving, start by making eye contact with someone who looks friendly and approachable before moving round the rest of the room.

Remember also to target people at the back and sides, or those who appear less enthusiastic. If you remain too nervous, look between two heads or scan the room – never avert your eyes from the audience. Not only will you lose their trust, your voice may become muffled and indistinct too.

Holding the audience

Novelty and expectation will keep your audience focused through the early parts of your presentation. But keeping their attention once they are accustomed to the sound of your voice and your presentation style can be more of a challenge. Look out for signs of disengagement, and be prepared to act quickly to bring the audience back on track.

Keeping interest

You have prepared an interesting presentation. You are delivering it with conviction using a good range of visual materials and rhetorical devices. Yet when you look out, you don't get the reassurance of attentive expressions on the faces of the audience; you may even detect signs of distraction.

Perhaps your audience is tired, or your presentation is the last in a gruelling day, or maybe you are delivering some difficult material. In any case, you need to take action fast:

- **Ask the audience** if they can hear and understand your words and if they are comfortable. Take remedial steps if necessary.

Reading signs from the audience

POSITIVE SIGNS

O Chin resting on hand

O Legs relaxed and parallel

O Clasped fingers

O Making eye contact

O Nodding in agreement

O Leaning forwards

Tip

TURN ON CAMERAS
When presenting **remotely,** request that your audience members **switch on** the cameras on their devices, if possible, so that you can judge their **level of engagement.**

Get **interactive and pose questions** to the audience and **invite answers**

- **Consciously change** your delivery; slow your pace, or introduce pauses after key points. Change your voice pitch or volume.
- **Get interactive** and pose questions to the audience and invite answers. Field questions. Leave your position behind the podium and walk out into the audience, making extensive eye contact.
- **Don't get frustrated** with the audience. Compliment them so that they feel valued.
- **Tell your audience** what's coming up, and when – "we'll work through a few examples before moving on to a question-and-answer session in five minutes". This will help them feel more involved in proceedings.

NEGATIVE SIGNS

O Tapping feet

O Crossing legs

O Talking to a neighbour

O Looking around the room

O Folding arms across the chest

O Leaning away from the speaker

O Camera switched off

Taming nerves

Public speaking ranks at the top of many people's list of worst fears. Be assured that this fear is understandable and normal – and even highly experienced presenters sometimes feel some anxiety. Rather than fighting your fear, try to harness it so it works for you; as ever, this requires preparation, practice, and persistence.

Channelling your energy

Before your presentation, you will be brimming with nervous energy. Start by giving that energy a release: vent any concerns to a trusted colleague, then go for a walk, or do some gentle stretching and warm-up exercises. Your body's physical response to stress tends to work against your mental preparations.

In focus

RITUALS AND CONFIDENCE

Repeating the same sequence of actions and thoughts before each presentation is a helpful tool in preventing nerves. Rituals are used by people to combat much stronger fears – such as agoraphobia and fear of flying – because they set up a safe zone of familiarity. Your ritual can be anything from cleaning your spectacles to arranging your papers geometrically on the desk – just make sure that it is a sequence of simple, undemanding tasks that won't cause stress themselves.

Tip

CONTROL THE SYMPTOMS

There are many **symptoms** of nerves: feeling "butterflies" in your stomach is common, as is dryness of the mouth; twitching eyes; fidgeting or playing with your hair or a pen; and rocking from side to side. Work on **controlling** the **external signs** so they are not visible to your audience.

Take the following preventative action before you begin your presentation:
- Take several deep breaths, holding each for a count of four, then slowly release through your mouth. This will help moderate a quickening pulse and heartbeat.
- Don't take your position too early. Keep your body moving in the moments just before your presentation.
- Shrug your shoulders to help ease tension.
- Give your voice a warm-up by humming; stretch and release your facial muscles

etting yourself shine

ce you begin the presentation, control the
ease of energy. Don't dissipate it too early by
cing around or rushing your delivery. Maintain
e contact with individuals in the audience; this
l help your nerves because it gives you a mental
cus, and you will probably get positive feedback
m your audience (smiles and nodding heads)
at will boost your confidence. Behavioural
search has found visualizing a stressful event
enough to trigger a real physical reaction.
nversely, we can all achieve a calmer state
rough positive images. So before your next
esentation, try visualizing your own success.

> Don't take your position **too early.** Keep your **body moving** just before your presentation

ow to visualize success

Tell yourself you are
well prepared.
You CAN do it!

Imagine yourself taking
the stage **confidently** and
speaking well. See
yourself **enjoying**
the moment.

Remember how you feel
at your most **confident.** Tell
yourself you can and
will **succeed.**

Tell yourself you don't
need to be **perfect;**
the audience is on
your side.

Picture yourself as **relaxed
and prepared** – you look
more confident than
you feel.

Speaking powerfully

How do you sound? In control? Authoritative? Dynamic? Voice is a powerful tool in the presentation arsenal. Don't worry – you needn't have the booming resonance of a stage actor to convince your audience that you are fully involved in what you are saying.

Using confident vocals

As you speak, your audience "reads" your voice – its nuances of pitch, volume, pace, and so on. This process happens imperceptibly, below the radar of consciousness, yet it shapes your audience's perceptions of your message. Sound hesitant and your audience will question your content. Sound confident and your audience will side with you. Try using the various facets of your voice (see right) when you practise your presentation and use them to effect.

INTONATION

Using an upward inflection (upspeak) at the end of sentences may signal you are uncertain. Using **declarative sentences** with the voice ending in a downbeat will give even neutral phrases an **authoritative** touch.

PACE

Vary the pace of your delivery. This helps keep your audience alert. Speak slowly when delivering **key** messages: **new ideas** need time to be processed.

Remaining calm

Slow and deep breathing enhances your performance. It boosts the supply of oxygen to your brain, making you more alert; it helps you stay calm; and it increases the flow of air over your vocal cords, enhancing the clarity of your voice. To avoid stumbling during your presentation, declutter your speech by removing unnecessary words and any trite expressions.

Finally, learn to be comfortable with silence in front of an audience: it feels odd at first, but "dramatic pauses" after key points add memorable emphasis.

TONE

Whether **presenting** good or bad information, do so with a **tone** that matches the content of what you are saying.

Master your voice

VOLUME

Be comfortable **projecting your voice** so that it can be heard everywhere in the room. Vary your projection to grab and **keep attention.** Your aim is not only to be heard, but also to **alert** listeners to the importance of what you are saying.

DICTION

Enunciate words clearly, adjusting the pace of your **delivery** where needed. Be careful with acronyms or unusual words your audience might misunderstand. Repeat important numbers for emphasis and to be certain they are heard.

Tip

STAY ANIMATED

People find it harder to focus for long periods when watching virtual presentations, so when you present remotely, it's a good idea to be more animated in your speech and talk at a slightly slower pace than normal.

Sound confident and your audience will **side with you**

PITCH

Slow your delivery and breathe deeply. Only then will you be able to use the **full range** of highs and lows of your voice. A confident speaker **varies pitch** more than a rushed one whose pitch is flat and unengaging.

Succeeding with formal speeches

Formal speeches such as keynote addresses, appearances at award ceremonies, and addresses to trade conferences and at company events follow structured formats and are often delivered in large group settings. Look on them less as a chance to inform – more to entertain your audience while enhancing your own reputation.

Crafting your content

Delivering a formal speech at an official or ceremonial occasion requires a particular method of preparation. Formal speeches may be read verbatim from a script, delivered from detailed cards, or delivered extemporaneously based on careful preparation. However, they lack important features of other presentations: visual aids are rarely used, and the speaker is usually physically present, but separated from the audience, limiting the degree of interaction.

As with other presentations, consider who will be in the audience and what they need, as well as the messages you want the audience to receive.

Tip

KEEP DOWN THE DETAIL
There is a limit to the **level of detail** people can **absorb** while listening as opposed to reading. **Test your speech** on someone who hasn't heard it and check that they understand.

Speaking naturally

Match your delivery to the nature of the occasion; evening receptions, for example, are not the time for complex content – the audience is more inclined to be entertained. Without visual aids, handouts, or interactivity, your words must carry the full weight of your message. Keep your sentences short and confine yourself to one point per sentence.

Emulate the natural rhythms of speech in your script, keeping your sentences flowing naturally. Although the occasion may be formal, don't use "sophisticated" vocabulary solely to try to impress your audience. Instead, use everyday language in a concise and accurate way.

90

hours and **two minutes** was the length of **the longest speech** ever given

dapting your delivery style

en though you will probably be reading ur speech, look for different ways in nich you can show personality and mmitment to your message. Use hand stures as you would naturally when u speak, to emphasize your points. simple device such as this will help to ep things interesting for your audience.

Don't feel you have to read each word or phrase exactly as written. You should feel free to depart from your speech as required; this will give your delivery a much more spontaneous feel. Aim for a style of delivery that does not call attention to itself, but that conveys your ideas clearly and precisely without distracting the audience.

ips for speaking with confidence

Break up your sentences more than usual so you can deliver them more easily.

Write **delivery reminders** to yourself on your **script** – for example, highlight words you want to **emphasize** or write in "pause" to remind yourself of **pacing.**

Err on the side of **brevity.**

Practise your speech until it becomes **second nature** to you.

01

02

03

04

Teleprompters allow you to appear **more engaged** with your audience by **looking** in their general direction and **delivering** your text more naturally

Tip

ACT NATURAL
To make your **delivery** more human and **natural**, imagine a member of the audience (or a friend) on the other side of the teleprompter.

Tips for speaking with confidence

Practise reading ahead so you can speak with your **eyes on the audience** for as long as possible.

If someone else has drafted your speech, rewrite or **adapt** it so that it **reflects your own "voice"**. Add a few personal references to make it seem **less formal.**

Visualize yourself as a **professional TV presenter** – try to inhabit the role.

Ask for and **learn** from **feedback.**

05| 06| 07| 08|

sing teleprompters

xt-display devices such as hidden reens and teleprompters can avoid e need for a podium. They allow u to appear more engaged with ur audience by looking in their neral direction and delivering ur speech more naturally.

However, it takes practice to use ese devices well. You need to be fficiently at ease with them, so ey aren't a distraction, either to u or your audience.

4.5

the average number of **blinks per minute** when **reading**. The average resting rate is **8–21 blinks per minute**

How to use teleprompters

Follow these simple steps in order to ensure a smooth, professional performance:

O Teleprompters do vary. **Rehearse** with the actual device you will be using.

O As with every visual aid, make sure you are in **control.** Be sure to **set your own pace** of delivery.

O If your script is hard to read in this format, rewrite it. Adjustments now will **pay off** later.

O Build in and script pauses to **sound natural.**

O Read ahead in **phrases** to look more natural.

O Deliberately **increase** your **blink rate** in order to prevent "teleprompter stare".

USING A PODIUM

Dos	Don'ts
O **Placing papers high up on the podium to reduce "head bobbing" as you read**	O Maintaining a "death grip" on the sides of the podium
O **Sliding rather than turning pages to reduce noise and distraction**	O Leaning on the podium
O **Allowing the audience to respond; pausing to acknowledge applause or laughter if interrupted**	O Tapping fingers on the podium or near the microphone
O **Varying voice, tone, and pacing throughout the speech**	O Allowing your voice to trail off at the ends of sentences
O **Testing and adjusting podium height before beginning**	O Turning your head away from a stationary microphone
O **Standing squarely balanced on both feet at all times**	O Fiddling with pens, paper clips, or anything else on the podium

Speaking from podiums

Speaker podiums give the presenter a place to stand, room to place a hard copy of the speech, and, sometimes, a stationary microphone and in-built multimedia capabilities. However, podiums can also pose problems. While they do provide some comfort, they may also create a physical barrier between speaker and audience that is a challenge to overcome. Even transparent podiums, designed to mitigate this problem, still force the speaker into a small, tightly constrained space, making it difficult for the audience to gauge their commitment and belief in what is being said.

Working the room

To counteract the constraints of a podium, exaggerate your gestures so you can be seen clearly. Use a hand-held or lapel microphone to avoid obstructing

Tip

MAKE IT READABLE
Print out your speech in a **large, clear font** as single-sided pages. Mark your script for **points of emphasis,** but make sure you can easily read any handwritten edits or notes.

the audience's view of your face. Plan moments where you can move towards the audience, however briefly, to address a point – question-and-answer sessions following the speech can offer this opportunity. Freedom of movement will signal your willingness to engage with your audience.

If you are stuck behind the podium, keep in mind that you must still find ways to connect with the audience. Make eye contact at points around the entire audience, and find a natural delivery that lets people know that the words and thoughts you are speaking are indeed your own.

Running the Q&A

The question-and-answer part of your presentation is a great opportunity to drive home your key points and cement the bonds you have established with your audience. Q&A sessions keep an audience engaged and provide you with an invaluable insight into how they have received and understood your communication.

Making time for questions

Always allow time in every presentation for questions and answers or some other form of audience feedback. If your format doesn't allow for a session following your presentation, consider addressing questions as they come up.

Audiences often look forward to the question-and-answer session more than to the presentation itself. This is when their needs move to centre stage – they can engage with you directly and test the strength with which you hold your ideas. You should welcome the Q&A because the questions will indicate if you have been effective, and if you have addressed what the audience really wants to know. Consider the Q&A as feedback – a way of strengthening your presentation content and delivery.

> ### Tip
>
> **MAINTAIN OPENNESS**
> Stay away from defensive **language** – phrases such as "You misunderstand my point" – and seek to be **empathetic:** "I can certainly understand your objections".

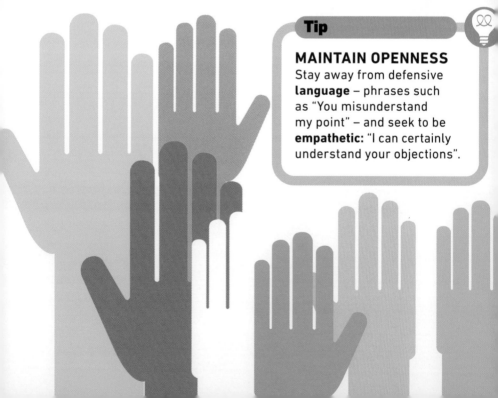

WRAPPING UP

Signal in advance your intention to close off questions with a statement such as, "We have time for two more questions and then I'll wrap this up". Don't just end abruptly after the last question is answered. Instead, take a moment to summarize your key points and offer your audience next steps or actions they can take. Be succinct in this closing, and restate without repeating what has come before. Remember to leave on an upbeat and positive note, and thank people for their time and their attention.

taying in control

early signal the start of the Q&A ssion not only with your words t through body language; an open sture indicates you are ready for estions. Stay in control of the session all times by directing the format and cus of the questions. Although this rt of the presentation is unscripted, ere are techniques to help keep the ssion focused:

Keep questioners on track: if they start to make a speech rather than ask a question, you could say, for example, "We're running short of time and I want to make sure we return to the immediate issue at hand".

GOOD QUESTION!

Don't overuse the **response:** "That's a good question!" or it will lose its meaning with your audience.

- Don't allow audience members to engage in their own separate debates, or to interrupt one another. Step in and direct the process with a quick assertion of control: "Ayesha, I'd like to hear your question, then we will turn to the issue Brian is raising".
- Seek to find common themes, or larger points that will get the discussion back to a message: "These are good points that deal with different ways to reach the goal we've been talking about".
- Don't dismiss questions even if it is clear that someone missed a key element of your presentation. Graciously repeat a quick summary for the questioner without making them feel awkward.

USE TOUCHSTONES

Keep returning to **key words and phrases** – or touchstones – in your answers. This will **emphasize crucial points** and help audience retention.

Answering tough questions

Even the best-prepared presenter will come up against hard questions, or difficult questioners. How you deal with these challenges can win or lose you the presentation, as the audience waits to see just how confidently and competently you can defend your position. In many cases, just staying calm and remaining in control under pressure is more important than having all the answers.

Anticipating situations

It is easier to appear confident when you have done your research, so be prepared for your Q&A session. Although it is unscripted, you should be able to anticipate the questions you are most likely to be asked, and those you hope not to be asked. Be ready with suitable answers to both types, but also prepare to be surprised by unconventional

> **Tip**
>
> **REPEAT THE QUESTION**
> In larger rooms, when wearing a microphone, **repeat or summarize** each question for the **benefit** of others in the audience before offering an answer.

questions. No one expects you to have all of the answers all of the time, so don't be afraid to say, "I don't know".

Maintaining poise

The key to handling difficult questions is keeping your poise. Maintain a calm demeanour, even if the questioner does not. Avoid signalling any discomfort through body language – stepping back from the audience or breaking eye contact, for example. If you have been standing up for the duration of the presentation, remain standing for the Q&A session.

Answering calmly

Keep a level tone, even if your answer is candid "I don't know". If caught off guard by a question, buy some time; ask for the question to be repeated, or say that you will return to the question later. Even if your audience perceives the question as hostile or unfair, they will still want to see how you handle the response. Try not to take statements or questions personally, and address the answer to the entire audience while responding. Avoid being provoked and remember, you are in charge of your presentation.

Responding to questions

PROBLEM	SOLUTION	EXAMPLE
Long-winded or unfocused questions	Pose the question differently	"So what you're saying is there's been a lack of progress – is that right?"
	Ask for clarification	"I want to be sure I understand the question. Are you asking why we haven't made progress?"
Sceptical or hostile feedback	Validate the concern	"You're right about this approach carrying some risk, but we can mitigate that risk by the way we handle this."
	Empathize with the concern	"I understand your frustration. This has indeed been a long process. We'd all like to move forward now and get on with implementation."
	Stand firm	"I hear your concern, but let me respectfully disagree with your statement. Here's why."
Questions that stump	Keep your cool	"That's a good question. I don't have the answer for it. Here's what I can tell you though..."
	Return the question	"Let me ask you how you would answer that?" or "Can you clarify why you're asking that question?"
	Delay	"We can certainly discuss it after the session."

Dealing with the media

Media interest carries more credibility with audiences than advertising because it is perceived as being less partial and not paid for. It can help your organization to advance ideas or products, and build awareness and credibility with a targeted audience. However, not understanding media priorities can have negative consequences, even for smart businesses.

Understanding your role

Dealing effectively with independent media means recognizing the nature of the relationship that you are about to enter into. When you are interviewed, your role is not just to passively answer questions, it is to shape the agenda so that you can present your key messages succinctly and effectively. While you can't control the questions asked or the context, you do have control over access and over what you say. Maintaining a balance of control in interviews is a matter of delivering your messages well, through preparation and practice.

> Every media interview can **impact** on your organization's **image;** think about **training** for all staff likely to come into **contact** with the media

> **Shape the agenda** so that you can **present** your key messages succinctly and **effectively**

Investing in training

Having expertise on a subject doesn't mean you are media-ready. In fact, being close to a topic often makes it difficult to speak in the broad and brief terms media interviews demand. Given that every media interview can impact on your organization's image and reputation, it is worth thinking about investing in training for all staff who are likely to come into contact with the media. Media training often provides managers with the best possible means to prepare for interviews. Training also helps managers to shape a story through their careful responses to the reporter's questions, and to meet the organization's requirements and the demands of reporters at the same time.

Ground rules for media interaction

AN INTERVIEW IS A BUSINESS TRANSACTION

Set yourself **a goal** for each interview, then **accomplish** it as briefly and as **memorably** as you possibly can. Know when to stop talking.

EVERYTHING IS ON THE RECORD

Reporters will **assume** that you know this. Anything you say **can and will** be **quoted**. (Unless you have agreed to an off-the-record interview and trust the reporter to respect the deal.)

BE CONCISE AND CONSISTENT

Understand your own message, and its **context.** Be firm when communicating it to the reporter.

AN INTERVIEW IS NOT A CHAT WITH A FRIEND

Reporters are **focused** on getting **a story.** They do not work for you and will **report** a story whether it serves your interests or not.

Talking to reporters

Anyone in business is a potential interview subject for a reporter searching for an expert opinion. Whether it is TV, radio, print, or other media, that opportunity, provided you get it right, can win you a wider platform to gain attention for a product or service, or to raise your own profile.

Preparing for the interview

Reporters are always under pressure to produce their stories. You will need to respect their deadlines while allowing yourself time to prepare thoroughly for an interview. Before the interview takes place, ask the reporter for the following information:

- What was it that captured their interest?
- What do they think that you can add to the story?
- What approach is being used – do they want a personal story, or a balancing opinion?
- What other sources will they be using – what can you uniquely add?
- Who is their primary audience?

Tip

FORM CONNECTIONS
Let the **reporter** know if there are others you are aware of who can provide information or **points of view** that can **aid** in understanding. Help the reporter get in touch with those resources.

Keeping it in context

Speaking to reporters under such circumstances – especially about controversial or news-based subjects – makes many people worry that they will be taken out of context. You can reduce the likelihood of this happening by planning ahead:

- Work your messages into a short, memorable form – sound bites for broadcast and quotes for print/online media. These are what you want the reporter to take away with them.
- Formulate "bridges" – ways of moving between an answer to an anticipated question and a sound bite that you have prepared.
- Seize the initiative by telling the reporter what you have to say about the subject, even before the questions begin. This is your opportunity to influence the direction of the interview

Tip

MAKE INDEPENDENT STATEMENTS
Make sure everything you say to a reporter can **"stand alone"**; that is, make sure your statements are not entirely dependent on a specific context to be **understood correctly.**

BEING INTERVIEWED

Dos	Don'ts
O Setting a clear goal for every interview	O Assuming the reporter will explain your points for you
O Taking the initiative in getting your points across	O Hoping the reporter asks the right questions
O Keeping answers short and memorable	O Giving detailed responses and letting the reporter select the relevant parts
O Staying focused on your messages and speaking about what you know	O Guessing at a correct response or the views of others
O Keeping your voice natural and lively	O Speaking in a monotone
O Anticipating the obvious questions as well as the toughest	O Winging your way through and hoping for an easy ride
O Correcting any inaccurate assumptions posed within questions	O Letting inaccuracies stand

Getting your message across

A standard line of questioning for reporters concerns the "worst case scenario". Reporters who are seeking interesting comments are prone to press subjects to speculate on what might happen in a given case that the public might need to know. However, speculation – no matter how carefully phrased – is likely to create problems if you are quoted out of context. Replace speculation with an interesting comment about what you do know. You will be in a good position to do that if you understand what the reporter wants and develop your own well-crafted messages to provide it.

NEGOTIATING

Preparing to **negotiate**

Negotiation is a skill that you can learn and develop through practice and experience. By framing the process correctly and by searching in advance for creative options, you will be able to find solutions that satisfy the interests of all parties.

19

Becoming a negotiator

Many people shy away from negotiation because they think it implies conflict. In fact, negotiation is what you make it. When undertaken with confidence and understanding, negotiation is a creative interpersonal process in which two parties collaborate to achieve superior results.

Seeing the benefits

When you become skilled in negotiation, you can create real value for your organization. Negotiation allows you, for example, to secure cost-effective and reliable flows of supplies, enhance the financial value of mergers and acquisitions, settle disagreements with government officials or union reps, or resolve internal conflict constructively. Increasingly recognized as a core competency, it can take place in a variety of ways: in-person; remotely by email, phone, or video chat; or via a mix. Many firms develop their own approaches and methodologies, and offer training and mentoring programmes for negotiators.

80%
of a negotiator's
efforts should go
into **preparation**

Tip

LEARN YOUR ART
Developing the **skills** needed to be a **successful negotiator** can take time, so be patient. Try to **learn** from every negotiation you undertake, both for your organization, and in your life outside work.

Understanding the basics

Good negotiators are made rather than born. Although some may be naturally gifted and intuitive (possessing, for example, the ability to empathize with others), most have developed their principles and tactics over time and recognize that negotiating is a largely rational process.

To be a successful negotiator, you have to feel psychologically comfortable in the negotiation situation, whether it occurs in-person or remotely. This means being able to adapt your approach, tolerate uncertainty, deal with unexpected behaviour, take measured risks, and make decisions based on incomplete information.

You need to think about solving problems and creating opportunities rather than winning or losing: if you are confrontational, you are likely to have a fight on your hands. And if you "win" there will necessarily be a loser, with whom you may have to work in the months to come.

BUILDING A FOUNDATION

Dos	Don'ts
O Keeping an open mind to learning new techniques	O Believing that negotiating is an innate ability
O Treating negotiation skills as a mixture of rationality and intuition	O Negotiating from a fixed viewpoint
O Developing trust slowly	O Appearing too eager
O Expressing empathy while negotiating assertively	O Behaving assertively without expressing empathy
O Having a strategy and sticking to it	O Chasing haphazard opportunities

Understanding negotiation dilemmas

The negotiating task is very complex because it embodies a number of fundamental dilemmas. To be successful in your negotiations, you need to understand the difference between the true dilemmas that you need to address, and the many myths that surround negotiating.

Identifying true dilemmas

Over time, a number of myths have evolved about the nature of negotiations. Many negotiators continue to hold to them, failing to recognize the difference between these myths and the real dilemmas they face. For example, it is a popular misconception that a negotiator must either be consistently "tough" or consistently "soft" if they are to be successful. In reality, effective negotiators do not need to choose between these approaches, but are flexible and use a repertoire of styles.

Using processes

Some believe that negotiation is largely an intuitive act, rather than a rational process. Many effective negotiators will use their intuition to a certain extent (to know the right moment to make a concession or present an offer, for example). However, most of the negotiating task requires systematic processes such as masterful due diligence, identifying interests, and setting clear objectives.

Skilled negotiators are able to recognize the myths and focus their energy on the true negotiation dilemmas, balancing their approach and making the difficult decisions needed to achieve the most successful outcomes in their negotiations.

The five negotiation dilemmas

THE STRATEGY OR OPPORTUNITY DILEMMA

Unexpected opportunities sometimes arise in negotiation. It can be tempting to divert from your **well-planned strategy,** but be aware that this may distract you from achieving your objectives.

Many **effective negotiators** will use their **intuition** to a certain extent

THE HONESTY DILEMMA

How much should you **tell the other party?** If you tell them everything, they may exploit the information and take advantage of you, so you need to **strike a balance** between honesty and transparency.

THE EMPATHY DILEMMA

If you **develop empathy** with the other party, it may stop you from acting assertively and negotiating for your interests. Try to do both well – maintain good relationships, but **protect your interests** too.

Skilled **negotiators** recognize the myths and **focus** on the **true negotiation dilemmas**

THE TRUST DILEMMA

Trust is needed for a negotiation to **move forwards,** but if you trust the other party completely, you put yourself at risk of being taken advantage of. **Invest in building trust,** albeit with measured caution.

HE COMPETE OR OOPERATE DILEMMA

u must compete for the benefits the table, but also **cooperate to eate** them with the other party. u therefore need to be **skilled** both, to be able to create and en claim value.

Being prepared

Your success in a negotiation depends largely on the quality of your preparation. Start by thinking through your position and your objective. Having clear goals will protect you from making too many concessions and motivate you to perform better. Objectives should be specific, quantifiable, and measurable. Only then can they be used as valuable benchmarks to measure your progress during the negotiation process.

Setting the limits

You should always go to the negotiating table with clear answers to the following questions: why do you want to negotiate the deal? How will this deal create value for you? What are your "deal breakers"? What must you have from the deal, what would you like, and what are you willing to give away? There may be alternative outcomes that you would be willing to accept – what are they?

Tip

DO THE RESEARCH
Information is power. Find out as much as you can about your counterpart before you sit down to negotiate.

Knowing your objectives

Set your objectives high but not outrageously so. It is tempting to censor your aspirations, setting them too low to protect yourself from the prospect of failure, but in doing so, you will almost certainly achieve less than was possible. If you fail to set clear objectives, there is also a danger that you could get trapped in an "escalation of commitment" – an irrational urge to "win" the negotiation at any cost.

Escalation of commitment is a real hazard in negotiation, and happens when you refuse to give up your pursuit of a negative course of action when the wiser choice would be to cut your losses and move on. Always set a limit for how far you are prepared to go and prepare an exit strategy (a means of walking away from the deal).

Tip

VALUE THE ISSUES
Draw up a list of **potential negotiating points,** starting with the most critical. Give each issue a **value,** and estimate the value that your counterpart is likely to place on it.

Case study

AVOIDING ESCALATION OF COMMITMENT

It can be easy to fall into the trap of competing with the other party at all costs, to "win". For example, in the 1980s, Robert Campeau, a Canadian businessman, made a hostile bid to acquire Federated Department Stores (FDS). Macy's, a competitor of FDS, was also interested and a bidding war began. Determined to win, Campeau kept increasing his already high bids to a point where he offered to pay an additional US$500 million. Campeau won the competition, but two years later he declared bankruptcy. This is a classic case of escalation of commitment and a lesson for all negotiators in keeping a sense of perspective in their negotiations.

Preliminary research

O Who will come to the table? **Research** their personality, and their history of negotiation. Have they been previously successful or unsuccessful and **what approaches did they use?**

O What can you find out about their **negotiating style,** life history, hobbies, and interests?

O If you have more than one counterpart, do they **share the same backgrounds** and functional area, and are they likely to be **united** in their desired outcome?

O Are they **authorized** to make binding decisions? If not, who are the "players" behind the scenes who will make the **final decision?**

Looking across the table

A negotiator was once asked if he could formulate a proposal that took into consideration both his and his counterpart's interests. He was puzzled. "Why should I care about the other party's interests?", he asked, "his interests are his problem". Such an attitude of blinkered self-interest characterizes the unprepared negotiator. In order to succeed, you not only need to understand yourself and your interests, but also the other negotiating party, and the situation as a whole. Ask yourself the questions listed above when preparing for a negotiation.

Understanding your counterpart

It is important to understand the issues and interests of the other party before you start the negotiations. Negotiators come to the table because they each need something from one another, so you must identify your counterpart's key issues and interests. How important is each one? Which are the deal breakers and which may they be willing to concede?

Try to assess whether it is you or your counterpart who holds the power. What are your counterpart's strengths and weaknesses? What is their level of information and expertise? How badly do they want to make a deal with you? Do they have other attractive options? Are they pressed for time? If you know the other side has a tight deadline that you are able to meet, you may be able to negotiate a better price. Similarly, if you know that your counterpart has recently expanded production capacity, you may be able to gain better terms for larger volumes of orders.

Can your counterpart walk away from the table and exercise a Best Alternative To a Negotiated Agreement (BATNA)? This term is used by negotiators to describe the course of action taken if negotiations break down.

Tip

CONSIDER THE TIMESCALE
Shape your **negotiating strategy** with respect to the **timescale.** You can be more blunt in a short, one-off negotiation than in a long negotiation that is part of an ongoing relationship.

Thinking strategically

Much of what occurs during the actual negotiation – whether it takes place in-person or digitally – is determined by what happens outside of it. This requires you to think strategically about your situation in relation to that of your negotiating counterpart. For example, in some negotiations, you and the other party may be representing others.

Make sure you are clear about the identi of your constituency, and that of your counterpart. What are their expectations and can you influence them?

If there are several negotiating parties analyze all of them and begin to think in terms of coalitions. With whom and how can you build a winning alliance and how can you block a threatening one?

Advantages of knowing your counterpart

O Better understanding of what can be **accomplished.**

O Proposals are more likely to be **accepted.**

O Ability to **adjust your strategy** as the situation changes.

O Successful negotiations and **superior outcomes.**

O **Better trade-offs** between the issues.

62%

of respondents in a **global** survey believe that most people can be **trusted**. In Denmark, that figure rises to **86%**, making it the **most trusting nation** in the world

Tailoring your strategy

Make sure that your negotiating strategy and behaviour reflects the other party's situation and approach. For example, in many negotiations, the other party is free to leave or join the negotiating table as they wish. In some cases, however, the parties are bonded together over the long term and cannot simply walk away, and your strategy should reflect this.

Some negotiators prefer to negotiate away from the public eye, while others insist on keeping all stakeholders and the public informed. Consider which mode is more advantageous to you, taking into account the sensitivity of the issues, the history between the parties, and the legal and governance systems of each party.

Some negotiation counterparts observe formal protocols in negotiations, while others are freer in what can and cannot be said. Take particular care to do your research when negotiating internationally to learn the formalities expected of you.

Designing the structure

Before producing a blueprint for a building, an architect first studies the functionality of the structure – the purpose it will serve. When you are planning a negotiation, you need to think like an architect and devise a structure and a process that will best fit the purpose of the negotiation.

Structuring your approach

Every successful negotiation starts with a clear structure: defined roles, agreed rules, a set agenda, and a schedule for action. A framework for the negotiation will most likely be suggested by each of the participants. It is then subject to negotiation and joint re-creation so that all parties are satisfied that it reflects their concerns. Consult with your opposite number before you negotiate to agree all procedures that you will use. If you cannot agree on the procedures, it may be better to postpone or abandon the negotiations altogether.

Basic ground rules These need to be agreed with your counterpart. For example, is it acceptable to change negotiators mid-stream? Are observers allowed? Is the meeting open or closed? How should people be addressed and how should priority of speech be given? What will be the course of action if you cannot reach agreement? All parties should agree to listen respectfully to one another, attempt to understand the positions of others, and refrain from legal proceedings for the duration of the negotiation.

> **Negotiation** starts with defined **roles,** agreed **rules,** a set agenda, and a schedule

Tip

CREATING THE RIGHT TEAM
In **team negotiations,** carefully **consider** the size and composition of your team so that you include all necessary **skills** and represent all key constituents.

Making a framework

Your agreed framework needs to be sufficiently flexible to accommodate changes in circumstance, but should at least cover the elements below:

> A **framework** for the negotiation will most likely be suggested by **each** of the **participants**

Elements of a successful framework

An agreed venue Will your negotiations take place in-person or in a virtual venue? Chinese philosopher Sun Tzu's *Art of War* states that one should "lure the tiger from the mountain" – that is make your counterpart leave their comfortable environment. Ask yourself how the choice of venue will affect you and your team. At the very least, ensure that you will have access to the necessary support (computers, secure phone lines, and the necessary advisors).

A clear agenda This should include all the substantive issues and interests that you and your opposite number wish to negotiate. Clarify the level of importance of each issue and decide the order in which issues should be discussed. Some negotiators prefer to start with easy issues, others tackle everything together.

Managing processes

Once you have an agreed framework in place, you also need to structure the processes that will steer the negotiation through its various phases. There are three distinct processes – the negotiation process, the temporal process, and the psychosocial process – that come together in any negotiation. Each requires a different set of skills.

The negotiation process involves managing all the information and communications during the discussions, planning and re-planning, coordinating efforts between negotiators, making moves and countermoves (all in real time), and making important decisions under conditions of uncertainty and time pressure.

The **negotiation** process

The **temporal** process

The **psychosocial** process

Structure **the processes** that will **steer the negotiation** through its **various phases**

28

nonths is the **average time** takes for countries worldwide agree terms for **regional rade agreements**

Keeping time

The temporal process involves managing time and the way in which the negotiation moves from one stage to the next by appropriately pacing the speed of each stage and synchronizing the actions of the negotiators. Many negotiations (and sales presentations) stall because the negotiators labour points for too long and are unable or unwilling to move the process towards its closure phase.

Thinking straight

The psychosocial process requires sound knowledge of human behaviour and an understanding that people will take on "roles" during negotiations. You need to be able to overcome barriers to rational negotiation and avoid psychological traps, such as the illusion of optimism, a sense of superiority, and overconfidence. Other hazards include a reluctance to reverse a decision that produces poor results or intense conflict, and competition between negotiators in the same team.

Playing by the rules

The purpose of processes and structures is not to constrain the progress of the negotiation, but to give you tools to resolve challenges or impasses. Having clear rules will allow you to:

- Move from multiparty negotiations to one-on-one negotiations.
- Change the level of negotiation, upwards or downwards.
- Replace negotiators who are self-serving or too rigid.

Avoiding common mistakes

Never underestimate the risks associated with poor preparation: when you fail to plan, you plan to fail. The most common errors in forward planning include:

AVAILABILITY BIAS

It is very **easy to find** information that is widely available. So make an effort to **uncover** information that is obscure and not so easy to obtain.

CONFIRMATORY BIAS

Do not filter out **important information** because it does not fit with your existing **points of view** and **beliefs.**

OVERCONFIDENCE

If you underestimate your counterpart you will neglect to **plan well.** If you already think you know how a negotiation will end, you may exclude new sources of information and **creative solutions.**

51%

of people in a global survey say they **trust the media**

Expedite the process by issuing a deadline.

Change the venue or schedule.

Conduct some of the negotiations behind the scenes by introducing a back channel.

Never underestimate the risks associated with poor **preparation:** when you fail **to plan,** you plan to fail

RELYING ON SECONDARY INFORMATION

Always seek out reliable **sources** of **primary information.** By all means read industry report analyses, reports of management projections, and corporate annual reports, but consider that these may sometimes be inaccurate or biased.

INFORMATION ASYMMETRY

Do you **really know** as much as you think? To be safe, you should assume by default that you know less than the other party.

UNDERESTIMATING RESOURCES

In any negotiation you must be able to **present supporting facts, anticipate** how the other side will respond to your arguments, and prepare **counterarguments.** Do not underestimate how long it can take to assemble such information, especially if you require input from experts and colleagues.

Setting
your style

There are many approaches to negotiation. Some negotiators advocate a hard-line, uncompromising style. But skilled negotiators know that you are more likely to achieve a satisfactory outcome by taking the interests of the other party into account and trying to create win–win deals, develop mutual trust, and build relationships for the future.

Defining negotiation styles

Negotiators come to the negotiation table because they have needs that they believe may be fulfilled through negotiations. In order to fulfil these needs, negotiators use different styles and engage in a variety of behaviours that they trust will help them get what they want.

Spotting different approaches

There are three styles of negotiation: distributive, integrative, and mixed motive. Negotiators that mainly use the distributive style view negotiations as a competitive sport, a zero-sum game with a winner and a loser. Such negotiators compete fiercely for the distribution of the outcomes (the size of the pie) and engage in value-claiming behaviour.

These negotiators use competitive actions in an attempt to gain a win–lose outcome in their favour. They dismiss the value of building relationships and trust as naive, tend to make excessive demands and use threats to obtain concessions, and exaggerate the value of the small concessions that they make. They also conceal their needs, do not share information, do not look for possible creative ideas, and even use deceptive tactics.

Using the integrative style

In contrast to value-claiming negotiator integrative negotiators believe that the size of the pie is not fixed and can be expanded, and that the negotiation process is able to produce a win–win solution. The integrative style of negotiation is designed to integrate the needs of all the negotiators. Negotiators engage in value creation behaviours. They invest time and energy in building relationships and nurturing trust, share information openly, and are cooperative flexible, and creative.

Mixed-motive style

Distributive style

DISTRIBUTIVE TACTICS

If the other party is using a distributive win–lose approach, a negotiator who favours the win–win style must protect their own interests. Some respond with the same hard tactics, meeting toughness with toughness. Since the win–lose negotiation style is most likely to produce sub-optimal outcomes, first try to influence the other party to move towards a more integrative style. Value claimants often think the other party is oblivious to their tactics, and so some negotiators inform the other party tactfully but firmly that they know what they are doing and that it doesn't contribute to productive negotiations. If all attempts to deal with value-claiming tactics fail and if they do not require the deal, many negotiators will leave the table.

42%

more value may be gained in a deal when **zero-sum games** are abandoned

Integrative style

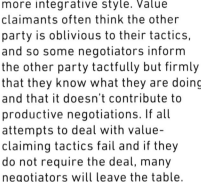

TAILOR YOUR APPROACH

Utilize all of the negotiation styles – **distributive, integrative, and mixed motive** – where appropriate, depending on with whom you are negotiating and what their negotiating style is.

Using mixed-motive tactics

The true nature of effective negotiations is often mixed, requiring both cooperative and competitive tactics. The rationale for this is that, through cooperation, negotiators create value; they put money on the table. Following this, once the value has been created, the parties have to split it among themselves. In order to secure the most profitable split, a negotiator has to switch from the cooperative mode to the competitive mode.

Defining interest-based negotiation

Negotiators often make the mistake of turning the negotiation process into a contest of positions. Some are hard bargainers, thinking of the other party as an adversary; others take a soft approach, considering the other person to be a friend and making concessions easily. Instead of utilizing hard or soft bargaining tools, effective negotiators tend to focus on the interests of both parties.

Focusing on interests

In interest-based negotiation, the negotiators come to the table with a clear understanding of what they want and why they want it, but also understanding that the other party has its own set of needs to fulfil. Knowing that both parties' needs can be satisfied in multiple ways allows for the negotiation process to be more about constructive problem solving – that is, collaborating to find out what they can do together in order to achieve their respective interests.

Understanding reasons

Focusing on interests concentrates on the "why" instead of the "what". People always have a reason for wanting something. For example, imagine that you and your friend are arguing over who should have the last orange in the fruit bowl. Your friend may want the orange to make juice, while you may want it because you need the peel to make cake. If, rather than arguing, you talk about why you need the orange and uncover the underlying interests behind your respective positions, you will discover that one orange can satisfy both of you.

AIM FOR JOINT GAINS

Instead of limiting the thinking to only one or two options, **work jointly** to **creatively explore** potential solutions.

FOCUS ON INTERESTS

Make sure that you have a **clear understanding** both of your own interests and those of the other party.

KNOW YOUR BATNA

Make sure that you have a clear understanding of your **Best Alternat To a Negotiated Agreement** – the **best option** available to you if the negotiation process falls apart.

onducting interest-based negotiations

People **always** have a **reason** for wanting something

SEE BOTH SIDES

Assess the situation from the other party's **perspective.** This improves **communication** and helps the other party understand how they stand to **benefit** from the deal.

SEPARATE THE ISSUES

Keep people issues, such as emotions, separate from **substantive issues** (such as price or delivery dates).

EXCHANGE INFORMATION

Before making any decisions, **exchange** information with the other party in order to **jointly** explore **possible solutions.**

USE STANDARDS

Base your negotiation on **precedents, laws,** and **principles,** rather than arbitrary judgements. This makes the agreement **fair** and makes it easier to explain the rationale to others.

Negotiating from the whole brain

We all think differently, and naturally bring our own "style" to the negotiating table. Understanding the strengths and weaknesses of your thinking style, and tailoring your approach to take into account the style of your counterpart, can greatly improve your success in negotiation.

Understanding your own style

Ned Herrmann, author of *The Creative Brain,* proposed that there are four thinking styles: the rational self, the safekeeping self, the feeling self, and the experimental self, which relate to dominance in different quadrants of the brain. Negotiating is a whole-brain task, requiring the ability to be diligent and rational (quadrant A activities), to plan and organize well (quadrant B activities), to interact well with others (a quadrant C trait), and to be bold and take risks (a quadrant D characteristic).

Improving your style

However, only four per cent of the population is dominant in all four quadrants. So, most negotiators have strengths and weaknesses in performing the negotiating task, and should work to improve in their weakest areas. Someone who has limited abilities in the feeling self (quadrant C), for example, can improve by developing their emotional intelligence. A negotiator weaker in the experimental self (quadrant D) can improve by developing their creative abilities by taking creativity workshops.

CHECKLIST...

Utilizing thinking style differences in negotiation

	YES	NO
1 Have you **determined** what your own thinking style is?	☐	☐
2 Have you **identified** your weaknesses in negotiation and are you working to **improve** in those areas?	☐	☐
3 If putting together a **team** of negotiators, have you taken each person's **thinking style** into account? Do they **complement** one another?	☐	☐
4 Are you able to **quickly assess** the thinking style of others?	☐	☐
5 Do you take your **counterpart's thinking style** into account when negotiating with them?	☐	☐

Influencing others

The whole brain model can sometimes help you to influence your counterpart negotiators. For example, if you believe that your counterpart's strength is in the feeling self (quadrant C) and their weakness is in the rational self (quadrant A), you will be more successful if you connect to him or her emotionally by building the relationship, and not by trying to connect cognitively through long speeches or rational arguments.

The four types of thinking styles

A: THE RATIONAL SELF

Individuals with brain dominance in **quadrant A** tend to be **logical,** analytical, **fact-oriented,** and good with numbers.

B: THE SAFEKEEPING SELF

Individuals with brain dominance in **quadrant B** tend to be cautious, **organized, systematic,** neat, timely, well-planned, obedient, and **risk-averse.**

C: THE FEELING SELF

Individuals with brain dominance in **quadrant C** tend to be **friendly,** enjoy human interactions, engage in **open communication,** express their emotions, enjoy teaching, and be supportive of others.

D: THE EXPERIMENTAL SELF

Individuals with brain dominance in **quadrant D** tend to think holistically and see the big picture. They are also often **creative,** comfortable with uncertainty, future-oriented, and **willing to take risks.**

Creating win–win deals

Some negotiators talk about wanting to create win–win deals, but when they hit major roadblocks leave the negotiating table prematurely, thus missing out on an opportunity to make a good deal. Effective negotiator utilize techniques to ensure they can create win–win deals.

Getting the conditions right

Effective negotiations, unlike competitive sports, can produce more than one winner. However, it takes motivation by both parties to find creative alternatives that fulfil their interests to create a win–win outcome. To promote win–win deals, effective negotiators focus on both the substantive issues of the deal (price, terms of payment, quality, and delivery schedule) and on formulating a social contract between the negotiators – the spirit of the deal. This involves setting appropriate expectations of how the deal will be negotiated, implemented, and re-visited, in case future disputes arise. If, by contrast, negotiators believe that negotiations are a zero-sum game that must inevitably be won at the expense of the other party, a win–win deal is not possible.

> To promote **win–win deals,** negotiators focus on the **substantive issues** and on formulating a **social** contract

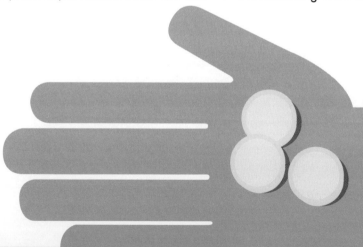

undling the issues

ffective negotiators do not negotiate single issue at a time because this mplies that there is a fixed pie and only ads to a win–lose scenario. Instead, ey bundle several issues together. ade-offs can then be made between egotiators because negotiators do not ace equal importance on every issue. he principle of bundling issues involves acing an issue that is of high value you (for example, price) with another at you consider to be of low value (for xample, warranty).

When you trade-off on issues, you can then keep your high-value issue (price) and give your low-value issue (warranty) away to the other party. The other party, in return, will allow you to have your high-value issue, because your low-value issue is, in fact, of a high value to them. If your low-value issue is also considered to be a low-value issue by the other negotiating party, then they will reject the trade-off. Therefore, it is important for you to know what the other party considers to be their high-value issues.

WIN–WIN NEGOTIATING

Dos

- O **Negotiating on multiple issues simultaneously**
- O **Understanding what is important to the other party**
- O **Identifying and leveraging differences in the interests of and the risks to the other party**

Don'ts

- O Negotiating on only one issue at a time
- O Focusing exclusively on your own interests
- O Ignoring differences in your counterpart's interests and risks

apitalizing on risk

ou can also capitalize on differences risk tolerance. Some negotiators re more comfortable with high-risk ituations than others. As a win–win nd risk-taking negotiator, it is possible r you to design a deal where you ssume more risk and receive more enefits while your counterpart, who is lso a win–win negotiator but risk-averse avoider), assumes a lower level of risk ut receives fewer benefits from the deal.

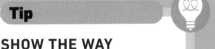

Tip

SHOW THE WAY

If you are dealing with a win–lose negotiator who thinks the idea of **win–win** deals is naive and unrealistic, show them how to **create value** and reach **superior** agreements by focusing on interests and **bundling issues** together.

Building relationships

Contract negotiators are typically task-oriented and pragmatic, tend to focus on negotiating specific issues, and do not invest in building relationships. Relationship negotiators, in contrast, invest first in building good relationships before negotiating on specific issues. Effective negotiators need to be skilled at both approaches.

Making a personal connection

Today, more and more negotiators from the West value what the Asian, Arabian, and Latin societies recognized thousands of years ago: the high value of good relationships. Experienced negotiators invest in building relationships because good relationships "oil" the negotiation process and make it more efficient. Once negotiators have a good relationship, even the most difficult and conflict-inducing issues can be resolved, simply because the negotiators are more transparent and flexible in their dealings with each other.

Making contact

Effective negotiators know that, in the long run, good relationships are best built via face-to-face interaction – whether in-person or in virtual meetings – rather than over the phone or email. Where possible, try to create opportunities to socialize with the other party before the negotiations begin. This is not to talk about the negotiations and "discover secrets", but rather to get to know the other person better and connect with them on a human level. The atmosphere of the negotiation process may be very different if you are not meeting your counterpart for the first time at the negotiation table.

In focus

CONNECTING REMOTELY

Building rapport can be more of a challenge when conducting negotiations remotely. In virtual situations the charismatic qualities that help you win a room in person, (gestures, quality of voice, how you dress...) carry less weight than the substance of what you say. Demonstrating your competence and professionalism early on (without being arrogant) can help establish trust. But also don't forget the human connection. As with in-person situations, take every opportunity to get to know your counterpart better – even a five-minute social chat ahead of negotiations has been shown to improve the chances of reaching an agreement. And if you're using video-conferencing software, switch your cameras on – seeing your counterpart face-to-face activates the parts of the brain that build goodwill, making win-win outcomes more likely.

teracting informally

your interactions with the other party,
ke advantage of any opportunities to
enuinely express your appreciation
ad congratulate them for their
chievements. Use small talk and
umour where appropriate – taking
opportunities to interact informally
ill help you build a relationship.
e cautious, however, and use "safe

humour" in order not to risk offending
the other party. Where possible, focus
on the common ground between you.
You may find that similarities are
personal (you may share the same
hobby, for example) or ideological,
such as a similar business philosophy.
These findings offer a solid start for
building a long-lasting, friendly, and
constructive business relationship.

hinking long-term

ou should also protect the "face",
dignity, of others and treat them
ith respect when you are taking
ore from a deal than they are.
his is especially helpful when
ou are trying to build long-term

relationships. In team negotiations,
it can work well to include socially
skilled negotiators in your team who
can take greater responsibility for
building lasting relationships, while
others (contract negotiators) focus
more on the specific issues.

Developing mutual trust

Trust is an essential component of success in all types of negotiation, whether business, diplomatic, or legal. Although developing it may mean making yourself vulnerable to your counterpart, the reward can be a more efficient negotiation, and a greater likelihood of reaching good and lasting agreements.

Understanding the benefits

Trust involves a willingness to take risks. It has to do with how vulnerable one is willing to make oneself to a counterpart. There are many benefits to having trust between negotiators: it promotes openness and transparency, and makes the negotiators more flexible. Negotiators who trust each other take each other's words at face value and do not have to verify their statements. This reduces emotional stress and other transaction costs, and makes the negotiation process more efficient. Trust also means that the likelihood of achieving good and lasting agreements is higher.

Tip

TREAD CAREFULLY
Although there are many **benefits** to a trusting relationship, it is not always possible to **build trust.** Some individuals and groups are simply untrustworthy, so be cautious in your efforts to develop trust.

Keeping your commitments

Building trust is difficult but losing it is easy, especially if you break your commitments. The French diplomat Francois de Callier, who wrote the first negotiation book in 1716, stated that a relationship that begins with commitments that cannot be maintained is doomed. Shimon Peres, the former president of Israel, said that promises have to be delivered, otherwise one's reputation is at stake. Although people do sometimes make genuine mistakes and promises in good faith that they ultimately cannot keep, if you want to build trust, you need to make every effort to keep your commitments.

Developing trust

Reciprocation is important for building trust. When negotiators offer information or concessions, they expect the other party to reciprocate. Without reciprocation, no further gestures of goodwill will be offered. With reciprocation, the negotiating parties will be able to find ways to collaborate and create value for both.

It is also important to be seen to be fair. As fairness is a subjective matter, however, make sure that you understand the standard of fairness that your counterpart adheres to. Past behaviour is often used as a predictor for future behaviour, so try to behave consistently

uilding your reputation

ne of the most important currencies
egotiators have is their reputation.
may sometimes be tempting to
aximize short-term gains by

overlooking the long-term
consequences, but experienced
negotiators know that people prefer
to do business with those they trust,
and guard their reputation fiercely.

Examples of actions used by negotiators to build trust

In 2015 India and
Bangladesh agreed to
exchange 162 tiny enclaves
straddling their mutual
border. Although a plan to
deal with the pockets of
land – 111 owned by India
in Bangladesh and 51 by
Bangladesh in India – had
been around since the
1970s, India finally decided
to ratify it as a goodwill
gesture ahead of talks
with its neighbour on more
testing issues, such as the
sharing of the waters of
the Teesta river.

When Disney CEO Bob Iger
negotiated the purchase of
LucasFilm, owner of the
Star Wars movie franchise,
for $4.05 billion from
George Lucas in 2012,
he won Lucas's trust by
conducting negotiations
personally, and by staying
patient (the process lasted
18 months). Iger also
requested treatments for
three new *Star Wars* films
in the acquisition, helping
assure Lucas that he
wanted to expand rather
than supplant his ideas.

Negotiating fairly

Fairness is an important characteristic in negotiations. Negotiators need to believe that the negotiation process and its outcomes are fair, otherwise they may choose to end the negotiations without coming to an agreement, or fail to put the agreement into action.

Ensuring fairness

There are several categories of fairness that contribute to creating successful negotiations. Distributive fairness relates to the distribution of outcomes (the splitting of the pie). Negotiators use three different principles of distributive fairness:

- Equality: this states that fairness is achieved by splitting the pie equally.
- Equity: this states that the outcome should relate to the contribution made by each party.
- Needs: this states that, regardless of their contribution, each party should get what they need.

Ways to ensure that the pie is sliced fairly

CLARITY
Be certain that the **final decision** is clear, without any potential misinterpretations.

CONSISTENCY
Make sure that you apply the **fairness principles** (equality, equity, or needs) in the same manner throughout the negotiation process.

CONSENSUS
Confirm that all parties in the negotiation are in **complete agreement** on the method of slicing the pie.

35%

of people in a survey assumed the **pie was fixed** and did not consider all the factors that would increase it

reating a fairness frame

addition, a negotiator's level of
tisfaction and willingness to follow
rough with an agreement are usually
etermined by their perception of the
vel of fairness of the procedure
rocedural fairness), and also the
ay they feel they have been treated by
e other party (interactional fairness).

Fairness is a subjective issue. When negotiating, if you first define what you consider to be fair, you can then use this "fairness frame" as a bargaining strategy in your discussions with the other party. Alternatively, if you state the importance of fairness at the beginning of the negotiation process, it may encourage the other party to be fair.

Define what you consider to be fair, you can then use this **"fairness frame"** as a **bargaining strategy** in your **discussions**

TISFACTION

ke sure that all
ties are **happy** with the
ults – they are then more
ely to follow through with
agreement.

JUSTIFIABILITY

Make sure that all parties are able to **explain** why you are slicing the pie this way to somebody else.

MPLICITY

sure that all negotiating
ties can **understand** and
scribe the **pie-slicing**
ocedures you use to
arantee smooth
plementation.

Conducting
negotiations

The negotiation process is a strategic interplay between the parties on either side of the table. To be successful, you need to know how to build a strong position, deal with difficult situations, influence your counterpart, and close your deals.

Negotiating with power

Power is a central factor in determining the outcomes of the negotiation process. Effective negotiators understand that power is not static and thus engage in continuously assessing and enhancing it. However, it is equally vital to know how to negotiate when you do not have power.

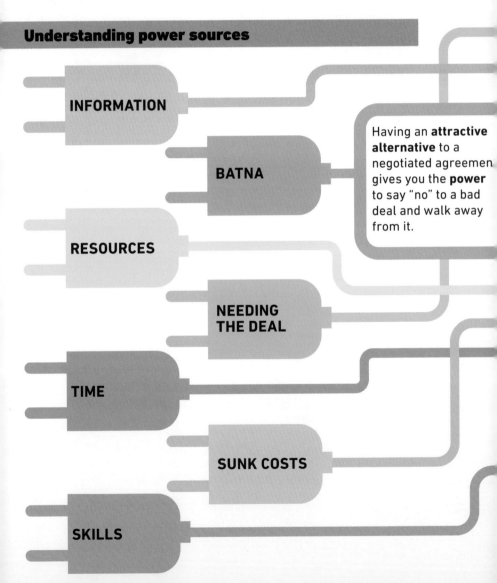

Understanding power sources

INFORMATION

BATNA

Having an **attractive alternative** to a negotiated agreement gives you the **power** to say "no" to a bad deal and walk away from it.

RESOURCES

NEEDING THE DEAL

TIME

SUNK COSTS

SKILLS

Being **well informed** enables you to **support** your arguments and **challenge** the other party's arguments.

The less badly you need the deal, the **more power** you have not to settle it.

The party that has **more resources** – financial, technological, or human – has more power

The more **willing** you are to let go of your sunk costs (such as financial and emotional expenses), the more **power** you have.

The fewer **deadlines** you are pressed with, the more power you have to wait and explore **opportunities** for **better deals**.

The more **skilled** you are in the **art of negotiation,** the more **power** you have to produce better **joint outcomes.**

Tip

RECOGNIZE YOUR TRUE POWER
Weak parties often underestimate their own **power** and overestimate that of powerful parties, so try to make an **objective assessment** of the amount of power you have.

Negotiating from a weak position

If your position is weak, never share this information with the other party. New opportunities or information may arise at any point, which may strengthen your BATNA and your negotiating position. Even if your position is weak overall, try to identify any areas of strength you have and use them as leverage. Even the most powerful party will have some weaknesses, so try to discover these and target them.

Never make "all or nothing" deals from a weak position – you may miss out on opportunities that would have arisen as the value of what you are bringing to the table increases during the negotiation process. Instead, make deals sequentially and in small chunks, to ensure that the other party will be more likely to recognize the added value that you bring to the table.

Even if your position is weak overall, try to **identify** any **areas of strength** you have and use them as **leverage**

Case study

CREATING POWER

In 2017 Masayoshi Son, the billionaire head of Japanese tech conglomerate SoftBank, was seeking to buy a stake in ride-sharing firm Uber and negotiations were stalling over the price. Son let drop to the press that he could happily invest in rival firm Lyft if the deal fell through.

Observers interpreted his comments, which suggested he was willing to walk away and place his substantial investment elsewhere, as a move to gain leverage. In January 2018 Son completed a deal for a 15 per cent stake in Uber worth $7 billion that made SoftBank the firm's largest shareholder.

Tip

USE LIKEABILITY AND INTEGRITY
When in a weak position, do not
underestimate the power of **personal
likeability.** People do business with
people they **like** and whom they can
trust to **keep their promises** and
deliver **good value.**

Making offers and counteroffers

Before you go into a negotiation, it is vital to plan your opening move. Do you open negotiations and make the first offer or do you wait and allow the other party to go first? Make sure that you have an opening offer in mind, and plan how you will respond to your counterpart's offers.

Knowing when to go first

Some experts suggest that you should not make the first offer and should always allow your counterpart to go first. Skilled negotiators, however, question the conventional "never open" rule. They choose to tailor their approach to each negotiation. How should you decide whether to go first or second? You should present your offer first when you are confident in the thoroughness of your due diligence and also when you suspect that your counterpart is ill-informed. By going first, you will "anchor", or set a benchmark, that will be used as a reference point for the counteroffer.

If you are not fully informed, do not go first. Consider the other party's first offer, do not respond to it, and do your due diligence. In some cases, two negotiators are equally skilled and well informed and neither wishes to go first. Such cases often require the involvement of a trusted third party to act as a neutral go-between and get the negotiations started.

> You should **present** your offer first when you are **confident** in the **thoroughness** of your **due diligence**

In focus

POSSIBLE RESPONSES TO TOUGH OPENING OFFERS

It is easy to be thrown if the other party's opening offer is extremely tough. Effective negotiators make sure they are not startled by an aggressive first offer, and avoid making a quick, emotional reaction.

It is vital that a tough opening offer does not become a benchmark for the negotiation. Possible responses include rejecting the offer as unreasonable; asking the other party to revise the offer; or asking questions and probing the other party to justify the offer.

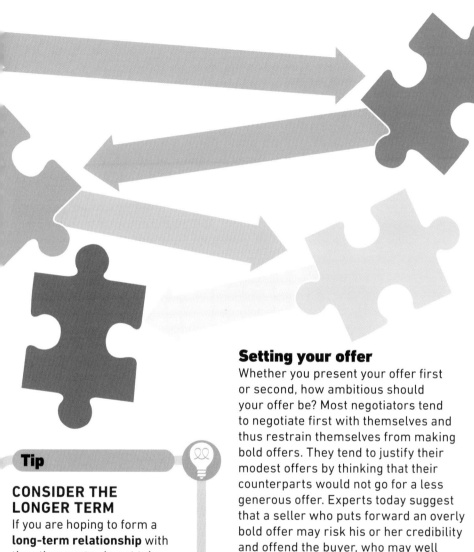

Tip

CONSIDER THE LONGER TERM

If you are hoping to form a **long-term relationship** with the other party, do not take advantage if they make you a generous first offer. You will **generate goodwill** and nurture the relationship if you instead respond with a counteroffer that is better for them, but still reasonable to you.

Setting your offer

Whether you present your offer first or second, how ambitious should your offer be? Most negotiators tend to negotiate first with themselves and thus restrain themselves from making bold offers. They tend to justify their modest offers by thinking that their counterparts would not go for a less generous offer. Experts today suggest that a seller who puts forward an overly bold offer may risk his or her credibility and offend the buyer, who may well walk away without even providing a counteroffer. Instead of coming up with offers that are either too bold or too modest, it is often better to make offers that are as close as possible to what you think your counterpart's BATNA would be. Such offers are reasonably bold, tend not to be acceptable, but are still negotiable.

Making concessions

Experienced negotiators know that successful negotiations involve a certain amount of give and take, and are well versed in the process of making concessions. They tend to develop offers that leave room for concessions, as these are the oil that lubricates the making of a deal.

Conceding in small steps

Each negotiation event is unique, so there are no absolute rules for how to make concessions that apply to all situations. However, it is generally true that people like to receive good news or benefits in instalments, rather than all at once. Skilled negotiators, therefore, tend to make multiple small concessions in order to increase the level of satisfaction of their counterparts.

> **Tip**
>
> **WATCH YOUR TIMING**
> Think carefully about the **timing** of your first **sizeable concession.** If you make it too soon after your initial offer, it will give the other party the impression that the initial offer was not a credible one.

Knowing what to concede

Inexperienced negotiators often make a first sizeable concession as an expression of goodwill. However, this can set the expectation that there are many concessions to be provided. Experienced negotiators, by contrast, tend to untangle the relationships from the concessions. Sometimes, in order to set the tone of reciprocating concessions, these knowledgeable negotiators concede first by making a concession on a minor issue.

Wait before you make the first sizeable concession. During this time, advocate for your initial offer and convey the idea that it is not that easy to make concessions. The second concession should be smaller in size than the first and be a longer time in coming. Making concessions in progressively declining instalments will then lend more credibility to when you finally say: "There is no more to give."

Wait before you make the first **sizeable concession**: **advocate** for your initial offer and **convey** the idea that it is **not that easy** to make concessions

Making and interpreting concessions

ENABLING RECIPROCITY
Label the concessions you make as ones that are costly to you and then reduce your value. This sets up the **expectation** that you will receive a concession in return, implying **value for value.**

USING CONTINGENCY
If you suspect that your concession will not be **reciprocated,** offer a concession that is contingent upon the other party providing a **concession in return.** For example: "I will be willing to extend the terms of payment to 45 days if you will increase your order by 500 items."

SETTING BOUNDARIES
Some negotiators put the deal at risk by asking for too much. Set boundaries for the other party by being **clear and precise** about what you can concede and what you absolutely cannot.

SETTING RULES
Sometimes negotiators make **final concessions** but then withdraw them or make them contingent on receiving a new concession. Set a **clear rule** that a concession cannot be withdrawn, unless it was explicitly offered as a tentative or conditional concession.

SPOTTING DEAL BREAKERS
Some concessions are deal breakers: without them, your counterpart will walk away from the negotiation table. Try to distinguish these from **value-enhancing concessions,** which are demands that will get a **better deal,** but if not provided, would not result in the other party abandoning the negotiations.

Being persuasive

A successful negotiation process requires effective persuasion. When attempting to influence your counterpart, it is crucial to identify your moments of power and take advantage of them. Seasoned negotiators understand how to use appropriate persuasion techniques to sell their ideas to the other party.

Influencing others

Effective negotiators use a range of persuasion techniques that take advantage of the natural responses of negotiators to certain types of information. For example, negotiators are generally more motivated to avoid losses than they are to obtain gains.

60%

of people **globally** say they **trust advertising** on TV and in the press

Negotiators use a range of persuasion techniques that take **advantage** of the natural **responses** to certain types of **information**

Emphasizing benefits

A group of home-owners in California was given the advice that "if you insulate your home, you will gain 50 cents a day". Another group was told that "if you fail to insulate your home, you will lose 50 cents a day". More home owners under the second set of instructions insulated their homes than under the first set of instructions. Similarly, you are more likely to persuade the other party of the benefits of your deal if you emphasize what they would lose if they don't agree, not what they could gain if they do.

Tip

SLIDE AWAY
When conducting negotiations **remotely** via video it can be harder to maintain focus. Here **visual aids** such as slides can help combat distraction and **boost** your persuasion powers. Use them to **emphasize** your main points, and keep both you and your counterpart **centred** on what's important.

Negotiators are generally more motivated to avoid losses than they are to **obtain gains**

Offering small concessions

Making small unilateral concessions can be a successful way to influence your counterpart. Negotiators feel obligated to reciprocate, no matter how big or small the concessions are. Even a small concession on your part can help the other party to comply. The more beneficial your concession is to the other side, the more likely they are to feel obliged to return the favour.

94%
of people will **agree** to a **request** if given a reason

93%
of people will **agree** to a **request** even if the reason does not make sense

Strengthening your hand with persuasion techniques

USE SCARCITY
It is human nature for people to **want more** of what they cannot have. When you present your offer to the other party, inform them of the **unique benefits** you are offering that they would not be able to get elsewhere.

GAIN COMMITMENT
Encourage the other party to agree to an initially modest request. They are then **more likely** to follow up with their **commitment by agreeing** to your key demand to justify their past decision to say yes to you.

GIVE A REASON
People are much more likely to **agree to a demand** if you have given legitimate justification for it. Try to give a reason that can be backed up with evidence, but using even a frivolous **reason increases** your chances of reaching agreement.

GIVE "SOCIAL PROOF"
People often use **"social proof"** when making decisions – they think that if many people are doing things a certain way, it must be good. Demonstrate how your product or service has been **successfully used** by others.

LET THEM SAY "NO"
Give the other party the **opportunity** to say "no" by making an outrageous demand, before retreating immediately and putting forward a more **reasonable demand.** This can also serve to make the other party feel obligated to make a concession.

SET A BENCHMARK
Negotiators who are not fully informed tend to compare the cost of an item to a **reference point or benchmark.** You can influence the way they make their decision by setting a benchmark for them.

Managing impasses

Negotiations do not always conclude with an agreement. You may encounter an impasse or a deadlock during the process. How should you deal with a deadlock? Should you leave the negotiation table, concluding that the process has failed, or should you encourage yourself and your counterpart to remain at the table and keep the negotiations going?

Dealing with deadlock

Skilled and experienced negotiators expect there to be impasses in the negotiating process. They anticipate deadlocks and develop counteractions to deal with them when they occur. They view an impasse as a natural ingredient in negotiations and do not give up easily in their attempts to reach an agreement.

Impasses usually generate negative emotions and sometimes deep feelings of resentment. Prior to and during the negotiation process, you should always be sensitive to the other party's concerns, feelings, and, particularly, their self-image. Research has suggested that negotiators have an image to uphold and that negotiations are less likely to be successful when either or both parties are not sensitive enough to each other's dignity, or "face". You should always be mindful not to harm the self-image of your counterpart, and this is never more important than during critical moments of an impasse.

12%

greater profits are **achieved** when parties negotiate over **a meal**

MANAGING DEADLOCK SITUATIONS

Dos	Don'ts
O Anticipating potential impasses and planning in advance how to deal with them	O Believing that you can just think on your feet if a problem arises
O Being open-minded and flexible, and finding creative solutions	O Thinking that deadlocks always lead to "no deal"
O Reacting calmly and using your emotional intelligence, because you know that deadlock situations can be resolved	O Leaving the negotiating table early because you are deadlocked with the other party

Oiling the wheels

If you are facing an impasse, experts suggest that, in the intensity of the moment, you should first take time out to cool down. This will help to defuse the emotional situation and you can resume the discussion at a later time.

Once you reconvene, start by trying to highlight any existing mutual benefits. Impasses usually occur after some progress has been made. So, it may be useful to frame the impasse in the context of what has already been achieved and highlight the potential losses to both parties if agreement is not reached.

If you are still deadlocked, you may need to try expanding the pie. If you maintain a zero-sum, fixed-pie mentality towards the negotiation, this will restrain your creativity in negotiating for the best deal. The purpose of negotiation is not to win an argument, but to find solutions that would maximize the benefits for both parties. Consider new ideas to help you reach agreement. Expand the issues you are discussing, but avoid making concessions. In this way, you may be able to overcome the impasse on one critical issue by adding another issue that is attractive to the other party.

Avoiding decision traps

Most negotiators believe that they are rational. In reality, many negotiators systematically make errors of judgement and irrational choices. It is important for you to understand and try to avoid making these common errors, as they lead to poor decision-making.

Making the right decisions

Understanding the decision traps that negotiators can fall into will help you avoid making the same mistakes yourself, and may allow you to use the other party's errors to leverage your own power. There are many tactics and strategies you can use to avoid decision traps or turn them to your advantage.

Hot and cold coginition

Psychologists have identified two approaches to decision-making: "hot cognition" and "cold cognition". High-speed, pressurized decisions use "hot cognition", while logical, slow decisions use "cold cognition". In high-pressure environments try to overcome your emotions and use "cold cognition".

Understanding decision traps may **allow you** to use the other party's errors to **leverage** your **own power**

Tip

WATCH YOUR TIMING
To avoid feeling that you have not made the **best possible deal,** never accept the first offer that is made, even when it is a **great offer.** Always negotiate a little.

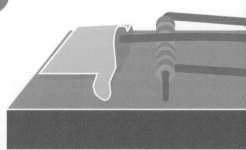

Strategies for decision-making

Do not hesitate to reverse your original decision and cut your losses; **create an exit strategy** even before you get involved in the negotiation process.

Set a **benchmark** that could give you an **advantage** when your counterpart is ill-informed, but be aware that they could do the same to you.

Engage a **trusted expert** who will challenge your overconfidence in your ability to negotiate and put pressure on you to do a reality check.

Make sure that your offer is based on **solid research.** When buying, demand a performance **guarantee** of the product.

Invest time and energy in looking for **information** that is not easily available. You will often find accessible information that can improve your position.

Present information more or less vividly to influence others, but be wary of overvaluing information that is attractively presented to you.

As a negotiator, be aware of how the other party **frames the situation** and presents its offers.

Approach each negotiating event as a **unique case.** They are never identical.

Understanding decision errors

ERROR	DESCRIPTION
Non-rational escalation of commitment	O **Acting contrary** to your self-interest by increasing your commitment to an original decision, despite the fact that this decision produces negative outcomes ("throwing good money after bad").
Anchoring and adjustment	O **Using a faulty anchor** as a benchmark from which to make adjustments and decisions. An ill-informed home-buyer, for example, may use the seller's asking price as an anchor for their counteroffer, rather than solid due diligence on home values.
Overconfidence	O **Believing that you** are more correct and accurate than you actually are. This leads to an overestimation of your power within the negotiation, the options open to you, and the probability of your success.
The winner's curse	O **If you settle quickly** on a deal when **selling,** feeling that the "win" was too easy and that you could have got more from the deal.
	O **If you settle quickly** on a deal when **buying,** thinking "I could have got this for less" or "What is wrong with this item? I must have got a bad deal."

ERROR	DESCRIPTION
Information availability bias	O **Making a decision** based on limited information, even though information is readily available or would have been available if enough effort had been put in to finding it.
Vividness bias	O **Recalling and assigning** more weight to information that was delivered in a vivid fashion, and giving less weight to equally important, but dull, information.
Framing and risk	O **Making decisions** based on how the issues were framed (for example, a glass may be described as being half empty or half full). Risk-averse negotiators are more likely to respond positively to offers that are framed in terms of losses, for example, because they are afraid of losing out; risk-seeking negotiators, by contrast, will respond slowly, because they are willing to wait for a better offer.
Small numbers bias	O **Drawing a conclusion** based on a small number of events, cases, or experiences, believing that your limited experience allows you to generalize from it.

Managing emotions

In the heat of a negotiation, the emotions you display can significantly influence the emotions of the other party. Effective negotiators try to synchronize their behaviour with the other person's, developing an interpersonal rhythm that reflects a shared emotional state.

Understanding the approaches

There are three types of emotional approach in negotiations: rational (having a "poker face"), positive (being friendly and nice), and negative (ranting and raving). Of the three emotional strategies, the positive and rational approaches are more effective than the negative approach in achieving targets in an ultimatum setting. The positive approach is more helpful in building a long-term, constructive relationship than the rational or negative methods.

POKER FACE

Some negotiators believe that exposing their emotions to the other party makes them vulnerable and will result in them giving away too much of the pie, and so try to always keep a "poker face" when they are negotiating. They also believe that emotional displays may result in an impasse or in defective decision-making, or cause negotiations to end.

In focus

STRATEGIC USE OF ANGER

Some negotiators successfully use displays of anger strategically to try to encourage the other party to agree to their demands. They aim to gain concessions from their opponent because the other party takes their anger as a sign that they are close to their reservation point. Inducing fear in their opponent pushes that person to cave in and agree. It sends the signal that they would rather walk away from the table without reaching an agreement than settle for less than what they want. The opponent may also wish to end the unpleasant interaction by giving in.

BEING POSITIVE

Some negotiators believe that displaying positive emotions enhances the quality of the negotiated agreement, because a good mood promotes creative thinking, leads to innovative problem-solving, and smoothes out communication. Negotiators with a positive approach use more cooperative strategies, use fewer hard tactics, engage in more information exchange, generate more alternatives, and come to fewer impasses than negotiators with a negative or rational mood.

BEING NEGATIVE

Negotiators who use the negative approach display anger, rage, and impatience in order to influence the other party. Anger is sometimes used strategically, but negotiators who are genuinely angry feel little compassion for the other party, and are less effective at expanding and slicing the pie than positive negotiators. They tend to achieve fewer win–win gains when angry than when they experience positive emotions. Angry negotiators are also less willing to cooperate and more likely to seek revenge.

85%

of our **success** is based on our **ability** to understand human **behaviour**

Monitor and **regulate** your **emotions**

You **need to** find ways to **empathize** with the **other party**

Using emotional intelligence

When negotiators are emotionally overwhelmed, their mental capacity to negotiate effectively is impaired. To overcome this, you must manage your emotions intelligently. You need to be aware of the emotions you are experiencing and be able to monitor and regulate them, and you need to find ways to empathize with the other party. When negotiating with any other group or individual, it is important to make a conscious attempt to modulate your irritation. For example, while it might be frustrating if your counterpart retracts from an earlier commitment, you could disguise your irritation and use the term "misunderstanding" instead of openly displaying your anger.

ASK YOURSELF...

Do I use emotional intelligence when negotiating?   **YES   NO**

1 Am I able to make an **emotional connection** with my counterpart, even if I do not know them very well? .... ☐ ☐

2 Am I able to **judge** when my own emotions threaten to affect my ability to make **rational decisions?** .... ☐ ☐

3 Can I **manage** my emotions to ensure that I am always **effective?** .... ☐ ☐

4 Am I able to react in a **measured way,** keeping my emotions under control, even if the other party is using value-claiming tactics or behaving in a manner that I do not agree with? .... ☐ ☐

Dealing with competitive tactics

In competitive win–lose position-based negotiations, negotiators use various manipulative tactics to maximize their interests while disregarding the interests of their counterparts. They usually believe that these tactics are quite effective. Often, however, these tactics can backfire, escalating the level of negotiation or even leading to an impasse. Skilled negotiators recognize these tactical traps and know how to avoid and neutralize them.

Competitive tactics and how to avoid them

MAKING A HIGHBALL OR LOWBALL OFFER

A negotiator assumes that you are not fully informed and tries to take advantage by making a very high offer as a seller, or a low offer as a buyer. Their objective is to replace the benchmark you have in your mind with one in their favour.
To avoid: Be confident in your benchmarks and try to see clearly through this ploy.

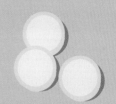

PLAYING GOOD GUY/BAD GUY

One negotiator plays tough and uses aggressive tactics, such as threats and ultimatums. Another empathizes to make you believe that he or she is on your side. Neither is on your side – both are trying to maximize their own interests.
To avoid: Focus squarely on protecting your own interests.

APPLYING TIME PRESSURE

The other party uses the pressure of time to try to get you to concede by setting tight deadlines for an offer, or using delaying tactics to reduce the time free for the negotiation.
To avoid: Use your judgement to decide whether a deadline is real or not.

SEPARATING THE ISSUES

A negotiator insists on reaching an agreement on a single issue before moving on to the next issue. This prevents you from bundling issues and creating opportunities for trade-offs.
To avoid: Negotiate multiple issues at once, stating that 'nothing is agreed upon until everything is agreed upon".

USING EMOTIONAL BLACKMAIL

A negotiator tries to intimidate or influence you by fabricating anger, frustration, or despair. They try to emotionally shake you and make you feel responsible for the lack of progress.
To avoid: Use your emotional intelligence. Stay calm and centred, and try to steer the negotiations back on track.

NIBBLING

The deal is done, but at the last minute the negotiator asks for another small concession. Most negotiators concede, fearing that the last-minute demand might derail the deal if it is not fulfilled.
To avoid: Remember that refusing to budge on a small concession at the last minute is not usually a deal breaker.

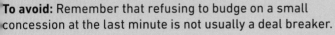

97%

of **concessions** were won in a survey when **threats** were made late in the **negotiation**

Closing the deal

Closing the deal after reaching an agreement is the last but most critical part of any negotiation process. It is certainly not simple, and is not just about outcomes. It also has to do with building relationships and making sure that the negotiated agreements can be carried out smoothly. Closing the deal properly is especially important when negotiated agreements are complex and multi-dimensional.

Preparing to close

Before you close the deal, both you and your counterpart need to understand that the purpose of making the deal is not to sign the contract, but rather to accomplish what the contract specifies. What goals is each party pursuing through the deal and what will it take to accomplish them? As you depend on each other to accomplish your goals, it is important to make sure that both parties are signing the contract wholeheartedly. Review both parties' key interests and ensure that nothing has been neglected. It is quite possible for the other party to decide to overturn the entire deal if he or she feels pushed into an agreement without having their own needs taken care of.

Considering implementation

Most negotiators underestimate the importance of implementation. If not considered, the intense process of negotiation can undermine your ability to achieve your goals after the deal has been signed. For example, if you have used hard negotiation tactics to push the other party to agree to the deal, the other party may feel, upon signing the contract, that they have been unfairly treated and sabotage the deal, or fail to deliver.

Before you put pen to paper, discuss the implementation of the deal with the other party. What you agree must fulfil the needs of both parties if you are to ensure successful implementation. Unless both parties have confidence that the deal can be successfully implemented, there is no point in continuing the discussion.

Treat closing as **the start** of a collaborative process between you and the other party.

When **closing the deal,** make sure that neither **party** over-commits.

HOW TO ENSURE EFFECTIVE IMPLEMENTATION

Reaching agreement

A written agreement usually marks the closure of a negotiation. The agreement, which includes solutions for both parties, may be summarized and you may ask the other party to sign this document. This is

Continue to work with the other party until implementation is completed.

Share any concerns you have as the process progresses.

Include all **stakeholders** in the implementation process.

the most simple and natural way to conclude a negotiation. Changes should be allowed after the agreement has been signed. In other words, if circumstances change, both parties should feel quite comfortable contacting the other party to discuss these changes. Upon mutual agreement, such necessary changes can be incorporated into the new agreement. Make sure you include this last point in the agreement, as a deal is not done until it is done – it is better to allow for some flexibility than to force the other party to overthrow the entire deal, should the circumstances change.

CHECKLIST...
Closing a deal

		YES	NO
1	Have you **considered** all possible stakeholders?	☐	☐
2	Have you **clarified** the purpose of the deal?	☐	☐
3	Have you made sure that **both parties** understand what it takes to implement the agreement?	☐	☐
4	Have you built a relationship with the other party, to pave the way for **future collaboration**?	☐	☐
5	Have you made enough **arrangements** for another team to implement the agreement, if another team is taking over?	☐	☐

Developing
your technique

However experienced you are at negotiating, there are always ways to improve your technique. Negotiating in groups, in an international arena, and using your skills to mediate conflicts all require a tailored approach to achieve the best results.

22

Negotiating as a team

Many business situations are too complex for a solo negotiator to be fully informed about every aspect of the deal. In such cases, working in a team may give better results, though this requires a high degree of internal coordination and a smooth flow of information between members.

Deciding when to use a team

Some negotiations demand a diverse set of abilities. In addition to sound negotiation and psychosocial skills you may need specific technical expertise, for example, in areas of law, drafting joint ventures, or the planning system. You may need to exercise leverage on your opposite number through the use of PR, or require a keen appreciation of politics and strategy in order to identify the multiple stakeholders in the negotiation and figure out their interests. If you lack any of these abilities, you will probably benefit from the collective wisdom of a team.

You may **need** specific **technical expertise,** for example, in areas of **law,** drafting **joint ventures,** or the **planning system**

MAKE TIME TO PREPARE

Make sure that you have enough time to **create a cohesive,** trustworthy team, and allow time to prepare your **strategy as a group** before you enter into a team negotiation.

3%

of **men** in negotiations lied to men, but 24% **lied** to women

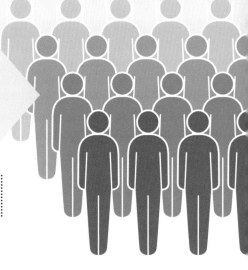

You may **need** to **exercise** leverage

DECISION TIME

Negotiating as a team begs the question of how to decide on a course of action. Broadly, there are three ways to reach a decision: first is unanimity, in which all team members must agree on a given issue. This is a tough rule and not recommended for most situations. The second is the majority rule.

The majority will decide and the minority comply with the decision. The hazard here is that the majority may impose a tough solution that the minority cannot live with. The third, and usually best, decision-making rule is consensus: making a decision that not all the team members agree with fully, but that all can live with.

Advantages and pitfalls

Understanding the advantages

There are many benefits to negotiating as a team. Being part of a team provides for multiple creative trade-offs and options and has other advantages, too. Sheer "strength in numbers" makes a team feel secure and powerful and sends a clear message to the other party that you are serious about the deal. You are also likely to feel less pressured when negotiating as a team, and unlikely to make too many concessions too early in the process.

Avoiding the pitfalls

Working in a team can lead to a lack of focus and consistency, so appoint a chief negotiator to lead your team and agree in advance each member's role and responsibilities. Avoid falling into "groupthink", when team members feel pressured to conform to an existing group mindset and reluctant to present ideas that conflict with it. It can also be easy for a team to create a false sense of cohesiveness: "us", the good team, versus "them", the bad team. If this happens, genuine conciliatory attempts made by the other party can be dismissed as dishonest "tricks" and rejected, resulting in missed opportunities to make a deal.

Dealing with many parties

Many business partnerships or deals involve agreements between three or more different parties, each with their own positions, needs, and goals. Negotiating in this environment requires dexterity and a constant eye on the pitfalls, such as coalitions between the parties opposing you

Balancing complex issues

Multiparty negotiations are in many ways similar to two-party situations but require a wider set of skills to deal with their additional complexities, which include those listed here:

Social complexity With more negotiators involved, the social context becomes complex. In a two-party negotiation, your focus is on one counterpart, but multiparty negotiations require you to understand, analyze, and build relationships with each negotiator. You must learn to resist social pressure and protect your interests, even when faced by a coalition of parties in the negotiation.

Strategic complexity Multiple parties have many interests, and often conflicts of interest, between them. Each party has its BATNA (Best Alternative To a Negotiated Agreement) which may change as alliances are formed. To be prepared for a multiparty negotiation, you must constantly reassess your own and your counterparts' BATNAs.

Emotional complexity Negotiating in a multiparty context can be very taxing. Hold your emotions in check; emotional distress often results in poor decisions.

SUCCEEDING IN MULTIPARTY NEGOTIATIONS

Do's	Don'ts
O **Forming or joining coalitions**	O Insisting on acting independently
O **Resisting group pressure to modify your core interests**	O Settling too easily when faced by a coalition
O **Being clear when you disagree**	O Keeping quiet: silence may be interpreted as assent
O **Monitoring the positions of all the parties**	O Focusing on only one part of the negotiations

Informational complexity The number of parties involved produces multiple exchanges of information, proposals, and multiple trade-offs. You need to develop a solid information system that can record and recall all the information exchanged in the negotiation room.

Procedural complexity The design of the negotiation process may be fraught with difficulty. Its structure – the rules of engagement, selection of venue, sequence of issues, and how decisions will be made – must be perceived to be fair. In high-value negotiations, it is wise to employ an expert to facilitate the process more effectively.

Case study

CHAIRING MULTIPARTY TALKS

How do you gain the trust of 196 different negotiating parties? That was the challenge Daniel Reifsnyder and Ahmed Djoghlaf faced as they prepared to co-chair the UN climate talks in Paris in December 2015. Ten months before the international summit, they invited delegates to Geneva to help create a first draft of an agreement, allowing anyone to add any proposals they wanted. This made sure everyone had a voice and built trust in the co-chairs. After further meetings, delegates became confident in allowing the co-chairs to edit the document alone. The result in October was a 20-page draft that served as the starting point for what would become the historic Paris Agreement to reduce emissions and slow climate change.

Building winning coalitions

The moment there are more than two parties in a negotiation, there are opportunities to make coalitions. To protect your interests and remain in the negotiating game, one of your major objectives will be to think well in advance about offence (how to build a winning coalition) as well as defence (how to put together a blocking coalition).

When attempting to build a stable coalition, there are three essential factors to consider. The first is the issue of agreement. Some parties will agree and others will disagree with your vision and the strategies and tactics you plan to use to achieve it.

To build a coalition, there are **three factors** to consider

Tip

DIVIDE THE PIE
Make it clear to your coalition partners how the **benefits** – the proverbial pie – will be divided if you achieve your goals. The division certainly must be fair, but **fairness** does not necessarily mean an equal share.

Gaining influence and trust

The second important factor to consider when building a coalition is influence. Some potential partners may be highly influential and can use their positions of power to assist you in moving your agenda forward, while others will be weak and unable to help much. The third factor to consider is trust. Coalitions are temporary entities driven by self-interest, so partners are easily seduced to defect once the pay-offs elsewhere become higher. Your main objective should be to recruit potential partners who are trustworthy and will remain loyal to the coalition.

Tip

GAIN POWER
Consider **building a coalition** if you think you hold a weaker hand than one of your opponents. Being part of a **successful** coalition may help you shift **the balance of power.**

Recruiting coalition partners

When building a coalition, start by identifying all stakeholders, both supporters and opponents of your objectives. Classify each stakeholder according to their level of agreement (high, medium, or low, on a scale from one to 10), the degree of influence they could bring to the coalition, and their level of perceived trustworthiness. First, approach your best potential allies – the parties who agree with your vision and agenda and are very influential and trustworthy.

First, **approach** your **best potential allies**

ASK YOURSELF...
About forming a coalition

		YES	NO
1	Do you know your **agenda** for the negotiation and what you are trying to **achieve?**	☐	☐
2	Have you considered the **main factors** that you need to consider in building your coalition?	☐	☐
3	Can you **identify** potential coalition **partners** that are most likely to work with you to allow you to **jointly** fulfil your objectives?	☐	☐
4	Should you **sequence** the recruitment of each potential coalition **partner?**	☐	☐
5	Do you know the **best way** to approach potential partners?	☐	☐

> Focus on the
> **allies** who **agree**
> with your **vision**

Gaining allies

Next, focus on the allies who agree with your vision and are trustworthy, but who do not hold positions of power at the moment; they may gain influence as the negotiation proceeds. Ignore the weak adversaries: those who disagree with your agenda and have little influence. At the same time, think how you could block your powerful adversaries.

Can you make a coalition with one of their potential partners? Coalition partners are often motivated solely by gains. Once the gains elsewhere are higher, they may defect, so you should attempt to cement integrity within the coalition. One way to do this is to ask each partner to make a public commitment to the coalition, making it harder for them to defect.

Negotiating internationally

In today's global economy, ever more business deals are made across national borders. Negotiating international deals is a challenge because you must be familiar with the complexities of the immediate negotiation context, such as the bargaining power of the parties and the relevant stakeholders, as well as the broader context, which may include currency fluctuations and government control.

Understanding the differences

You are likely to experience significant differences in several key areas when you engage in international negotiation:

Agreements Western negotiators expect to conclude the process with a comprehensive bullet-proof legal contract. In other countries, and notably in Asia, memorandums of understanding, which are broader but less substantial agreements, may be more common.

Time sensitivity In countries in which a "doing" culture is prevalent, people believe in controlling events and managing time strictly. In some countries, time is not viewed as such a critical resource, and negotiations can be slow and lengthy.

Degree of formality Negotiators from informal cultures tend to dress down, address one another by their first names, maintain less physical distance, and pay less attention to official titles. In contrast, negotiators from formal cultures tend to use formal titles and are mindful of seating arrangements.

Factors to consider in international negotiations

01

POLITICAL RISK

While some countries have long traditions of an abundance of resources and **political stability,** others have scarce resources and are marked by volatile political changes.

02

IDEOLOGY

In individualistic cultures like the US, the purpose of the business is to serve the **interests of its shareholders,** but in collective cultures, the business has a larger purpose: to contribute to the **common good** of society.

03

CULTURE

Different cultures have starkly **different cultural beliefs** about the role of individuals in society, the nature of relationships, and the ways in which people should communicate. These have a fundamental effect on how you need to **approach** a negotiation.

04

INTERNATIONAL FINANCE

Currencies fluctuate and affect the balance of **expenses and profits.** The **stability** of the currency your investment is made in affects the risk to you. Many governments also control the **flow of currency,** limiting the amount of money that can cross their borders.

05

BUREAUCRACY

Business practices and government regulations vary from country to country. In some countries, the government bureaucracy is deeply **embedded** in business affairs, and businesses are constantly required to secure **government approval** before they act.

06

POLITICAL AND LEGAL SYSTEMS

Different countries have different tax codes, labour laws, legal philosophies and enforcement policies, laws that govern joint ventures, and **financial incentives** for attracting business **investments.**

Negotiating in Asia

Succeeding in any international negotiation means taking the time to understand the complex negotiating environment, being sufficiently flexible to be able to change your ways of working, and learning to work within different governmental bureaucracies. The overall cultural and business landscape in Asia is especially unfamiliar to Western organizations, and, with the region's rapid rise to economic prominence, every manager needs to be aware of how it differs. But bear in mind that not everyone will conform to stereotypes, and also that non-Western counterparts are likely to be just as, if not more, familiar with Western methods of negotiating as Westerners are with non-Western styles. The best negotiators move slowly and do not assume anything.

The Asian style of negotiation

RELATIONSHIPS ("GUANXI")

EMOTIONS

FAIRNESS

TRUST FROM THE HEART

FACE

LEGALISM

DECISIONS

Tip

BE PATIENT
Indian negotiators are more concerned with getting **good outcomes** than with the efficiency of the negotiation process, and may negotiate for weeks or even months to get the **best deal.** Never put pressure on your counterpart to reach agreement more quickly or you may lose the deal.

Chinese business leaders invest heavily in making **interpersonal connections** and creating a dependable **social network,** known as **"guanxi".** They prefer to do business within their trusted network.

The Confucian teaching **xinping qihe,** meaning **"being perfectly calm",** makes it difficult for Western negotiators to "read" their counterparts and to know where they stand.

The concept of **fairness** is based on needs: those who have more should give to those with less.

Asian businesses like to do business with **trustworthy individuals** rather than faceless organizations. The lengthy process of building trust is based on openness, **mutual assistance, understanding,** and the formation of **emotional bonds.**

Dignity and prestige are gained when individuals behave **morally** and achieve accomplishments. Face is a **formidable force** in the Asian psyche that negotiators in Western organizations must be particularly aware of.

You risk insulting your Asian counterpart if you emphasize penalties for dishonouring commitments in detail. Contracts are short and merely a **tangible expression** of the relationships being created. They are not treated as "fixed" legal instruments.

Although Chinese and Japanese societies are hierarchical, they use the **consensus** style of decision-making. Lead negotiators refrain from dictating a decision in order to **preserve relationships** and give face to others.

Acknowledging differences

Asian culture is characterized by concern for people's feelings. It emphasizes interdependence, cooperation, and harmony, while Western culture tends to be more competitive and achievement-oriented, and rewards assertiveness. Like Asian culture, in South America good relationships are vital, but so is emotional expression.

Asian and South American societies tend to give a higher priority to collective goals; self-sacrifice for the good of the whole is a guiding principle. Also, there is a greater acceptance of unequal power distribution, and relationships are built based on differences of status, age, and gender.

> **Tip**
>
> **MAKE A CONNECTION**
> Present your partners with a **long-term vision** of the **mutual benefits** of a deal, stressing your **personal relationship** rather than legal obligations.

Asian and South American societies give a **higher priority** to **collective goals;** self-sacrifice for the **good of the whole** is a **guiding principle**

Business people in China and Japan like to avoid uncertainty, preferring **structured and clear** situations, in which they make decisions after **careful evaluation** of information

Avoiding uncertainty

Another cultural differentiator is the level of comfort that individuals have with ambiguous situations. Business people in China and Japan like to avoid uncertainty, preferring structured and clear situations, in which they are able to make decisions after careful evaluation of a large amount of information. Contrast this with some Western societies, where people are more comfortable with ambiguous situations and are prepared to make quick decisions based on a limited amount of information. In South America, people may be deliberately ambiguous to avoid being directly negative.

Be aware too that there are differences in communication styles: Asians may be "high context" (indirect, implicit, and suggestive), while those from the West are "low context"– more direct and specific.

Understanding emotions

South American business people often seek to form close, friendly relationships at the outset of any negotiation. They may talk and express their emotions with a level of intensity that many Asian and European cultures avoid.

The South American style of negotiation

GREETINGS
A close, **personal greeting** to every team member at the start of each meeting will make people feel valued and important. In South American cultures, being **open and welcoming** is part of professional life.

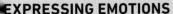

EXPRESSING EMOTIONS
Using **expansive gestures** and speaking loudly and with passion is considered usual in many **conversations**. Do not wait for a pause to join the debate – a **continuous flow** of conversation builds bonds and **deepens trust**.

FAMILY TIES
Extended families form the **core** of South American society. Often there is limited distinction between personal and business life, so **expressing interest** in the families of South American colleagues and discussing your own family is important when negotiating.

RESPECT
Treating people with the **correct level of respect** in relation to both their role in a company and **standing in society** is equally important. A **chain of command** guides business processes, but at each level team members work together with **mutual respect**.

AVOIDING CONFLICT
The word "no" is rarely expressed in conversation. Refusing a **request** or being negative is considered impolite, so many South Americans will avoid certain subjects or use reserve and closed expressions to imply their **true intentions**.

Using a coach

Many negotiators have blind spots, hold false assumptions, and are prone to repeating their mistakes. Some continually fail to fully understand the other party's perspective; others are unable to convert positions to interests, or to manage their emotions. Working with a coach is an excellent way to gain perspective on your weaknesses and strengths and develop your skills for greater success.

Understanding the benefits

Many negotiators do not realize that they could improve their techniques. They continue to make the same type of mistakes because they filter information, hearing only what they want to hear, rather than absorbing the complete information that is required to perform well. Another self-serving trap is attribution. Negotiators often attribute problems in negotiations to their counterpart negotiators. An objective coach who is willing to challenge you can help raise your awareness of your limitations and improve your negotiating performance.

57%

of people who thought they ha been **assertive** in negotiation were **seen** as under-assertive

WORKING WITH A COACH

Do's	Don'ts
O Embracing coaching as a way to become more successful	O Rejecting an offer of coaching because you can't improve
O Respecting your coach's assessment of your weaknesses	O Believing that your coach doesn't understand your superior approach
O Using the feedback your coach gives you to improve your skills	O Dismissing your coach's advice because you know better

ROLE PLAY

Scenario role play can be an effective method of preparing for negotiations. A coach helps you rehearse your role and make sure there are no gaps or weaknesses in your case and in the negotiation process. For example, the coach may help identify your BATNA or make sure that you are not so enamoured with the potential deal that you are unable to walk away from it. Although it is impossible to perfectly script a negotiation process ahead of time, it is helpful to "know your destination and all the terrain" so that even if the other party takes the process off track, you can still find a way to achieve your goals.

...eing assessed

...hen you first work with a coach, ...ey will make an assessment of your ...erformance. This often starts with a ...50-degree feedback session, in which ...ur coach collects data from people you ...egotiate with, in order to identify your ...rengths and weaknesses. The coach ...ay also "shadow" you in some actual ...egotiations, to take note of your existing ...erformance. Witnessing you in action ...lows a coach to provide relevant and ...sightful suggestions for improvement. ...he key outcome from the diagnosis is ...r the coach to identify patterns in your ...eliefs and behaviours, giving you a ...gher level of self-awareness.

A **good coach** helps the negotiator to **test** his or her **own assumptions,** consider **different perspectives,** and reach a **conclusion** about how to proceed

Fine-tuning your style

The coach then works with you to identify the skill sets and attitudes you want to focus on throughout the coaching period. Coaches are experienced in diagnosing possible pitfalls in your negotiation styles, and can help you be proactive in preventing them from occurring. They can also help you to uncover issues and resolve them on your own. They can expand your repertoire of behaviours by trying out different approaches and styles with you. Coaches ask a lot of questions. A good coach helps the negotiator to test his or her own assumptions, consider different perspectives, and reach a conclusion about how to proceed. Many coaches will use scenario role play to help you practise new ways of doing things.

Once you have used the new ideas and approaches in a real negotiation, a coach can provide a non-threatening evaluation and help you learn from your mistakes, achievements, and missed opportunities. Your learning can then be applied in your next round of negotiations.

Being a mediator

As a manager, you will often have to negotiate directly with people within your organization, but you may also be asked to get involved as a third party to help others engaged in disputes to resolve their conflicts. You therefore need to understand the principles of effective mediation and how your role as a manager mediator differs from that of other mediator

Defining mediation

Mediation is a structured process in which an impartial third party facilitates the resolution of a conflict between two negotiating parties. For mediation to be successful, the person selected to mediate a dispute must be acceptable to both of the parties. They must be entirely happy that the mediator is unbiased and will assess the circumstances of the dispute objectively.

Acting appropriately

If you are asked to mediate a dispute, you need to be certain that you will be able to remain impartial and not let yourself get swept up in the emotional side of what is taking place. Your role will require you to look at the situation from the perspective of each of the disputing parties to find areas of common ground between them, and use this information to make some recommendations that would be acceptable to both parties.

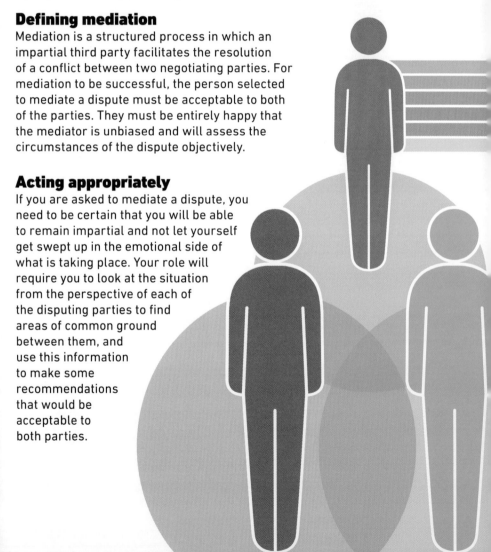

Principles of effective mediation

ENCOURAGE SELF-DETERMINATION

Ensure that the disputing parties **recognize** their differences and know that their **participation** in the mediation process is **voluntary** and they are free to leave at any time.

GIVE OWNERSHIP

Let the disputing parties know that they must take **responsibility** for the conflict and for its **resolution,** and are expected to identify the issues and **engage creatively** in **solving** the conflict.

REMAIN NEUTRAL

Ensure that you remain **neutral** and help to **facilitate** the mediation process, rather than actively trying to influence the outcomes of the conflict.

ADVOCATE CONFIDENTIALITY

Make it clear to all parties that the mediation process is **confidential.** Disputing parties are only likely to share important information if they believe that the mediator is **neutral and trustworthy.**

USE AN INTEGRATIVE APPROACH

Try to understand the **interests** of each of the disputing parties, and help them reach an integrative **(win–win)** resolution that they would both find acceptable.

KEEP THE GOAL IN MIND

Always remember that the **aim** of mediation through **integrative negotiation** is not to achieve absolute justice, but to develop options and find the most **workable** and **satisfactory option.**

Remaining impartial

The manager's role as a mediator is similar to that of other neutral third-party mediators. He or she is working to the same goal as other mediators: to help the disputing parties resolve their disputes. However, as the types of conflict a manager has to deal with often affect organizational goals and performance, he or she may sometimes find it difficult to remain neutral to its consequences. In order to protect the organization's interests, the manager may sometimes have to exercise more control over how the conflict is mediated and also over how the dispute will be resolved. In addition, managers will often have a shared history and possibly a future relationship with the disputing parties. Given these challenges, a manager must do his or her utmost to mediate the dispute in an unbiased manner.

To protect the organization's **interests,** the manager may exercise **control** over how the conflict is mediated

80%

of business disputes are estimated to have been **resolved** through **mediation**

MEDIATING AS A MANAGER

Dos	Don'ts
O Ensuring that the disputing parties reach an integrative agreement that is satisfactory to all	O Failing to take the time to fully listen to and understand the interests of the disputing parties
O Trying to resolve the conflict as quickly and efficiently as possible	O Allowing the conflict to disrupt the organization's day-to-day business
O Ensuring that the mediation process is fair to both parties	O Introducing your own biases
O Allowing disputing parties to express their feelings	O Disregarding the emotions of the disputing parties

Understanding the process

The mediation process is a step-by-step, structured process. However, unlike the rigid legal process used for mediation, the process used by managers is flexible. It involves five main steps:

Initial contact Start by meeting with each party to identify the issues and provide general information about the mediation process and principles.

Assessment and preparation Next, you need to introduce your role as the mediator, and talk to each disputing party to obtain information about the nature of the dispute. You should also make an assessment of your ability to mediate this dispute, by deciding whether the disputing parties are ready for mediation. You also need to get the parties to commit to engaging in constructive mediation, by asking them to sign a contract. Finally, make a list of the issues in dispute for later discussion.

Joint opening session Once fully prepared, you must establish a psychologically safe environment – whether physical or virtual – in which the mediation can take place. Clarify the rules of engagement, such as mutual respect, taking notes, and meeting privately with each disputing party. Educate the parties on the differences between each of their positions and interests and begin to work on the issues.

Joint sessions Facilitate a productive joint problem-solving situation by continuing to move the disputing parties from positions to interests. Prioritize and narrow down the issues, identify areas of agreement and areas of disagreement, and encourage the disputing parties to make realistic proposals. This may take one or a number of sessions.

Agreement Write down aspects of the agreement as the disputing parties begin to agree on more issues. Ensure that the final agreement is very precise, is owned by the disputants, and is forward-looking.

Learning from the masters

Irrespective of the field in which they ply their trade, be it business, law, diplomacy, labour, or sports, master negotiators possess a unique set of combined characteristics that clearly differentiate them from common negotiators, and define their success. Every negotiator can benefit by understanding the skills and attitudes of a master negotiator.

Becoming a winning negotiator

Master negotiators have superior negotiating capabilities in three major areas: the ability to understand and analyze issues (cognitive skills); the ability to manage emotions, especially negative ones (emotional skills); and the ability to connect with others by developing relationships and trust (social skills). These are the areas that you need to work on if you are to hone your negotiating skills and work towards becoming a master negotiator.

Defining key attributes

Using masterful due diligence
Master negotiators understand the dangers of being poorly prepared, and invest ample resources in planning and gathering useful information.

In focus

BAD DEALS

Master negotiators know that negotiations are not about making the deal and signing the contract, but rather about diligently pursuing their interests. No deal is better than a bad deal, so they condition themselves mentally to walk away from the table if their interests are not met. Inexperienced negotiators tend to be biased towards securing a deal and often tend to stay at the table and get a poor deal.

There are two reasons for this: first, negotiators do not want to let go of the sunk costs (expenses) involved in attempting to make the deal. Second, they do not want to face the fact that it is not possible to make the deal and thus feel that they have failed. Master negotiators, in contrast, are willing to let go of the sunk costs and do not feel that they have failed in the negotiation task if the deal does not go through.

Thinking strategically
Negotiations are rarely a one-on-one business, so master negotiators spend time analyzing the interests of the "players" who are not at the table, how the power balance lies, and what opportunities exist to increase their own power.

Seeing the other side Master negotiators know that they can only present a good offer or trade-off if they know what their counterpart's interests are. They are able to easily shift from seeing things from their point of view to seeing things from that of the other party.

Being firm and flexible
Master negotiators are firm and clear about the issues they must have, and flexible on the issues they would like to have.

Investing in relationships
Master negotiators use all possible opportunities to nurture trust and develop relationships, and make sure that those connections remain intact over time.

Managing emotions
Master negotiators make an active choice to always monitor and constructively control their emotions.

Appreciating uniqueness Master negotiators approach every situation afresh and are always ready to modify their practices and adapt to the specific conditions of any on-going negotiation.

Index

Acknowledgments

Stats

p.21 "Seventy-One Percent of Employers Say They Value Emotional Intelligence over IQ, According to CareerBuilder Survey", CareerBuilder, 18 August 2011

p.47 Living to Work: Employee Motivation Report, Motivates, 2018

p.60 Mission & Culture Survey, Glassdoor, 2019

p.64 "What Does It Mean to Be a Manager Today?", Brian Kropp, Alexia Cambon, & Sara Clark, Harvard Business Review, 15 April 2021

p.70 State of the Global Workplace, Gallup, 2017

p.75 "Your Employees Want the Negative Feedback You Hate to Give", Jack Zenger & Joseph Folkman, Harvard Business Review, 15 January 2014

p.76 Coaching: A Global Study of Successful Practices – Current Trends and Future Possibilities 2008-2018, American Management Association, 2008

p.82 IWG Global Workspace Survey 2019

p.95 The imposter phenomenon in high achieving women: Dynamics and therapeutic intervention, Pauline Rose Clance & Suzanne Imes, 1978

p.110 "Founder-Led Companies Outperform the Rest – Here's Why", Harvard Business Review, 24 March 2016

p.115 Leadership & Management in the UK – The Key to Sustainable Growth, Department for Business, Innovation & Skills, July 2012

p.122 "Delegating: A Huge Management Challenge for Entrepreneurs", Gallup, 15 April 2015

p.124 State of the Workplace Empathy, Businessolver, 2018

p.134 Feedback on Feedback, Eagle Hill, 2015

p.137 "3 Ways to Improve Performance Management Conversations", Gartner, 20 December 2019

p.153 Succeeding in Disruptive Times: Global Transformation Study, KPMG, 2016

p.159 "The Right Culture: Not Just About Employee Satisfaction", Gallup, 12 April 2017

p.162 The True Value of Customer Experiences, Deloitte, 2018

p.167 "The Productivity Advantage of Serial Entrepreneurs", Kathryn Shaw & Anders Sørensen, ILR Review, 17 July 2019

p.169 "Fostering Creativity at Work: Do Your Managers Push or Crush Innovation?", Gallup, 19 December 2018

p.173 Global Human Capital Trends, Deloitte, 2019

p.175 "Follow the Leader(ship) Spending", Mike Prokopeak, Chief Learning Officer, 21 March 2018

p.186 "Personality Can Make or Break Your Next Interview Reveals New Survey", Resume-library. com, 23 July 2019

p.188 "Study focuses on strategies for achieving goals, resolutions", Dominican University of California, 2015

p.197 "A large-scale experiment on New Year's resolutions: Approach-oriented goals are more successful than avoidance-oriented goals", Martin Oscarsson, Per Carlbring, Gerhard Andersson, Alexander Rozental, *PLoS ONE* 15(12), 2020

p.197 "Writing about personal goals and plans regardless of goal type boosts academic performance", Michaéla C. Schippers, Dominique Morisano, Edwin A. Locke, W. A. Scheepers, Gary P. Latham, Elisabeth M. de Jong, *Contemporary Educational Psychology*, January 2020

p.199 "Are SMART Goals Dumb?", LeadershipIQ.com, 2021

p.203, p.205, p.206 "The State of Work Life Balance in 2019", RescueTime.com

p.216 "How Many Words Do We Read Per Minute? A Review and Meta-analysis of Reading Rate", Marc Brysbaert, PsyArXiv.com, 12 April 2019

p.220 *Women: Confidence at Work*, My Confidence Matters, 2017

p.223 "Optimism is associated with exceptional longevity in 2 epidemiologic cohorts of men and women", Lewina O. Lee, Peter James, Emily S. Zevon, Eric S. Kim, Claudia Trudel-Fitzgerald, Avron Spiro III, Francine Grodstein, Laura D. Kubzansky, *PNAS*, 10 September 2019

p.225 *Hacking Diversity with Inclusive Decision Making*, Cloverpop, 2017

p.226 "The Decision-Driven Organization", Marcia W. Blenko, Michael Mankins, Paul Rogers, *Harvard Business Review*, June 2010

p.236, p.240 "Eighty-percent of professionals consider networking important to career success", LinkedIn.com, 22 June 2017

p.242 "Business mentoring in the UK – Research & Infographic", Paymentsense.com, 23 October 2017

p.260 *Capitalizing on Effective Communication: How Courage, Innovation and Discipline Drive Business Results in Challenging Times 2009/2010*, Tower Watson

263 "Your Scarcest Resource", Michael Mankins, ris Brahm, and Greg Caimi, *Harvard Business view*, May 2014

276 "The Facts on How People Create resentations – Based on Real-World Survey ata", Presentationpanda.com, 2018

279 "Do Your Slides Pass the Glance Test?", ancy Duarte, *Harvard Business Review*, October 2012

285 "Bad Writing Is Destroying Your Company's roductivity", Josh Bernoff, *Harvard Business view*, 6 September 2016

300 "The Discipline of Listening", Ram Charan, arvard Business Review, 21 June 2012

303 "Nonverbal signals", Judee K Burgoon *Handbook of Interpersonal Communication*, ark L. Knapp and Gerald R. Miller (Eds.), ageEditors, 1994

321 "How Users Read on the Web", ob Nielsen, Nielsen Norman Group, September 1997

322 *Social Trends 2021*, Hootsuite

346 "Presentation Habits Presenters Don't ke To Admit", Prezi.com, 15 June 2016

355 "First Impressions: Making Up Your Mind ter a 100-Ms Exposure to a Face", Janine Willis nd Alexander Todorov, *Psychological Science*, 2006

358 "[INFOGRAPHIC] The 2018 state of tention",Prezi Blog, 28 August 2018

366 "Longest speech marathon", ww.guinnessworldrecords.com

369 "It's Time to Think About the Blink", view of Opthalmology, 13 June 2011

384 "Why negotiation is the most popular usiness school course", Leigh Thompson, eoffrey J Leonardelli, Ivey Business Journal, ly / August 2004

391 "Social trust in advanced economies lower among young people and those ith less education", Pew Research Center, December 2020

395 "Why Do Trade Negotiations Take So ong?", Christoph Moser, Andrew Rose, KOF wiss Economic Institute, ETH Zurich Working aper No. 295, 17 January 2012

396 Trust Barometer, Edelman, 2021

401 "Why Negotiators Still Aren't 'Getting To s'", Keld Jensen, Forbes, 5 February 2013

412 "Negotiation Strategy: Seven Common tfalls to Avoid", Barbara Buell, Stanford aduate School of Business, 15 January 2007

p.424 Global Trust in Advertising: Winning Strategies for an Evolving Media Landscape, Nielsen, September 2015

p.426 "The Mindlessness of Ostensibly Thoughtful Action: The Role of 'Placebic' Information in Interpersonal Interaction", Ellen Langer, Arthur Blank, Benzion Chanowitz, Journal of Personality and Social Psychology, 1978

p.428 "Should You Eat While You Negotiate?", Lakshmi Balachandra, Harvard Business Review, 29 January 2013

p.436 How To Win Friends And Influence People, Dale Carnegie, 1936

p.439 "Hot or Cold: Is Communicating Anger or Threats More Effective in Negotiation?", Marwan Sinaceur, Margaret Neale, Gerben A. van Kleef, Christopher Haag, Journal of Applied Psychology, June 2011

p.445 "Not competent enough to know the difference? Gender stereotypes about women's ease of being misled predict negotiator deception", Laura J. Kraya, Jessica A. Kennedy, Alex B. Van Zanta, Organizational Behavior and Human Decision Processes, November 2014

p.460 "Pushing in the Dark: Causes and Consequences of Limited Self-Awareness for Interpersonal Assertiveness", Daniel R. Ames, Abbie S. Wazlawek, Personality and Social Psychology Bulletin, 28 February 2014

p.464 "Mediation Secrets for Better Business Negotiations: Top Techniques from Mediation Training Experts", Program on Negotiation at Harvard Law School, 2010

Acknowledgments

Managing People
Written by Philip L. Hunsaker
and Johanna Hunsaker
Working Remotely chapter was written by
Lara Kavanagh and Wes Nicholson
This book would not have been created without the
initiation, guidance, perseverance, and flexibility of Kati
Dye at Cobalt id. We also want to thank Peter Jones at
Dorling Kindersley for his assistance and adaptability in
managing the schedule and business side of this project.

Leadership
Written by Christina Osborne
Writing a book for Dorling Kindersley immediately
involves you in teamwork at its best – a combination
of many talents, much patience, and great commitment.
I would like to thank Adèle Hayward and Peter Jones
for their vision and stewardship throughout and Marek
Walisiewicz for his inspiring leadership in bringing
about the meld of visual impact and words, with his
team of editors and designers, which has made this
such an interesting project.

Achieving High Performance
Written by Mike Bourne and Pippa Bourne
We would like to acknowledge and thank Mike's friends
and colleagues at the Centre for Business Performance,
Cranfield School of Management for their support and
ideas incorporated into this book. We would also like to
thank the Institute of Chartered Accountants in England
and Wales for giving Pippa the time to write this book
and in particular Charles Carter and Debbie Kimpton
for their support.

Effective Communication
Written by James O'Rourke
My thanks to the good people at Cobalt id who have
helped me condense decades of experience, teaching,
and research into an interesting, readable volume. Had
Marek Walisiewicz not called and asked me to consider
this project, I'd never have gotten it done. My
appreciation goes, in particular, to Kati Dye and the
other talented artists, editors, and designers who've
transformed my thoughts and observations into a lovely
book. My thanks, as well, to Daniel Mills and the very
professional staff of Dorling Kindersley whose diligence
and professionalism with this title and this series have
been nothing short of remarkable. Thanks to you all.

Presenting
Written by Aileen Pincus
The author would like to thank the editors at Dorling
Kindersley and Cobalt for their sure hand in guiding
this project. This book is dedicated to: Scot, Benjamin
and Anna, for their love, support, and patience; and
to my father, Meyer Pincus, whose love of words and
ideas lives on.

Negotiating
Written by Michael Benoliel and Wei Hua
Our thanks go to the business associates at the Centre
for Negotiation (USA) and the International Perspective
(Singapore), to the academic colleagues at Singapore
Management University, to our editor Amrit Kaur,
and to our research assistant Deborah NG Sui Ling.
We appreciate your support. Thanks to the many
managers and executives in USA, UK, China, India,
Singapore, Thailand, Malaysia, Indonesia, and the
Philippines. Your active participation in our negotiation
training and coaching workshops put our expertise to
the ultimate test of relevancy and precision. Thanks to
our students at Johns Hopkins University, Singapore
Management University, and Nanyang Technological
University, Singapore. Your inquisitive nature helped us
crystallize our thinking. Thanks to Marek Walisiewicz,
Peter Jones, Kati Dye, and many other talented
designers and editors. Your commitment to publish
this book gave light to our negotiation and coaching
ideas. This collective endeavour will promote the best
practice of negotiation.